TA926707

SHOWBOATS

SHOWBOATS

THE HISTORY OF AN AMERICAN INSTITUTION

BY

PHILIP GRAHAM

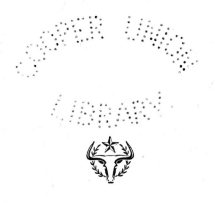

AUSTIN: 1951

UNIVERSITY OF TEXAS PRESS

UNIVERSITY OF TEXAS PRESS
AUSTIN 12

THOMAS NELSON AND SONS LTD
Parkside Works Edinburgh 9
3 Henrietta Street London WC2
312 Flinders Street Melbourne C1
5 Parker's Buildings Burg Street Cape Town

THOMAS NELSON AND SONS (CANADA) LTD
91–93 Wellington Street West Toronto 1

SOCIÉTÉ FRANÇAISE D'EDITIONS NELSON
25 rue Henri Barbusse Paris V^e

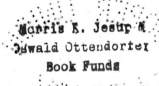
Copyright, 1951, by Philip Graham

Printed and bound in the United States of America by
Vail-Ballou Press, Inc., Binghamton, N. Y. Offset Illus-
trations by Meriden Gravure Company, Meriden, Conn.

DEDICATED
BY THE AUTHOR
TO
Captain Ralph Emerson, Tommy Windsor, Harry High,
Captain Bill Menke, Captain Callie French,
Captain John McNair, Miss Clarkie McNair, John S. Cobb,
Clark B. Firestone, Norman Hanley,
Alexander Clark, Lon Burrowes, LeRoy C. Oetter,
William E. L. Bunn, Franklin J. Meine,
Mabel Bartenhagen, Clair Brewer, J. Mack Gamble,
Wesley Stout, Captain Billy Bryant,
Sidney Snook Haman, Fred G. Neuman,
William J. Peterson, Bert Potter, Glenn Hughes,
Carroll Coleman, Paul Meyers,
T. A. Prichard, Jean T. Selby, Raymond Sillito,
Donald T. Wright,
AND TO THE MANY OTHERS
WHO HAVE GENEROUSLY CONTRIBUTED
TO THE MAKING OF THIS BOOK

CONTENTS

[vii]

CONTENTS

ILLUSTRATIONS

Facing page

SHOWBOATS

I

BEFORE THE SHOWBOAT

The River Frontier

A BOISTEROUS American frontier by 1825 had already reached the Mississippi, and the rivers had carried it there. Even at the beginning of the century, before Napoleon's sale of the Louisiana region in 1803, the vast Mississippi basin contained half a million settlers from beyond the Alleghenies. These were widely scattered, clustered in small villages and sprinkled in remote homesteads and shanties over the far-reaching territory. Only New Orleans could be called a city, and very few of its inhabitants spoke English.

By the end of the first quarter of the century, however, five million newcomers had joined these scattered holders of the land, as hardy Americans as ever went westward, all intent upon transforming a shabby present into a glorious future. The big half-moon of territory was in the process of an astounding development. Pittsburgh, St. Louis, Cincinnati, and Louisville quickly took form as cities. The rivers brought homeseekers by the thousands. These cleared land, built houses, established businesses, founded families. Most important of all these men of the valleys built boats: light fast canoes and bull boats, long substantial keel boats, awkward flat-bottomed, square-nosed, heavily loaded barges, and a few of the luxury river steamers that soon were to clutter the Western waters like floating castles. For the rivers carried the whole burden of this remarkable development. On their surface came the ever increasing wealth of supplies, as well as the constant stream of humanity. They brought life and at the same time brought the means of sustaining life. The physical development that the region was undergoing, remarkable both in rapidity and extent, resulted from the union of vast natural resources and almost boundless human energy. The rivers were the agents for bringing together these two important elements of empire-building.

The men who furnished the energy for this great project came, with few exceptions, from the East. The metamorphosis which they underwent was even more remarkable than that which came to the region itself, for this violent Eden seemed to have a near-magic power of changing all within its bounds. A young man of Boston, New York, or Richmond made his way to the headwaters of the Allegheny, the Monongahela, or the Kanawha, and down the rivers into the heart of the new country. Immediately the ferment of material growth seemed to enter his blood, and he was no longer the same person. All energy of mind and body centered on matters of physical existence. Engulfed in an empire being built on very material foundations, he himself became a builder or a cog in a giant machine that was building. In a region that had temporarily forgotten everything except its own growth, he necessarily shaped his own life by the same simple and direct pattern. If he had enjoyed a cultured environment in the East, he was likely to become in the West either a professional gambler (a tribe notorious wherever there was running water), or, if he was more sensitive to social obligations, a man of great courage and greater action—perhaps a Henry Shreve who dared to tame the vicious Mississippi herself, or a James Eads who built bridges where none had been possible. If he had come from the middle classes, he would likely become a landowning farmer, smelling of the soil and belonging to it, or a skilled mechanic or builder, capable of more work in a day than he could have done in a week in the old environment. Or perhaps he would prefer the river, to become a boat captain or a mate, in charge of busy water traffic. If he had belonged to the less privileged classes in the East, he, and his sons after him, were certain to take to the river, to become one of that remarkable new breed of brawny, bullying, truth-telling rivermen, who swore mightily, drank deep, and shot straight, performing incredible physical labor and for recreation enjoying the sweet and continuous battle against the river and its pirates. Nowhere else has man's physical activity been greater, and nowhere else has human life been held cheaper or property more impersonal.

Some have thought that the surging rivers with their great volume of muddy and powerful water caused all this emphasis on the outer realities of life. Whether a man of the Middle West happened to be a builder of cities or a shanty boatman, he was dependent on the rivers and inevitably became a part of what they were. As the great streams had been the means of man's penetrating and subduing the new regions, so the rivers set their stamp upon the men that came, to create the roughest, the most energetic, the most physical-minded frontier that America has known. Because it was a river frontier, it moved rapidly, constantly re-establishing itself in hitherto inaccessible sections, and leaving behind an ever increasing semi-literate area.

Such a region, with its Herculean and exhausting labor, its harassing and dangerous experiences, and its bombastic primitivism, especially needed emotional outlet and some escape from itself. Liquor was the frontier's first and least satisfying solution to the problem. The whiskey barrel was considered as essential on the busy river boat as food itself. Even on the better passenger steamers liquor was made generously accessible to crew and patrons alike.

As life on the river frontier grew slightly less strenuous, cultural entertainment became gradually another answer to the great need. Wholesome pleasure of any variety doubtless would have served well. But the stage, with its world of make-believe and its music and its dance, was best adapted in this region to furnish relief to an overworked and emotionally repressed people.

As the rivers had brought the necessities of physical life—calico, cooking utensils, and grist mills—so they were to bring the beginnings of culture to the region. Certain forms of entertainment were as old as the settlements themselves. Every flatboat hand could play a comb solo or bring minor-keyed music from an empty whiskey jug. James Hall, who drifted down the Ohio in 1820, records entertainment that filled those tediously long days when the current guided the boat, songs "with poetry dressed in rags and going on crutches." He remembers, too, how liquor put life in the dancer's heels, while Old Pap made the music on Katy, his faithful fiddle. When this same crew tied up to a village landing, more than likely they put on their little act for a sufficient fee to pay for a new supply of drink. River entertainment even became commercialized when a few early medicine and whiskey boats lured their customers with songs, wrestling, and acrobatics. Semi-professional itinerant musicians, dancers, tricksters, and mimics gave their exhibitions in the cabins of river steamers, on the flatbottoms, and at the landings. Concerning the excellence of such efforts, one can only guess. These softer-textured things of life introduced into the wilderness must have appeared glamorous by virtue of contrast alone. And then, too, these adventurous spirits from habit craved excitement, and therefore accorded an eager though perhaps rude welcome to such meager glimpses of the ideal. Whatever the worth of the performances, certainly the avidity with which river people patronized even the crudest entertainment is a comment on the cultural starvation of the frontier.

When Mike Fink, king of the keelboatmen, was still ranging the bayous of the Southwest, entertaining his crew and others at the landings with his harmonica and fiddle, a professional actor and his company appeared on the Mississippi. Noah Ludlow and eleven associates steered their keelboat, with its rude superstructure, into Natchez-under-the-Hill on December 10, 1817. The little band had traveled over three thousand miles, by wagon and by boat, with numerous losses and additions in personnel, since it had started for the West two years before.[1]

In spots the great course of the Mississippi had already acquired some appearances of civilization. Thriving towns like St. Louis, Natchez, and of course New Orleans, had built their first theatres, and local thespians and even a few professionals were whetting an appetite for the drama. As the population increased, so grew the desire for more than the joys of shelter and food and security from the Indians. Most of the settlers had nostalgic memories of the dramatic performances in the East from which they had come. The region needed a little relaxation from the strenuous business of building empire, and its inhabitants were beginning to seek public amusement.

Noah Ludlow and his company had arrived in the Valley for the purpose of satisfying this need. The company, at first under the leadership of Samuel Drake, Sr., had set out from Albany, New York, in December of 1815, bound for play-hungry (according to rumor) Kentucky, especially to entertain the legislators at Frankfort. At Olean on the Allegheny River, two hundred and sixty miles above Pittsburgh, they purchased a broad-horn, a flatbottomed boat twenty-five feet long, with a sheltering superstructure. In this they drifted down the Allegheny, steering with oars and poles when the danger was greatest. They suffered the hardships of the river and began to learn its strange drama. They were hungry, they were cold, they

[1] Noah Miller Ludlow, born in Albany, N.Y., 1796, began playing genteel comedy roles in his native city when he was eighteen. From 1815 to 1853 he barnstormed the West, with a short interval in New York in 1830. He was manager (with Sol Smith) of the St. Charles Theatre, New Orleans, 1845–1853. In 1880 he published *Dramatic Life As I Found It*, a record of his experiences in the West, vivid, though not always accurate.

Chapman's FLOATING THEATRE

Spaulding and Rogers' FLOATING CIRCUS PALACE

French's First New Sensation

French's Fourth New Sensation

listened to the weird symphony of the wolves. On some nights they were lucky enough to find lodgings in a tavern. On one such occasion, when the only available room was fully occupied by a crew of ill-smelling mule handlers, they secured possession of the coveted quarters by frightening away their competitors with a hurried acting of the ghost scene from "Hamlet." On other occasions, they slept aboard their boat, tied up to a tree in the mouth of some secluded creek, to avoid the notice of those who would have murdered them for their small craft. Through it all Samuel Drake, the moving spirit of the expedition, insisted on waking the members of the company each morning "with a touch of Shakespeare," some appropriate passage quoted, just as the sun rose, in not too soft a voice!

The players remained at Pittsburgh for almost three months, performing to full and appreciative audiences in the Luke Usher frame theatre, and then they again drifted down the river, this time the Ohio. At Limestone, Kentucky, they disembarked, purchased a wagon, and started the long anticipated Kentucky tour.

They timed their arrival in Frankfort to the meeting of the legislature—incidentally the same legislature that a little later was to witness the notorious "Kentucky tragedy" in real life—for they had heard that that body was most desirous "of observing play spectacles." But Frankfort proved disappointing, and soon the company played its way through Kentucky into Tennessee, stopping wherever they could secure a hall, an empty store, a commodious tavern dining room, or even a deserted brewery. Usually it was first a comedy, often Tobin's "The Honeymoon," followed by the short afterpiece, "The Lying Valet." If they remained for a second performance (there was seldom a third night), they tried "The Poor Gentleman" or "The Weathercock." If the church element, small but vocal, raised moral objections to "play people" visiting the town, they put on "Catherine and Petruccio" ("The Taming of the Shrew" as altered by Garrick), for Shakespeare's name had a quieting effect on objectors, even in the roughest of the frontier towns.

At Nashville these hardy troupers again took to the rivers, this time with New Orleans as their objective. They changed their name to the American Theatrical Commonwealth Company—a phrase suggesting a curious mixture of Western democracy and English tradition—purchased a keelboat for two hundred dollars, christened it NOAH'S ARK, and formally elected Noah Ludlow their captain. Significantly, the boat was larger than their last, for, though Ludlow does not state the dimensions, its type would indicate a length of approximately one hundred feet. It would seem that some acting on board was contemplated.

After one evening's instruction by an experienced river man—not to tie up near caving bluffs, not to pass, unaccompanied, the pirate-infested localities, not to leave the swiftest current—"drama" once more set out on the rivers. Down the Cumberland into the Ohio, down the Ohio into the Mississippi, with only an occasional stop for a saddle of venison or milk for the Drake baby. Only by working to exhaustion did they avoid the numerous snags and sawyers.[2] For it was a danger-ous passage, especially for those untutored in the ways of the River. Often all hands—actors and actresses alike—had to turn out to pole the boat around a sand bar, and at such notorious spots as Plum Point, Rowdy Bend, or St. Francis River, every man and woman were armed with sabers hastily unpacked from the stage properties to repel possible attack by river robbers.[3] The raft was nearly wrecked a few miles above what is now Vicksburg.

And that is the sum of the adventures of the American Theatrical Commonwealth Company, if we are to believe Ludlow, before it reached Natchez-under-the-Hill on December 10, 1817, almost a month after leaving Nashville. It is altogether probable, however, that the players had performed on their boat at various landings as they drifted down, to sustain their meager fortunes. Yet it is not strange that Ludlow in his account of the voyage should make no mention of this fact. Both he and Sol Smith wrote extensively of their theatrical experiences in the West, but neither ever admitted having performed on a boat.[4] They were anxious to make it appear that they acted only in the best theatres of the region at a time when the boat-shows had

[2] Ludlow records this definition of a sawyer: "For the information of such as may never have had the pleasure (?) of coming in contact with these peculiar institutions of the West, I will merely say that a Western 'sawyer' is a huge monster called a tree! Many of these not infrequently made sudden departures for lands unknown *via* the Mississippi River and the Gulf of Mexico; and after pursuing their course an indefinite number of miles, and having divested them-selves of certain superfluous leaves and branches, they often suddenly stop to rest on some conveniently arranged submerged sand-bar, and modestly drooping their heads, with an outstretched limb endeavor to admonish all incautious boat-men not to rub against and disturb them in their repose."—*Dramatic Life As I Found It*, 125.

[3] One authority states, without citing sources, that the Ludlow Company played one night at Plum Point, and two nights at St. Francis River (Memphis *Commercial Appeal*, July 3, 1938).

[4] N. M. Ludlow, *Dramatic Life As I Found It;* Sol Smith, *Theatrical Ap-*

none too savory a reputation. Also Ludlow's later fame as actor and manager has perhaps helped to obliterate his early connections with the showboat.

Therefore it seems altogether probable, though no record exists, that as the play-boat tied up to the "Gold Coast" of Natchez-under-the-Hill in the twilight of that December night in 1817, Ludlow and his associates lost little time in announcing that they would perform "that good play, *Catherine and Petruccio*," since several days later they did "that amusing comedy, the *Honeymoon*," in the main town on the Hill.

Ludlow would have hesitated to take the ladies of his company into the saloons of the "Coast," and therefore he would have chosen the boat for the performance, especially since he had been warned that these people under-the-hill "were safer to be encountered in the day-light than after dark." Furthermore the Company was in no hurry to get to New Orleans until that city should get well rid of the yellow fever.

If these suppositions are correct, then Ludlow's NOAH's ARK was the first of the showboats. It did not serve for long in that capacity, however, for five days later the troupe sold it as a cotton transport and took passage for New Orleans, at $20 per head, on the ORLEANS, the first steamboat on Western waters, after happily performing the "Honeymoon" and the "Lying Valet" in the amateur theatre on the Hill. The money-minded manager was elated that the people had been so eager to have a company of "regulars" that the use of the theatre had been offered without charge.

Nor were Ludlow and his fellow actors the only strolling players to take to the rivers. Joseph Jefferson in his *Autobiography* tells of his journey down the Cumberland in a flatboat, with a cargo of drama. Sol Smith was likewise beginning his career of barnstorming, mostly by boat, over territory extending from Pittsburgh to New Orleans and Atlanta. Almost every actor of the time with courage, ingenuity, and a crusading love of his art wanted to play the West. The river and boats were ready to provide transportation. Plays, both English and native, were to be had for the taking. Most of the wealth of the region gravitated toward the rivers, and audiences along their banks needed entertainment and were anxious to pay for it. The one factor

prenticeship and *Theatrical Management in the West and South for Thirty Years*. Yet both men record seeing the Chapman showboat a little later.

lacking was an adequate playhouse that could be made readily accessible to a widely scattered population. The showboat supplied this need.[5]

[5] Principal Sources: Newspaper files, manuscripts, and Noah Ludlow's *Dramatic Life As I Found It.*

Other Sources: Items listed in the bibliography under T. A. Brown, Hodding Carter, Joe Curtis, Florence Dorsey, Esther Dunn, James Hall, Carl Holliday, Joseph Jefferson, Deck Morgan, C. D. Odell, Constance Rourke, Lyle Saxon, Sol Smith, Wesley Stout, and Francis Wemyss.

II

Here Comes the Showboat

William Chapman and His Family

A LITTLE more than a decade after Noah Ludlow had left the River for the more pretentious land theatres, the first deliberately planned showboat was launched, in the summer of 1831, at Pittsburgh.[1] The boat had been designed by William Chapman, Sr., formerly of London, since 1827 of New York and Philadelphia. In reality, the whole Chapman family had planned it. That master craftsman, Cyrus Brown, had built it. With little ceremony but with much pride both builder and family watched the small craft, no larger than a keel boat, slide off the ways and bob jerkily onto the Ohio. William Chapman, Sr.; his wife, Sarah; their two sons, William, Jr. and George; their two daughters, Caroline and Therese Sarah; William, Jr.'s wife, Phoebe, a gifted musician whom he had married three years before leaving England; Grandmother Chapman; the grandson, Harry, aged nine, son of Samuel who had died in Philadelphia the year before: they were all there, tense, tired, and happy, for this boat was to be not only their profession but also their home and their great adventure.[2] "Mama Chapman" probably said least and

[1] This date has been ascertained from the stage records of the New York and Philadelphia theatres. There the Chapman names consistently appear from 1827, the date of the family's arrival from England, until the Spring of 1831, after which date they are absent. The father's name never reappears, and the children's names only after 1840, and then with the statement that they have been on their father's river-theatre.

[2] George Chapman three years later married a newly acquired member of the cast, Mrs. Mary Ross Parks, and several years later Therese married the actor William B. Hamilton at Jackson, Mississippi. Bernard and Elizabeth Chapman had remained in England. In 1838 Pud Stanley, of Texas sojourn before and after, joined the cast to play the lead role in "Richard III."

[9]

felt most when the white flag took the breeze and proclaimed in her red-piquéd letters the name Floating Theatre.

These Chapmans, America's first showboat family, were labeled by early dramatic critics also America's most remarkable theatre family. Noah Ludlow wrote that he had never met elsewhere in the profession of the stage a group possessing such versatility and unusual ability. Certainly few families could boast of a richer theatrical back-ground or of more talent in the immediate home circle. William Chapman, Sr., whose ancestors had played lead-roles in London thea-tres for more than a century, had been born in England in 1760, and had himself played with Mrs. Siddons at Covent Garden as early as 1803. As a young man he had joined Richardson's Travelling Theatre, at that time one of the principal road-shows of its kind in the British Isles. This company visited fairs throughout England, traveling, ex-hibiting, and lodging in their own vans, a significant fact which un-doubtedly contributed the basic idea of the "river-van" to Chapman.

Financial distress amounting to famine came to English actors in 1826. As the elder Booth wrote from England to his father in America in February, 1826:

The distress is so excessive . . . that men look upon each other doubtful if they shall defend their own, or steal their neighbor's property. Famine stares all England in the face. As for the theatres, they are not thought of, much less patronized. The emigration to America will be very numerous, as it is hardly possible for the middling classes to keep body and soul together.

William Chapman and his family became a part of this histrionic exodus to America, arriving in New York during the summer of 1827. The next two seasons found him playing numerous roles at the Bowery Theatre—*Billy Lackaday* ("Sweethearts and Wives"), *Henry* ("Richard III"), *Iago* ("Othello"), *Polonius* ("Hamlet"), and *Sir Arthur* ("Metamora"). He was a steady, respectable actor in por-traying all the heavy or declamatory old men, though he was capable of infusing life and spirit into characters of a more humorous cast. His contemporaries never forgot the night he was playing the *Ghost* ("Hamlet"), in armor, and walked on the stage still wearing his spectacles. The titter in the audience swelled to a roar before Chap-man became conscious of the cause of the laughter!

The children of William Chapman were as gifted as their father. The oldest, Samuel, born in London in 1799, had appeared, like his father, at Covent Garden Theatre. He came to the United States with the family in 1827, bringing his own five-year-old son, Harry. From his arrival he was a great favorite in Philadelphia, where he played almost constantly until his untimely death, caused by a fall from a horse, in 1830. The year before, he had married a second wife, Elizabeth Jefferson, daughter of "Old Joe" Jefferson of stage fame, and had become co-manager of the Walnut Street Theatre in Philadelphia. Both facts suggest quick recognition of his ability.

Samuel had a twin brother, William B. Chapman, Jr. He, too, began his dramatic career at the Covent Garden Theatre and came to America with his father in 1827. In the same year he was received as "an excellent comedian" when he made his first American appearances as *Crack* ("The Turnpike Gate") and as *Billy Lackaday* ("Sweethearts and Wives"). Critics of the day credit him with more than ordinary ability, and twenty years later he was to achieve fame as the finest comedian in California. The third son, George, who took the stage name of "Mr. Greenwood," essayed heavy roles, appearing during 1830 in both New York and Philadelphia. He and his youngest sister Therese Sarah were the least talented of all the Chapman clan. Of him Noah Ludlow could only say that as a melodramatic actor he "was not bad," scant praise from that usually enthusiastic and voluble gentleman. Therese was too young to have had stage experience before the launching of the floating theatre at Pittsburgh.

Caroline, next to the youngest Chapman child, born in England in 1818, was the most gifted member of the family. At the age of twelve she appeared, under the stage name of "Miss Greenwood," as *Betty Finniken* in "Gretna Green" at the Philadelphia Walnut Street Theatre, where her brother Samuel was manager. Later dramatic critics, from New York to San Francisco, never tired of praising her through a vivid and versatile career.

By 1831 the characteristically American belief that happiness and success lay in the West prevailed everywhere. Some even suggested that the achievements of the East might be merely a prelude to a fuller and a final accomplishment in the regions beyond. Andrew Jackson, already two years in the White House, was emphasizing the West, the section from which he had come.

The stage, particularly of New York and Philadelphia, shared this intense interest in the vast region on the other side of the Alleghenies, much of it only recently purchased from Napoleon. Such well-known actors and managers as Drake, Macready, Forrest, Booth, Sol Smith, Ludlow, and Caldwell had toured the Mississippi Valley and had brought back to the East glowing accounts of stage opportunities.

It is not surprising that the Chapmans determined to go West, for here was that very lure which four years before had drawn them from their native England. Furthermore they were clannish, with a strong desire to remain together, and no single theatre was willing to give the whole family employment. They set out by stagecoach for Pittsburgh, hoping to work their way on beyond into the heart of the frontier, as far as people lived who loved a play. Arriving early in June, they found a thriving Pittsburgh of about twenty thousand people, "sunk in sin and sea-coal," where England's Mrs. Frances Trollope, that frank critic of American culture, could hear only the splashing of tobacco juice, a sound that formed "a running accompaniment of thorough bass" to all other activities.

Pittsburgh was no more hospitable to Chapman than it was to be to his successors.[3] The city's first brick theatre was not to be constructed for another year, and the Luke Usher frame theatre, in which Drake and Ludlow had performed fifteen years earlier, was temporarily occupied, Chapman found, by a machine shop. Indeed all Pittsburgh seemed similarly transformed. A boom was on. The whole city had become a great workshop, with only one thought, and that was to build boats—flatboats, keelboats, barges, and the newest and finest of them all, steamboats. Since the ORLEANS had been launched in 1812, enthusiasm and capital had combined to make the young Pittsburgh the boat-building center for the nation. Apparently the new occupation had left scant thought or space for the drama.

According to legend, William Chapman with difficulty persuaded the keeper of the Old Red Lion Hotel, on the bank of the Allegheny River on the north side of town, to rent him lodgings for his family, and, each evening after supper, also the dining room for the presentation of plays. The good landlord feared that the presence of actors, especially since their number included women, might injure the reputation of his house, but he was reassured when Chapman promised that the chief fare would be Shakespeare.

No record exists of the plans and the arguments of the Chapmans

[3] Pittsburgh is the single large city along the rivers to preserve only scanty records of the showboats. It early acquired a reputation of being a difficult place for actors: it was here that the worldly-wise Sol Smith had most trouble in eluding the bailiffs, and it was here, years later, that the showboat GOLDENROD's villain got himself tossed into the river. Yet the city must be given credit for producing Stephen Foster, born there July 4, 1826, who was to create some of the showboats' most treasured songs.

between their first performance in the Old Red Lion dining room and the launching of their theatre boat three months later. Yet the imagination easily bridges the gap. The conditions were these: a clannish family, well trained in the drama with a strong professional ideal that looked not so much toward stardom as toward a warm and unified domestic arrangement; a past that included both traveling and lodging in vans; an immediate environment difficult in the matter of available lodgings and theatres, but very enthusiastic in the matter of river boats and the new uses to which they were being put; a desire to travel through a region where the rivers were almost the only means of transportation and where the inhabitants were said to be drama-hungry. The showboat was the inevitable result. Certainly it represented a characteristic development on the frontier, the adapting of an Eastern institution to the Western environment. Few families ever realize so completely their ideal as the Chapmans probably did when they climbed aboard their FLOATING THEATRE.

Eleven people embarked on the drama barge on that July evening in 1831. For in addition to the nine members of the family, there were two unidentified persons, one a riverman and the other an unnamed extra actor. The plan was to drift with the current down the Ohio and the Mississippi, stopping for a one-night performance at each river landing where an audience seemed likely, and in late winter to sell or junk the boat at New Orleans. If the experiment proved enjoyable and self-supporting, they planned to return to Pittsburgh by steamer, build another boat, and repeat the trip the next year.

A surviving woodcut shows that the boat was crudely constructed, resembling a large garage set down on a small barge. It was a little more than one hundred feet long and sixteen feet wide. A contemporary, the redoubtable Noah Ludlow himself, writes his impression of the boat into his sparkling *Dramatic Life As I Found It:*

I beheld a large flat-boat, with a rude kind of house built upon it having a ridge-roof, above which projected a staff with a flag attached, upon which was plainly visible the word "Theatre." This singular object attracted my attention as it was lying tied up at the landing in Cincinnati, and on my making inquiries in regard to it, I learned that it was used for a theatrical company, under the management of a Mr. Chapman, "floating down the ribber of de O-hi-o," as the negro melody has it. They did not play while there . . . They were on their winding way to New Orleans, and, as I heard afterwards, stopped at every town or village on the banks of the river where they supposed they could get together a sufficient audience.

The enclosed portion of the boat, measuring one hundred feet long and fourteen feet wide, was divided into a narrow, shallow stage at the stern (the front of the theatre), a pit in the middle for the white audience, and a small gallery at the bow (the rear of the theatre) for colored people. White muslin draw-curtains and tallow candle footlights equipped the stage. Hard board benches, securely fastened down, ran the entire width of the boat. Though these were without backs or cushions, audiences have testified that the only undesirable seats were exactly in the center, under the tallow-dropping chandelier, which was a hogshead hoop with candles attached.

This hardy British family adapted itself to the river with remarkable ease. No Chapman boat ever suffered fatal difficulty with sand bars, sawyers, traffic or any of the other numerous dangers of the river. The whole cast—men and women—lent a hand with the large scoops or sweeps when the boat was to be moved in to shore. Since at first there was no advance advertising and therefore no schedule to meet, if either fish or friends in a particular cove proved attractive, the Chapmans were likely to tie up for several days. Living seemed far more important to this gay and irrepressible family than wealth or professional success, and tales of their adventures spread all up and down the rivers. Their chief diversion was fishing. Sol Smith records that during the "waits" the actors amused themselves by dropping a line over the stern. At Friar's Point, Mississippi, during a performance of the "Stranger," when father Chapman was playing the *Stranger* and son William the role of *Francis,* there was a longer-than-usual stage wait.

"Francis! Francis!" called the *Stranger.* (No reply.)

"Francis! Francis!" he called again. (A longer pause.)

"Francis!!" and this time it was the irate father calling rather than the play-character.

A very distant voice: "Coming, Sir!" (A considerable pause, interrupted by an audible thud on the deck above, during which the *Stranger* walks up and down, *à la* Macready, in a great rage.)

Francis (entering): "Here I am, Sir."

Stranger: "Why did you not come when I called?"

Francis: "Why, Sir, I was just hauling in one of the damnedest biggest catfish you ever saw."

It was some minutes before the laughter of the audience allowed the play to go on.

At one settlement on the Indiana shore, a group of village dandies became offended because they were not admitted for half-price, the regular price being half a dollar for adults. They hung around, nursing their disappointment, and when the play was well under way they cut the boat loose from its moorings, and it drifted more than a mile down the current before it could be brought to shore. The disgruntled spectators trudged home as good-humoredly as could be expected, and probably dealt out justice in the village next morning.

The Chapmans always started their annual tour at Pittsburgh, drifting down the Ohio and the Mississippi. Sometimes they poled their boat up the wild Arkansas and the still wilder White River, where occasionally they had to use bird shot to repel ruffians who would have boarded them by force. They *bushwhacked* and *cordelled* their way up the narrow and picturesque Green River, which was in later years to become showboaters' paradise. They tied up at hundreds of landings for one-night stands, where the inhabitants had never seen a play. A peck of potatoes or yams, two gallons of fruit, a side of bacon, or fifty cents, preferably the last, was the usual price of admission; children and negroes, half price. Sometimes they stopped also at larger towns, such as Point Pleasant, Memphis, Port Gibson, and Vicksburg, where usually they gave a series of performances. One gentleman in Natchez records in his diary that he attended the "Chapman Boat Show" four times between February 7 and February 22, 1834, and labels the entry for February 20, "50¢ to Miss Chapman's benefit." [4]

The Chapmans soon learned that, in order to avoid the morning winds, which seriously impeded the progress of the boat with its expanse of bulk above the water-line, they should start as early as 3:00 A.M. on their next jump, normally not more than twenty miles. When they arrived at the new stand, well before noon, two of the men, usually William, Jr. and George, went ashore to advertise the performance. A "town crier" was employed to walk through the streets, blowing a trumpet—the calliope had not been invented—and announcing the play and a free concert. Circulars prepared by Phoebe Chapman were tacked on trees or at prominent corners in the village. These were modest announcements of facts, not in the least resembling the extravagantly phrased posters of a later date. The

[4] The trail of the Chapmans is clearly marked in such sources as the Memphis *Enquirer*, the Port Gibson *Correspondent*, the Vicksburg *Register*, the Natchez *Free Trader*, and the Johnson Memorial Collection (Louisiana State University Archives, Baton Rouge).

afternoon was devoted to laying in needed supplies at the village store, rehearsing, and fishing. The concert began at 7:30, the first four numbers from the top deck, the last three from the front of the stage; the curtain was pulled at the ringing of a bell at eight, and all was over by ten o'clock. The elder Chapman liked to stand at the exit to bid each of his guests goodnight. Then he raised the gangplank, and all hands slept until three the next morning.

The Chapman boat emphasized drama more than any other show-boat ever on the rivers, for William Chapman was an actor long before he was a riverman. The program for an evening's entertainment was likely to consist of a play, followed by a monologue elocutionized in the manner of the day, sketches and impersonations, and musical numbers and dances. The play most frequently performed was Dunlap's version of Kotzebue's "Stranger," [5] a comedy rich in a great variety of emotional effects. Less frequently it was "Cinderella," the old fairy tale—not the opera—embellished with music and additional story-characters. A typical playbill reads:

This Evening, Saturday, 1st Oct., will be
performed Kotzebue's play of the
STRANGER
With a variety of Singing. To conclude
with the farce of
PERFECTION
Great care has been taken to render the
Wharf commodious for ladies.
Memphis, Oct. 1.

On rare occasions, and only by the special request of the community, the play performed was "Hamlet," with the emphasis on the emotional Ophelia rather than the intellectual Hamlet. Thus did these British Chapmans, with the tradition of Covent Garden in their keeping, slip into the mold of the new locale, adapting their presentation, even the very substance of the plays, to the peculiar requirements of the new region. The medium must be, they found, emotional rather than intellectual.

Acting on the boat was better than mediocre. William Chapman, Sr. had the rich ideal of the English stage behind him. His forte was serious and sentimental old men. His son, William, Jr., was labeled by

[5] William Dunlap's Americanized version was first performed December 7, 1798, in New York. During the 1830's it was made immensely popular by the acting of Thomas Barry.

the critics of later years as one of America's most capable comedians. He was at his best in such characters as *Billy Black*, "with original conundrums," in the "Hundred-Pound Note." But the star of the boat was undoubtedly Caroline Chapman, playing under the name "Miss Greenwood." She and her brother made a splendid comedy team. Though her features were plain and rather irregular, she was slender and radiant, while her lovely dark eyes "could convey at a glance more meaning," says one admirer, "than any contemporary feminine optics on the New York stage." Her vibrant personality, as well as her exquisite dancing, probably accounts for her unprecedented versatility; on one occasion she played seven parts in one performance. Her best roles, however, were characters of low-life comedy, chambermaids and rustics, and comic singing characters. When occasion demanded, she did not hesitate to resort to Italian *bravura* and burlesque. Her half-comic, half-sentimental songs, such as "Suzanne," high-lighted an evening's entertainment for many a man and woman who had never before heard a song from behind footlights. After she left the rivers, to become immensely popular at McGuire's palatial Jenny Lind Theatre in San Francisco and at Burton's Chambers Street Theatre in New York, the critics were amazed that she could have been trained under her father's "aquatic management," and further amazed that New York had not found her earlier. Certainly her genius for delighting common people could have had no better maturing than her experience on the Mississippi showboat. Though past master of all the rules and traditions, she had learned from her river experience that most of this ritual could be laid aside.

With such a star and such a family on board, it is little wonder that the Chapman FLOATING THEATRE was successful. Both the acting and the showboat itself were nicely adapted to the environment. Only the difficulty of navigating upstream remained.

Tyrone Power, writing from Bayou Sara in 1835, neatly summarized contemporary opinion of the Chapmans:

This floating theatre, about which I make constant inquiry, and which I yet hope to fall in with, is not the least original or singular speculation ventured on these waters. It was projected and is carried on by the Elder Chapman, well known for many years as a Covent Garden actor; his practice is to have a building erected upon a raft at some point high up the Mississippi, or one of its tributaries. Whence he takes his departure early in the fall, with scenery, dresses, and decorations, all prepared for representation. At each village or large plantation he hoists banner and blows trumpet and few who love a play suffer his ark to pass the door, since they know it is to return no more until the next year; for, however easy may prove the downward course of the drama's temple, to retrograde, upwards, is quite beyond its power. Sometimes a large steamer from Louisville, with a thousand souls on board, will command a play whilst taking in fuel, when the profit must be famous. The *corps dramatique* is, I believe, principally composed of members of his own family, which is numerous, and, despite of alligators and yellow fever, likely to increase and flourish. When the Mississippi theatre reaches New Orleans, it is abandoned and sold for firewood; the manager and troop returning in a steamer to build a new one, with such improvements as increased experience may have suggested. This course Mr. Chapman has pursued for three or four seasons back, and, as I am told by many who have encountered this aquatic company, very profitably. I trust he may continue to do so until he makes a fortune, and can bequeath to his kin the undisputed sovereignty of the Mississippi circuit.

Prosperity did come to the Chapmans. In 1836 [6] they were able to substitute for their drifting flatboat a fully equipped, though small, steamboat, "fitted up very comfortably after the manner of a theatre," with a stage twenty feet wide and six feet deep. River traffic was already getting too heavy for safe drifting. Furthermore they could now make the return trip upstream instead of junking their boat at New Orleans and building a new one at Pittsburgh each spring. The new arrangement meant, too, the adding of much rich territory, for now they could ascend such tributaries as the Wabash, the Green, the Tennessee, the sluggish Yazoo, and even tiny Bayou Sara. At last the showboat was on even terms with the rivers.

But the new boat brought new troubles. Along with the painted scenery came also a new curtain, a real drop, on which was painted in oils a girl dipping her bare foot in the cooling waters of a spring. This daring picture of a woman's naked ankle and ten inches above shocked the women so badly, especially when their men remarked on it, that some left before the show was over. The scene was painted out before the end of the season.

Probably the most disturbing adventure ever to befall the Chapmans occurred at Natchez, Mississippi, on July 29, 1837. The FLOATING THEATRE had visited the town first in 1834, tying up at Natchez-under-the-Hill, and playing to a rowdy audience. Since that engagement they had drifted far and wide along the Great River and its tributaries and had learned much about river audiences. They were

[6] This date is established by a notice in the Memphis *Enquirer*, Sept. 29, 1836, p. 2, announcing the coming of "Chapman's Theatrical Steamboat." Earlier advertising had announced "Chapman's Floating Theatre."

no longer operating on a shoestring, for along with their new steamboat they had acquired a crew and cast of twenty-one, of whom five
were actresses and eight actors. Furthermore their reputation for
good performances had spread abroad, for the *Picayune* promised
that the St. Charles Theatre would be filled for them if they would
visit New Orleans. The Natchez *Free Trader* of July 14, 1837, announced that the "Ark of the Drama" would soon be moored below
the city. The Chapman corps, the editorial continued, "are well
trained and have succeeded in extracting as many 'grins' from the
semi-civilized hunter and mountain boatman as they have witching
smiles and sighs of sentiment from the accomplished belles of the
famed sunny clime." The editor facetiously added, "They have
enough comedy on hand to make the banks resume specie payment
and banish the pressure of the times" (1837 was a depression year),
and "they will certainly be as welcome as was Noah's household on
the top of Ararat after they had *done* the drama of the deluge."

But Chapman did not plan to perform on his steamboat at Natchez.
Because the river landing was "a little way out of the elite and
fashion," and probably also because he was remembering his former
visit,[7] he hoped to rent the Main Street Theatre, which was certainly
more commodious than his boat. The renting of that theatre brought
on the whole trouble.

The company did not arrive promptly, because of an unscheduled
engagement up the river. They had stopped at Fort Adams for a one-
night stand, and while there they were induced to play almost a week
at nearby Woodville. From that village Chapman sent J. Hamilton
to Natchez as his agent to rent the theatre. But Hamilton found that
the man who had the legal right to rent the building, a Mr. Burns,
was out of town, and therefore applied to Horace Gridley, another
stockholder, who was proprietor of a hotel next door to the playhouse. Gridley, with or without legal right, was nevertheless anxious
to have the theatre in operation because of the increased business for
him in the sale of "iced punch and delicacies," and agreed with Hamilton on a rental of sixty dollars per week for the building.

In due time Chapman arrived. The usual printed bills were distributed, and as evening approached, the theatre was lighted and the

---

[7] It is entirely possible that Chapman had not heard of the purging of Natchez-
under-the-Hill by fire and flood. The blacklegs had been expelled, their rookeries
annihilated, and the character of the section largely changed since his former
visit.

acting corps installed in the dressing rooms. At this moment Burns, who believed that he had the sole right to rent the theatre, returned to town, apparently hysterical with rage. He had Chapman arrested on a twenty-thousand-dollar damage suit, and hurried him through the streets to the city jail in full view of the theatre-goers, who were by this time strolling toward the playhouse to see the expected performance. Chapman remained in prison until midnight, when he was bailed out by Gridley. At the hearing next day Chapman agreed to pay all costs and surrender the playhouse, and Burns agreed to withdraw the damage suit. The episode cost Chapman a total of $348— including $200 for Burns' lawyers (apparently Chapman had none of his own), $108 for "jail fees," and $40 for advertising performances which did not take place. These figures do not take into account the expenses of the idle crew and cast.[8]

Two nights later Chapman opened on board his vessel, now advertised as the STEAMBOAT THEATRE. Perhaps he was trying to retrieve his serious financial loss. Certainly he found the complexion of the waterfront changed, and his entire audience this time came from the Hill and the surrounding plantations. After an unusually long stand, almost three weeks, he pulled out for New Orleans, hurried along by local rumors of yellow fever. He never again visited Natchez.

Exactly ten years after the elder Chapman had launched his first FLOATING THEATRE, he died on board his boat, near Cincinnati, where he was making plans to build a larger steamboat.[9] The new boat was nevertheless completed the next year, and was successfully operated by Mrs. Chapman under the name CHAPMAN'S FLOATING PALACE. She sold to Sol Smith in 1847, after the children had long since left the River, and retired with a modest fortune.[10]

The great adventure of the Chapmans did much to set the pattern for the American showboat. In the first place, they were a *family*, only semi-commercial in interests and strong in wholesome domestic relationships—a fact that operated to combat the unsavory reputation

[8] The Natchez *Courier*, unsympathetic with Chapman, stated that his jail fees were only $3.50, "which he never paid." Chapman's figure may have included sheriff's, justice's, and other fees. Sources include: Natchez *Free Trader*, June 23, July 14, and 28, 1837; *Tri-Weekly Free Trader*, August 1, 3, and 5, 1837; Power, *Impressions of America*, II, 177; Free, *The Theatre of Southwestern Mississippi*, I, 320.

[9] A few authorities, probably following the sparkling but erratic Ludlow, give the date as 1839 and the place as Manchester (now Yazoo City), Mississippi.

[10] The Chapman children continued their brilliant careers on the stages of San Francisco and New York.

Courtesy Miss Clarkie McNair

Capt. A. B. French in 1902

Capt. Callie French in 1907

of existing river entertainment, to restore the confidence of river-people in the drama, and to emphasize the restful, perhaps over-sentimental atmosphere of the future showboat. In the second place, these Chapmans, all born on British soil and trained in the British acting tradition, as they floated on American rivers, presented old material adapted to the new setting. And last, they performed honest service, providing many citizens of the new region with the only taste of make-believe they were ever to enjoy. Wherever they played and danced and sang, they spread the charm and geniality of the showboat in its purest form.

It all adds up to an ideal for the future showboat.

The success and fame enjoyed by the Chapman boat brought imitators and followers. Unfortunately, most of these forgot their model. During the 1840's and 1850's dozens of small showboats swarmed over the river systems of the Middle West, bringing entertainment to hundreds of river landings. These make-shift shows emphasized legitimate drama and professional acting far less than had the Chapman family, with a corresponding increase in song-joke-dance and even lecture entertainment. In fact, both on and off the rivers, the average American during the 1840's preferred to attend lectures on such subjects as mesmerism, animal magnetism, phrenology, and the new phenomenon of the electric telegraph rather than witness the legitimate drama. Religious revivals were in vogue, and the public was devoted to circuses, pantomimes, displays of fireworks, and museums of artificial and natural wonders. Accordingly the river shows had to temper their offerings more and more with "instructive and moral" features. These small boats—few of them seated more than two hundred—played at villages without newspapers or printing facilities—one reason that few records of them exist. Writers of the time, like Ralph Keeler, seemed to consider the showboat such a common occurrence as scarcely to merit individual mention.[11]

A few of these small boat-shows, however, managed to escape oblivion. Sol Smith [12] purchased the Chapman FLOATING PALACE in

[11] Keeler (b. in Ohio, 1840) in his *Vagabond Adventures* (p. 219) records seeing the showboat BANJO in 1849, and he himself played wench impersonations on at least two showboats. In 1873 he went to Cuba as special correspondent for the New York *Tribune,* and mysteriously disappeared, probably murdered and thrown into the sea.

[12] Solomon Franklin Smith was born in a log cabin at Norwich, New York, in 1801, the son of a fifer in the Revolutionary War. At nine years of age he

1847 at the time of Mrs. Chapman's retirement. This man, affec-
tionately called "Old Sol" throughout the South and West, was
the best known comedian in the section. He barnstormed from
Charleston to St. Louis, from Cincinnati to New Orleans. In partnership with Noah Ludlow he established and managed theatres at Louisville, St. Louis, Mobile, and New Orleans. He made the comic character *Mawworm* in "The Hypocrite" beloved throughout the play-
going nation. In spare moments he served as printer, editor, lawyer,
minister, and author. Versatile, thrifty, resilient, audaciously humorous, he was as much a product of the pioneer country as the showboat itself. In his Yankee wisdom, he remarked that money is

the talisman which unlocks all hearts; the balsam that heals all wounds;
the creator of respect, esteem, friendship, love!—Without it, a man is
neglected, abandoned, and scorned—with it, he springs into rank; is
courted, fawned upon, worshipped. . . . Money worthless! Nonsense!

It is characteristic of Smith that after hearing stories of the prosperity
of the showboats, he could not resist buying the Chapman FLOATING
PALACE, the best of them all.

But Sol was not to remain long in the showboat business. At Cincinnati he stocked up with provisions, new scenery, and a respectable
company of actors, hoping to carry his funny-man jokes and his character of *Mawworm* to every landing on the rivers. But when only a
day's journey below the city, he collided with a heavy steamboat,
which split his five-year-old showboat exactly into halves. Smith and
all members of the company managed to swim ashore, and with much
difficulty scrambled up the precipitous clay bank. But they had to
walk until daylight before reaching shelter and food. The boat was
a total loss. Small wonder that Smith omitted his showboat experiences

------

became self-supporting. He devoted the years from 1827 to 1853 to the drama,
most of them in the West. His tomb in Bellefontaine Cemetery, St. Louis, bears
the inscription:

Sol Smith, Retired Actor
1801–1869

"Life's but a walking shadow, a poor player,
    That struts and frets his hour upon the stage,
    And then is heard no more."

"All the world's a stage
    And all the men and women merely players."
Exit Sol

from his memoirs! [13] His only hope of avoiding the ridicule of Ludlow, his partner and rival, was to conceal this whole affair. Rumors
of other showboat activities both of Smith and of Ludlow were current on the rivers for years, but no further record has survived.

On the upper Mississippi the principal showboat during the pre-
Civil-War period was the steamer BANJO, which belonged to "Dr."
G. R. Spaulding, the owner and manager of several circuses of the
time. She first appeared in 1849 at Cape Girardeau on her way downstream to St. Louis and Alton. She was last recorded ten years later
at St. Paul. The little steamer, only eighty feet long, was fitted up in
theatre fashion, with a stage fully equipped with drops, scenery, and
footlights, and with a pit seating an audience of two hundred. She
carried what was then termed a "nigger show."

That last fact is significant. In the first place, it meant that the activity of the boat would necessarily be restricted to the Northern
rivers, for with such a program on board the BANJO would not dare
play south of Cairo. In the second place, it meant that some of the
showboats had picked up the newest in American entertainment, the
fast developing Negro minstrel show. "Daddy" Rice [14] in 1831 had
created his character "Jim Crow" from a Negro livery stable boy
with a queer old tune and a ludicrous limp. Soon all the Northern
portions of the United States, as well as England, were singing and
jumping:

> *Wheel about, turn about,*
> *Do jis so,*
> *An' ebery time I wheel about*
> *I jump Jim Crow.*

[13] It is ironically amusing that only a few months before this mishap, Sol Smith
had written his comic "Proceedings of the Convention of Snags and Sawyers,
held at the Grave-yard, in the Mississippi River, December 31, 1946," evidently
the kind of danger he had been warned of (*Theatrical Management* . . . , p.
203).

[14] Thomas Darmouth Rice (1808–1860), the creator of "Jim Crow," should not
be confused with Dan Rice (1823–1900), the American clown and owner of a
steamboat circus. Thackeray pays this tribute to the minstrelsy of the day: "I
heard a humorous balladist not long since, a minstrel with wool . . . who performed a negro ballad that I confess moistened these spectacles in a most unexpected manner. They have gazed at dozens of tragedy-queens dying on the stage
and expiring in appropriate blank verse, and I never wanted to wipe them. They
have looked up, with deep respect be it said, at many scores of clergymen without being dimmed, and behold! a vagabond with a corked face and a banjo sings
a little song, strikes a wild note, which sets the heart thrilling with happy pity."

Roustabouts on the rivers, between jobs, patted Juba and jumped Jim Crow; they cut the Pigeon's Wing and manipulated the Long Dog Scratch, often devising impromptu parts that later became traditional. Add a banjo, the fiddle, interject a few conundrums and jokes, and the minstrel pattern becomes complete.

It was much the same on board the BANJO. After an "overture" of music and repartee, the performers arranged themselves in a semicircle on the stage, with Bones at one end and Tambo at the other; in the catch-questioning and jokes that followed the pompous Middle Man was always worsted. Then came exhibitions of banjo and fiddle playing, interspersed with sentimental ballads and comic songs. The concluding walk-around, such as "Lucy Long," was likely to break up at the end into individual impromptu stunts. No formal drama was attempted, though on rare occasions burlesque skits, usually of a political nature, were added. Some of the players were Negroes, some white, yet all cork-blacked their faces. The show stopped at every landing that promised a crowd, with an average run per day of less than twenty miles. Certainly the little BANJO made a unique contribution both to minstrelsy and to showboat history.

The showboats HURON on the Little Miami Canal (Ohio), the first DIXIE, on the Wabash Canal, and the MISSISSIPPI RIVER BOAT MINSTRELS, on the Northern Mississippi, also featured minstrel programs, with such stars aboard as Willis Sweatnam and Fred Sprung.

The theatre-boats were also invading the East. With the opening of the Erie Canal in 1825—that great 400-mile artery between the Northeastern United States and what was then the West—the growth of towns between Albany and Buffalo was rapid. Troupes of actors filtered into the region, eager to profit from an amusement-hungry population, but to their disappointment they found very few theatres. What was still more disturbing, they found themselves, "for moral reasons," barred from suitable makeshifts, such as churches and school houses, which could be rented only by lecturers, elocutionists, and concert companies.

Henry Butler, an old theatrical manager who was attempting to operate a company in the Mohawk Valley, found a solution to the problem. A canalboat could serve for both transportation and theatre. Accordingly he fitted up a traveling theatre and museum and started out from Troy, New York, in the early summer of 1836. His stay at any one town varied from one day to a week, depending upon the size of the community and the volume of business. During the day he exhibited the museum part of his show, which contained the usual concomitants—stuffed birds and tigers, wax figures of General Washington, Captain Kidd, and the twelve apostles, and phrenological charts. In the evening his small company of actors performed a blood-red melodrama on the little stage at the stern of the boat.

For years Butler sailed up and down the Canal with his play-ship until advancing age and blindness forced him gradually to retire. He first dispensed with the theatre activities and devoted his entire boat to the museum. He did not let his blindness keep him from active duty, and exhibition hours always found him in the little ticket office, selling thirty-cent tickets to adults and ten-cent tickets to children. He ascertained the age of the buyer by placing a hand upon his head to judge his height, often with comic results.

In 1845, New York City got its first taste of showboating. Plans were made early in the year to convert a steamboat, lying at the foot of Spring Street on North River, into a floating theatre by sinking a pit through the main deck and raising a tier of boxes above the promenade deck, with a forty-foot stage in the stern. After a brief New York showing, it was to tour the Hudson and then Long Island Sound.

By the first of April all was ready, and the New York *Courier and Enquirer* carried this advertisement:

TEMPLE OF THE MUSES

The Public is most respectfully informed that this Novel and Splendid Establishment, erected in the form of a Theatre, on a large Man-of-War Built Steamship, at an enormous expense; and large enough to accommodate an audience of 2000 persons, will open for a few evenings before leaving New York, near the foot of Canal Street. On Wednesday Evening, April 2nd, 1845. Admission to the Dress Circle, 50 cents—Parquett, 25 cents—Private Boxes, $3.

Accordingly the doors of the TEMPLE OF THE MUSES opened at six o'clock, April 2, and the curtain rose at seven. The program, as printed in the New York *Evening Mirror* for that date, consisted of an original address spoken in character by Mrs. Sutherland; a laughable vaudeville, "The Alpine Maid," starring Mrs. Mossap and Mr. and Mrs. Sutherland; Saunders' Revolutionary sketch, "Our Flag; or Nailed to the Mast"; and a farce entitled "A Lady and Gentleman in a Peculiarly Perplexing Predicament." In other words, exactly the same fare as was being offered in the cheaper theatres of the city. (The

better houses were already featuring minstrel shows.) Evidently the
TEMPLE OF THE MUSES and its program were both well received, for
two days later the *Evening Mirror* reported that the audience on the
opening night had been "of fair size" and "highly respectable." For
more than a month the boat continued to present vaudeville, melodrama, and popular comedy at the docks of various streets touching
the East River. Suddenly it dropped completely out of the records.
We may suppose that it fulfilled its original purpose of playing the
Hudson River and Long Island Sound.

The success of the TEMPLE OF THE MUSES inspired another such
venture in New York, for in October of 1845 a floating theatre, "resembling a huge meeting house" and comfortably seating twelve
hundred persons, tied up at the wharf on Fulton Street. Palmo's
Burlesque Opera Company, under the management of D. S. Harris,
gave first a grand concert, and then played "La Som-Am-Bull-Ole."
Prices were popular: box seats twenty-five cents, seats in the pit
twelve and a half cents, and private boxes two dollars. Precautions
were taken that no charges of moral laxity could be made against the
enterprise, for the advertisement stated that the saloon of the theatre
would be opened with "Temperance Refreshments" and that an efficient police would preserve order. This floating company gave thirteen performances in Brooklyn, and then, as suddenly and as completely as the earlier boat, dropped out of sight.

These city boats, with their large seating capacity, had no part in
the earlier showboat's mission of serving the frontier, and lacked
entirely the ideals of the Chapman boat. In fact the showboat that for
more than three decades had brought wholesome entertainment to
the people along the rivers was suffering serious deterioration. River
grafters and medicine shows brought disrepute, for "putting on a
show" had become the last resort of the incompetent along the rivers.
Broken-down gamblers and deck hands who had learned ventriloquism became especially proficient as impromptu showmen.

Here is a true story: A gambler, a medicine peddler, a fiddler, a
house-painter and his wife were living in three shanty boats on the
southern bank of the Ohio. There was not a dollar among them all.
They tried selling medicine, picking cotton, drifting for logs, fishing,
trapping, and junking, without success. When they discussed the
very pressing matter of something to eat, they decided on a show.
The gambler knew some flashy card tricks, the medicine man could
make a stump speech and play the banjo, the woman could sing, the

fiddler was almost an artist, and the painter could sell tickets and keep order. They had a rehearsal in the morning, and in the afternoon two of the men went up the bank to advertise. That night they performed and took in ten dollars. A week later the "troupe" broke up, with money in every pocket.

The medicine boats were especially pernicious. Such a boat usually carried only a lecturer and music, dropping from landing to landing, attracting a crowd and then selling its wares. A few of these shows, however, were more elaborate. One boat gave a play featuring a woman in search of health as the heroine. She was portrayed as going from place to place seeking a remedy, without avail. The villain led her obviously away from the real cure, until at last the hero rescued her and gave her the magic dose—taking which she became wonderfully well and marvelously beautiful. And then the lecturer offered the same concoction at fifty cents the bottle, or three bottles for one dollar. Another boat sold a lotion guaranteed to turn colored people white.

Disreputable characters of every description were thus quick to take advantage of the opportunity created by the showboat, until the rivers became so infested with these cheap mountebanks and crooks that by the late 1850's the whole institution of showboating— the good along with the bad—was looked upon with disgust by all upright citizens. Many an honest showboat was warned away from the riverfront by a hostile posse of angry townsmen who had recently been fleeced by a quack performance. Perhaps it was just as well for the showboat that the Civil War silenced for a time all shows along the rivers.[15]

[15] Principal Sources: Newspaper files, scrapbooks and manuscripts, handbills, and the Chapman Collection (The University of California).
Other Sources: Items listed in the bibliography under T. A. Brown, Asia B. Clarke, Walter P. Eaton, Joseph M. Free, Alvin F. Harlow, Carl Holliday, Arthur Hornblow, Laurence Hutton, Joseph N. Ireland, Joseph Jefferson, Noah Ludlow, George MacMinn, Brander Matthews, C. D. Odell, Tyrone Power, Helen Pratt, Herbert Quick, LeRoy Rice, Otis Skinner, Raymond Spears, Francis Wemyss, Carl Wittke, and Charles Zuber.

III

Big-top on the Rivers

Circus Boats

THE URBAN centers of the Middle West, amusement-hungry
during the two decades preceding the Civil War, enjoyed
various forms of entertainment. Thousands in these fast growing
towns saw Charles Dickens, heard Ole Bull, or listened to Jenny Lind.
They gazed at P. T. Barnum's Tom Thumb and menagerie, which
local church elders endorsed as educational. They attended lectures
on electricity and mesmerism, and paid irregular visits to land theatres.
They even turned some of their religious gatherings into social occasions of great emotional significance.

Their favorite amusement, however, was the circus, with its multiple attractions of clowns, acrobatics, minstrelsy, wild animals, equestrian acts, curious freaks and wonders, feats of magic and pseudo-
science, and stirring music. Most of the important circuses of the
region traveled by boat as a convenient means of transportation. Some
of these unloaded their show at each river town and spread their big
tent on land for the performance. But this procedure was time-
consuming and expensive, and by 1850 several circuses were exhibit-
ing on their big boats, with no unloading, setting up, or reloading.
Their arena (one ring in those days!), their properties, seating, animals, and performers were kept on board, ready for immediate exhibition wherever they tied up. For a time such circuses were called
boat-shows to distinguish them from the earlier *showboats*, but all
distinction between the two types soon disappeared, especially after
the circuses included a dramatic performance as a side attraction.

Because of their size and the large amounts of money required both
for capital and for maintenance, these boat-circuses could not be
missionaries of enlightenment to out-of-the-way places. Their im-

mensity made generous patronage necessary, and this was available only at the larger towns. They were doing for the centers of population what the smaller boats were doing for the landings. These very facts meant a much fuller chronicling of the circus boats than of the smaller showboats, since cities had newspapers and landings usually had none.

The most completely chronicled, and also the largest of these circus boats was Spaulding and Rogers' FLOATING CIRCUS PALACE, built in Cincinnati in 1851.[1] This remarkable floating amphitheatre resembled a huge box, twice the size of the St. Charles Theatre in New Orleans, at that date the largest building of its kind in the Southwest. She was almost two hundred feet long and thirty-five wide, a little larger than the biggest river steamers of that day. She had two decks, besides the texas,[2] all elaborately supplied with windows. During her first year on the river she was towed[3] by the big side-wheeler NORTH RIVER, and later by the powerful JAMES RAYMOND. Many an observer watching the energetic towboat pushing the huge Noah's ark compared them to a nervous little man escorting a ponderous woman.

On board the circus boat, the big arena, where the equestrian exhibitions and similar acts took place, was well forward. The main deck, called the Dress Circle, was fitted with one thousand cane-seat armchairs, commodiously spaced and screwed down to prevent crowding. The first gallery, called the Family Circle, boasted fifteen hundred cushioned settees, and the second gallery provided seating for nine hundred, with a section designated for Negroes. A total capacity of thirty-four hundred, not counting the standing room outside the windows, which sold for half price after all available seats

[1] Gilbert R. Spaulding (1818–1886), known on the rivers as "Doctor" Spaulding, and his partner Charles J. Rogers had operated several circuses in up-state New York in the 1840's, and Spaulding owned also the little showboats BANJO and GAZELLE (the Hannibal *Missouri Courier*, May 12, 1853; the Memphis *Commercial Appeal*, July 3, 1938; the Wheeling *Intelligencer*, May 20, 1856; the St. Louis *Daily Missouri Republican*, Aug. 9 and 10, 1852, and Aug. 4, 1856).

[2] The *texas* was the large room on the upper deck. Staterooms on river steamers during the 1870's were named after various states of the Union, such as the Virginia, the Ohio, the Alabama. The largest of the staterooms, situated on the upper or hurricane deck, was always named the Texas. Long after this practice of naming the staterooms was discontinued, the quarters on the upper deck remained the texas.

[3] The term *towed* is misleading, for the steamboat actually pushed the barge-like structure, which could be managed more easily and economically in this fashion. This method, now so common on the river, was first practiced on the unwieldy showboats.

were taken. Off the main circus arena was a museum of "curiosities
and wonders," as well as dressing rooms for the performers and stalls
for the trained horses. The cabins above, with kitchen and dining
room, were at the stern, while the reception room, business office,
and staterooms were forward, with a hallway from bow to stern.

On the towboat, the JAMES RAYMOND, an elegant concert saloon,
called the "Ridotto," featured dramatic performances, vaudeville and
minstrel entertainments.

The two boats were well provided with music. A large pipe organ
supplied the rousing tunes for the main circus performance, and a
chime of bells across the hurricane deck provided free concerts for
the crowds that invariably collected on the river bank. On the steam
towboat a twelve-piece brass band gave the concerts and played the
interludes for dramatic performances, while, after 1858, a calliope
on the texas, the first to be installed on a showboat, announced the
coming of the circus for miles inland. The whole affair was so brilliantly lighted with gas that, according to the Natchez *Courier*, it
was worth a trip to the PALACE at night merely for the effect of the
unusual illumination, visible for a great distance on the bank.

The organization of the establishment must have seemed as im-
pressive as the boat itself. Almost a hundred persons—crew, business
staff, trainers, and performers—worked and lived on board, to say
nothing of innumerable trained horses and other animals. Van Orden
was the manager of the whole floating system, and an advance man
traveled in a boat of his own, several days ahead of the PALACE, to
advertise the show and to arrange licenses. The big boat carried her
immense cargo of entertainment, at popular prices of fifty and
twenty-five cents, up and down the Allegheny, the Wabash, the Ohio,
the Upper and Lower Mississippi, and even around to Mobile. The
rivers had never seen such an efficient and well-staffed showboat before, and they were to wait years after the Civil War before anything
comparable to it again appeared.

The amphitheatre exhibited the main circus. Here the "first man"
was the great American clown William Lake, who for ten years held
the official position of Leader of the Clowns. His controversies with
the ringmaster became classics of wit and repartee. Acrobatic stunts
were much in favor. Madame Olinza, a Polish lady whose quiet
domestic life aboard was in strange contrast with her daring acrobatics, performed the feat of walking the tightrope from one corner of
the museum to the roof of the farthest gallery of the auditorium, each

precarious step punctuated by the throaty power of the pipe-organ. (That was before the time of Blondin, when wirewalking was a new sensation.) The equestrian act, with forty trained horses in the arena at one time, always delighted the spectators, especially the Waltz, when fifteen blooded chestnut mares, with fifteen plumed "beauties" (men in feminine attire) daintily perched on sidesaddles, waltzed in formation for three minutes.

The Museum, which boasted "over 100,000 curiosities," charged an additional admission fee. Besides the usual stuffed tigers, puppet dancers, and figures in wax—the twelve apostles and an inebriate Tam O'Shanter were favorites—this sideshow exhibited "Mr. Nellis, born without arms." It also featured Professor and Madame Lowe's Invisible Lady Act. The Professor, described as "an ingenious, odd sort of Yankee," with his long hair braided in two tails down his back, was a great favorite on board until he acquired an especially mischievous bear cub. Madame Lowe had formerly been a Paris dancer. Their act used a hollow brass ball with four trumpets protruding from it, suspended inside a railing. Questions put by those standing around the railing were answered through a tube by a person in the compartment below. The imaginations of the spectators made the replies seem to issue from the brass ball. The answers of the "Invisible Lady," *alias* Madame Lowe, whose English was drolly mixed with her own vernacular, must have been amusing especially to the initiated. But if the responses were sometimes unintelligible, this fact only added to the mystery and success of the brazen oracle.[4]

In the "Ridotto," the concert hall on the steam towboat, the chief fare consisted of comedy skits, vaudeville, and minstrel acts. Here was Frank Lynch, who had been taught to dance, under Barnum, by the great John Diamond, the all-time king of American minstrel dancers. Lynch, now too heavy to exert himself, had declined into the fat and slippered end man, an adept banjo player and director of the minstrel performance. Here, too, were Dave Reed, later to gain fame as a writer of such popular character songs as "Sally Comes Up," and Johnny Booker, that inimitable master of minstrel repartee. The most interesting of the burnt-cork comedians, however, was Ralph Keeler, whose name was the biggest on the billboard. He was at one time offered a post with the celebrated Christy's Minstrels in New York, the ambi-

---

[4] Lowe later achieved fame as a balloonist with the Army of the Potomac during the Civil War. The Wheeling *Intelligencer*, May 20, 1856, describes the museum.

tion of every blackface on the circuit. Madame Lowe had taught him all the posturings and pirouettes of the Paris ballet girls, insisting on using her little whip whenever he "stepped out of the line of beauty." Spaulding and Rogers featured him in jig and female impersonation dances (Parisian ballet!), with an occasional juba thrown in. It is from his *Vagabond Adventures* that we get the keenest appreciation of life on the big boat. Those on board lived a rich and varied existence. Tied up at the bank, they knew the world of cities and hurrying people; on the boat, in their own world, they trapped mockingbirds or dropped a listless line over the side for catfish or soft-shelled turtles. It is Keeler also who assures us that jealousy may be as rife on a Mississippi showboat as in the antechamber of any court in Europe. "I have known," he says, "a *danseuse* to furnish boys with clandestine bouquets to throw on the stage when she appeared; not that she cared at all for the praise or the blame of the audience, but that she *did* care to crush a cleverer rival."

The FLOATING CIRCUS PALACE was unique among showboats in that it printed, not mere circulars, as did many of the boats, but also a daily newspaper, free to performers and patrons. The press and editorial desk occupied one corner of the Museum, and many visitors no doubt found the printing of the newspaper as interesting as the other curiosities. The editor was John McCreary, a brilliant but broken-down journalist, now reduced to printing this daily paper in the Museum of the PALACE, and, on the side, selling gingerbread, colored candy, and pale red lemonade at his stand near the editorial desk.

The most frequent contributor to the *Palace Journal* was a certain "Governor" Dorr, once business manager of Mike Mitchell's Minstrels. This individual took it upon himself to write most imaginative articles for McCreary's paper upon the wonders of the Museum. With picturesque joy he would pursue, with pencil and foolscap, the history of some bogus war club through the hands and over the heads of whole dynasties of savage kings. He would send his adventurous rhetoric upon sunny sea voyages to far tropic islands after some insignificant shell, which in reality had been picked up in Long Branch. He would pour his very soul into the meltingly tender history of the wax figures, especially the stolid blue-eyed lady with the excessive black lashes and pink cheeks, who had been purchased at auction in Albany and labeled "The Empress Josephine." Or, sprawled out upon his stomach on the floor of the museum, staring in a fine frenzy straight into the distended mouth and merry glass eyes of the stuffed alligator, the ecstatic historian would compose the heart-rending tragedy of the last man swallowed by the grinning saurian before him. Certainly the Governor's stories were better than the objects they described.

River life and wilderness country beyond brought strange occurrences and adventures aboard the FLOATING PALACE. There was the runaway couple in Kentucky who presented themselves and their minister, with the request that they be married in the Museum. Always on the alert for a new attraction, Manager Van Orden readily consented. And so, right in front of a perpetually smiling stuffed hyena and a hilarious alligator, while the barrel organ played a lively dance for the puppets, they were united in holy matrimony. The arrival of the bride's angry brother brought sudden excitement into the romantic scene.

In many sections—particularly Arkansas—men came on board with a pistol in one pocket, a whiskey flask in the other, and long bowie knives sticking from their boots. Sometimes trouble started. Every member of the showboat company was armed, and at a given signal was prepared to defend the boat. Their designated leader on such occasions was a giant of a man, the doorkeeper during normal times, whose aides were two professional New York prize fighters, ostensibly employed as ushers. Though these three fought only with their bare fists, they nevertheless left many an armed man with a broken head.

Sometimes the "law" itself caused trouble, usually over the matter of the license fee. At West Columbia, on the Ohio River, the authorities had agreed with the advance agent of the FLOATING CIRCUS PALACE that the fee for the right to exhibit should be two dollars and fifty cents. When the town officials saw the crowds on the banks waiting to purchase tickets, however, they suddenly decided that a license fee of twenty-five dollars must be paid. Van Orden objected, but finally offered a compromise fee of twelve dollars and a half. But the authorities stood firm on their new decision. The exasperated manager ordered the boat moved downstream a few yards, where it would be outside the corporate limits and the jurisdiction of local authorities. And the show performed, without paying any license fee whatever, to a large and sympathetic audience. This method, and also the trick of raising the end of the gangplank a few inches above "municipal soil," became the classic defenses of showboats against exorbitant license fees.

The gamblers, who had infested the rivers long before showboats were born, became another source of trouble. With the growth of passenger boat traffic, this menace had reached serious proportions. On many steamers staterooms on the captain's deck were reserved for these slickers, and they were encouraged systematically to ply their trade. When the FLOATING CIRCUS PALACE refused all gamblers access to the boat, these "preyers on purses" set up their tables on the bank, under bright kerosene torches. Van Orden first co-operated with shore authorities to disperse them, and when this attempt failed, he sent his pugilists up the bank to destroy their establishments. Showboats were thus permanently ridded of these pests.

With the exception of a few months when the Spaulding and Rogers' Circus took to land, the FLOATING CIRCUS PALACE continued to operate until 1862. At that time the Confederate Government took over the big boat, to convert it into a hospital ship, stationed at New Orleans. But it had finished its work, and good work, too. It had done much to establish a wholesome ideal of enjoyable entertainment along the Western waterways and had successfully combated the evil reputation that had threatened to engulf the whole institution of showboating. There was scarcely a community on the Mississippi and Ohio River system that had not welcomed the great circus. And what a sight it had been, for child and grownup, for slave and planter, for river-hand and frontiersman, as the smoke-belching towboat, all aglitter in red and gold, had pushed the big white-and-gold barge up to the wharf, with a flag flying from every standard and the calliope sending forth undulating announcements of arrival in screaming music! Children became hysterical, field-workers left their plows in the furrow, and stable boys' hands trembled as they harnessed horses for masters, who, for once, forgot to give orders. And anticipation did not prove greater than the experience itself. For the boat brought its welcome cargo of wholesome entertainment and pushed back many horizons. Perhaps Francis Wemyss, a contemporary historian of the drama, was right when he called it "one of the wonders of the age . . . perfect in every department."

The self-styled rival of Spaulding and the FLOATING CIRCUS PALACE was Dan Rice. From 1851 to 1865, and again from 1868 to 1886 this man traveled intermittently with river entertainment. During most of the time he transported his show by boat and performed under a big-top erected on the bank; for only three years did he show a circus on his boat.

Rice's career was long and varied. First as horse trainer and then as wrestler (Barnum's New York Museum) he came early into public favor. At twenty-one he was employed as a clown in the North American Circus, owned by Spaulding and Rogers, for fifteen dollars a month and board. After two years here, he started out for himself, apparently not satisfied with the treatment he had received. With his educated pigs Sybil and Lord Byron, his trick mule, and his trained horse Aroostook, which "occupied the disputed boundary between man and horse," he quickly rose to fame in the entertainment world, and by the middle of the century his circus was touring the rivers on the steamboat ALLEGHENY MAIL, which served for transportation only. In his own show he played the role of leading clown, advertising himself as "the modern Shakespearean jester," and "the original American white face clown."

He soon found that his old employers, Spaulding and Rogers, and their FLOATING CIRCUS PALACE were offering serious competition. Quick and bitter rivalry between him and them resulted, developing into a feud, talked about from New Orleans to Pittsburgh. Rice's outfit was considered small even by the standards of the 1850's; Spaulding and Rogers, with their greater capital, equipment, and personnel, offered a variety of entertainment that Rice with his small troupe of entertainers could not hope to match. Rice was full of tales of persecution, however, and constantly assumed with his audiences the role of underdog. He even accused Van Orden of moving the buoy lights near Caseyville, Kentucky, so that Rice's boat would run aground. On the other side, Van Orden brought slander charges against Rice, and succeeded in having him jailed for more than a week. During that period Rice composed his "Rochester Song," with which he was to regale many future audiences. One stanza runs:

> *In blowing up Van Orden I never will cease*
> *   As long as my name is Dan;*
> *He had me arrested for saying he's a thief,*
> *   Which I am to prove if I can.*
> *For he knows full well that it's the truth I tell,*
> *   A greater villain than he never run;*
> *So now on my fortune he cuts a great swell,*
> *   Which money was made by my fun.*[5]

[5] Maria Brown in *The Life of Dan Rice* (pp. 459–460) prints all eight stanzas as well as several other hate-ballads about Van Orden. The biography unfortunately states only Rice's point of view. Neither Spaulding nor Van Orden ever

Rice spread the rumor in front of Spaulding's FLOATING CIRCUS
PALACE that the big boat was a fire trap, and Van Orden countered
with the untimely rumor that Dan Rice had died. One agrees with
the editor of the Natchez *Courier* when he wondered in 1852 if New
Orleans was big enough to hold Dan Rice and Van Orden at the same
time. Somewhat ironically, memories of this quarrel between the
managers outlived both the circuses.

It was this same hardy Dan Rice who first resumed river-show
business after the Civil War.[6]

---

presented their side of the quarrel, which people along the Mississippi still
talk about.

[6] The last *bona fide* showboat circus was the GREAT AMERICAN WATER CIRCUS
(1901–1905). W. P. Newman, with money from the sale of his drygoods store in
Charleston, West Virginia, purchased and lashed together two large Pittsburgh
barges. He knocked out the adjoining bulkheads, filled the hulls with earth,
spread a big-top above, and there were both arena and seating space. This strange
craft carried forty horses and fourteen parade wagons up and down the Ohio
for four years. The show featured a troupe of horses, which dived from a high
platform into the river. When it was noticed, however, that they did not dive
of their own volition, but only when a trap was yanked from beneath their feet,
the S.P.C.A. intervened and the circus boat ceased operations.

The principal sources for this chapter, besides newspaper files, posters, and
manuscripts, are items listed in the bibliography under Charles Ambler, C. E.
Brown, Maria Brown, Coad and Mims, Joe Curtis, Florence Dorsey, Alvin
Harlow, Ralph Keeler, S. Kussart, Earl May, Dan Rice, LeRoy Rice, Gil Robinson, Francis Wemyss.

French's Fifth New Sensation

Capt. Edwin Price

IV

Bloody Waters

An Interlude

Between the launching of William Chapman's first showboat and the beginning of the Civil War, a space of only thirty years, the showboat as an institution had run a complete cycle of development. It had appeared and had grown rapidly in response to a need of the region; it had been perverted by undesirable elements in the environment that had produced it, and had declined; it had survived in slightly changed forms, such as the floating circus; with the coming of the Civil War it had disappeared.

During these years, while the land theatres were bringing the drama to the centers of population, the floating theatres were carrying the stage to that portion of the citizenry most characteristic of the region, outside the larger towns. The showboats had developed from a Ludlow ark, which could serve the hinterland, to Spaulding's mammoth floating establishment, usually city-bent. Their programs had changed from the Chapman legitimate plays, representing the best English acting traditions, to the Negro minstrelsy of the Banjo and the vast variety of the circus boat. The showboats of this period, like the land theatres, had come to grips with the fear of the immoral and the unconventional, voiced by those who believed that all stage entertainment was degrading, fit only for "the most abandoned of the human family—male and female." [1] The stage, with the help of the strong

---

[1] The Reverend Artemus Bullard, a Presbyterian minister of St. Louis, had used the occasion of the death of President Harrison to preach a bitter sermon against actors and the stage. Sol Smith answered the attack in his *Theatrical Apprenticeship* (p. 168). Smith's most illuminating remark, however, is his statement that a certain gentleman, since he was a member of the church, had to view the play from the wings of the stage (*Ibid.*, p. 120).

family traditions of the West, was finally to win the battle against the moral objectors.

The four bitter years of war had transformed the scene along the Western rivers. Manpower had been depleted. Local transportation was badly crippled, and commerce between the Northern and Southern districts had stopped altogether. The proud steamboats that in the old days had made a pageant-way of the Mississippi and Ohio had been sunk, and paralyzed trade held forth little promise to new builders. Where there were no cargoes, there was no need for boats. The rivers flowed by the same banks as in the days before the War, but beyond those banks was a horribly changed world. Many of the once prosperous plantations, each with its bustling landing on the river front, and the thriving river communities, crowded five years before, were now deserted and rapidly falling into ruins. Though the Western waterways were reopened for travel and commerce in 1865, men in utter discouragement saw in the rivers not visions of fortunes, as in the old time, but merely muddy streams.

The spirit of showboating had not died, however, and, as future events were to prove, time and more favorable conditions were to bring it back to life. Furthermore, though the War had temporarily put an end to show activity, it had also purged the rivers of those objectionable elements that had earlier menaced river entertainment.

The intrepid Dan Rice was the first to reappear after the Great Conflict. In 1869 he toured the rivers from St. Paul to New Orleans with his circus loaded on the steamboat WILL S. HAYES, which he had purchased for $10,000. He was traveling by boat, but showing on land. The next few years marked the peak of Rice's career. His success had attracted some wealthy partners, among them Avery Smith, John Nathans, and Gerald Quick, and together they launched the biggest circus afloat in America. Rice himself was manager. The chief attractions were a magnificent string of horses and the clowns. Rice became so intoxicated with his success, which he interpreted as his own justification in the old quarrel with Spaulding, that he even announced his candidacy for the presidency of the United States.

Financial disaster came in 1873. The partnership was dissolved, and Rice set out alone with a greatly reduced circus on board the sternwheeler DAMSEL. Business was slack, creditors were waging constant war against him, and his one wild animal, a mangy half-starved lion, was at the point of death most of the time. The circus did not venture out at all during 1877, but the next year, with the encouraging addition of the marvel milk-white horse Excelsior, "the one-horse show" and the Damsel again took to the rivers. The boat was snagged and burned near Decatur, Nebraska, on the Missouri River. The Damsel was a total loss, but local inhabitants saved Excelsior and some of the circus paraphernalia. Rice presented the boat's bell to the village church as a token of gratitude.

The old showman made one more attempt. Gradually he himself had become the most attractive exhibit in his circus. His vociferous quarrel with the Spaulding and Van Orden interests had become a legend up and down the rivers. His race for the presidency in 1868, taken by some as the greatest of all his jokes, brought him much publicity. Zachary Taylor had dubbed him a colonel, in recognition of "great service rendered in entertaining mankind." Certainly in 1886 when Rice constructed his Floating Opera at Cairo, Illinois, he was the most colorful figure in the Middle West. Even so, his tour of the Lower Mississippi, with performances on board his boat, was a financial failure, and Dan Rice retired both from the rivers and from the show business. During the forty years of an active career he had added little to the saga of the showboat, for his greatest contribution to American entertainment came through the circus in general. He did preserve and keep intact during those difficult Reconstruction years, however, the traditions—even the very possibility—of show-boating.

V

AT THE LANDING AGAIN

Re-establishment of an Institution

AN OLD showboater in Biblical mood, when asked about business after the Civil War, answered: "In the beginning was French, who begat McNair and Price, who begat all the rest except a few from the bullrushes—all of them a plague of competition." He might have added that this was the era when the showboat reached full maturity and yet remained small enough and honest enough, free from the pomp of size, to serve best the people who needed it most.

Augustus Byron French, as he was known to the public,[1] was certainly the Kingfish of the showboat world during the last quarter of the nineteenth century. He built his first boat in 1878, when he was already middle-aged, and his fifth one twenty-three years later, one year before his death. Each of the five was called FRENCH'S NEW SENSATION, and all were owned successively except the third and the fourth, which were operated simultaneously as FRENCH'S NEW SENSATION NO. 1 and FRENCH'S NEW SENSATION NO. 2.

French was born in 1833, only two years before Mark Twain, at Palmyra, Missouri, almost within walking distance of the great humorist's birthplace. He, too, early felt the spell of the Great River, only a few miles away, and at sixteen, an orphan compelled to shift for himself, he took a job as cabin boy on a steamer bound for New Orleans. It was his first trip among strangers, and he suffered acutely at the hands of the mate and the head cook.

Relief soon came. One morning above Natchez young French noticed a shanty boat tied beside the steamer. Perhaps it was the un-

---

[1] His real name was Augustus Byron Dolen. During his early show career he used his mother's name Mantanza. After his second marriage (to Callie Leach) he substituted French.

usual name painted on her side—it was QUICKSTEP—or perhaps it was the attractive girl on board that caused him to visit the tiny white-and-green craft. He found here a strange pair, a Mr. Church and his daughter Celeste. The father did magic tricks and the girl sang and danced. They explained to their visitor that they drifted from landing to landing, putting on their acts wherever they found an available wharf-shed or tavern room. It might be a precarious life, especially in bad weather, but it was also leisurely and, best of all, independent. On the QUICKSTEP no chief cook gave orders, and no mate made threatening gestures; instead the charming Celeste cooked catfish, and the genial Church told river stories. It is little wonder that French stole quietly back to the steamer to get his banjo and his bundle of clothes. He had joined up with the show.

For two years he sang duets and did a dance act with Celeste. His exhibition of banjo playing and Papa Church's magic (in which art French was taking lessons) completed a show that must have been acceptable at many landings. After leaving the QUICKSTEP, he was employed for a short time by Dan Rice to exhibit banjo playing and dancing, and then he joined the Spaulding and Rogers FLOATING CIRCUS PALACE as a magician. Here he was impressed with the basic showboat pattern—the performance actually on the boat, the free transportation, the general independence of the life. From that time on, the idea of a showboat of his own was constantly in his mind. When the War swept the big circus boat from the rivers, he traveled with wagon shows, and finally, with little except his banjo and Church's magic tricks, he set out with a one-wagon show of his own, which he named "New Sensation."

After the War—he was then nearly forty with only a spotted experience as river entertainer to his credit—he attempted to settle down. He bought a grocery store at Waterloo, Ohio, and later moved his small business to Clarksburg. Though he was financially successful, he could not forget the earlier show days, and in 1878 he purchased a small circus. In June of the same year he married Miss Callie Leach, back at Waterloo. French was forty-five, without fortune and without vocation; Callie was sixteen, and the belle of the town. Yet this was to prove a remarkably successful marriage through the remaining twenty-four years of French's life.

Together they refurbished the newly acquired circus, and by midsummer they were on the road with six wagons. They called their expanded show "French's New Sensation."

That summer was the wettest in the history of Ohio. Floods made travel almost impossible, and even after the wagons reached a stand, the torrents made life miserable both for performers and spectators. Disgruntled customers began asking for their money back. French, always deeply concerned about his patrons, became more and more nervous and impatient. After one particularly trying night—costumes were too wet either to be worn or to be packed, the water-soaked tent had collapsed, all the wagons except one had bogged down—he made his decision.

"If we have to float," he said, "we're going to have something that will turn the water. I'm going to get rid of this outfit, and build a showboat." Callie readily agreed with him, though she had never seen a boat except the barges on the Old Ohio Canal. She had faith in her husband, and she must have felt, too, that nothing could be worse than a water-soaked tent-show bogged down in Ohio mud with every-thing at a standstill except the ever growing expenses.

Once in Cincinnati, French found and bought a barge sixteen feet wide and eighty-five feet long, towed it to the point that is now the foot of Lawrence Street, and began work. It was not an easy job. Be-cause money was scarce, the boat must be cheaply built. It must be light enough to be manageable, and at the same time large enough for not only a stage and an auditorium but comfortable living quarters as well.[2] For this, like the earlier Chapman boat, was to be a family venture. By October, in spite of bad weather, bill collectors, and diffi-culty in getting materials, the NEW SENSATION, for of course that was her name, was ready for the perilous voyage downstream.

Even on the Mississippi of the 1870's this seemed an unusual craft. Her single-deck cabin extended over the entire barge upon which it had been built, with a runway about two feet wide on each side, at deck level. At both bow and stern, deck flooring and roof extended four feet beyond the ends of barge and cabin, thus forming a small covered porch at either end of the boat. Eight windows on each side promised ample ventilation. Two large sweeps, on swivels, were mounted on the top of the cabin amidships, one on either side. The handles were attached to long poles reaching down to the paddles in the water. At the stern a similar sweep served as a rudder. Two men, from the vantage point of the roof of the cabin, could handle the

[2] For an excellent and detailed account of building a showboat, see Pete Martin's story "River Singer," *Saturday Evening Post*, Aug. 16, 1947, p. 30.

boat with ease, and could even speed up slightly her progress down-stream, or could take her over to the bank.

Her color scheme made the New Sensation unique among river-boats. Callie proudly remarked that she got the colors from the river itself: the gleaming white paint on the outside was, she said, the re-flection of the white clouds in the water, the fine red trim was to her a burnt sunset in the ripples, and the light green of the interior was the cool color of shoal water. Between the windows French had painted in full color circus scenes, with wild animals, acrobats, and freaks, interspersed with characters from Shakespeare. Above the windows, painted in Callie's favorite dark red, was the name The New Sensation in letters almost three feet high, across the whole length of the cabin. With such vivid paint, the showboat was easily distinguished from the shabby shanty boats among which she often tied up.

Visitors were always surprised at the space on the inside of the little boat. At the bow, from the narrow sheltered porch the main entrance opened into a short corridor, with a small stateroom on either side. One of these served as ticket booth and business office. The corridor led directly into the back of the auditorium, a long, narrow room, fitted with eleven rows of benches for the spectators, with only a center aisle. The front six of these rows were thinly padded with red-and-white striped bed ticking, and were reserved at thirty-five cents each, ten cents more than regular admission. In the language of the river, "A bench with a rag on it for a dime."

The floor of the auditorium slanted slightly from the bow toward the stage, but leveled off a short distance in front of the footlights to furnish room for acrobatic acts. Above this was the elevated stage, only eight feet deep and fifteen wide. It had oil-burning lamps for footlights and a pull-curtain made of red-and-white checked cotton damask. There were no wings and no scenery.

Behind the stage was Mr. and Mrs. French's bedroom and living room combined, and back of this, opening on to the stern porch, was the kitchen and dining room combined.

After completing the boat, the new Captain had to get aboard pro-visions and a few utensils and furnishings, and last of all the cast. There were eight persons on board: Ned Martin, comedian; Maurice Dolen (French's cousin), blackface minstrel; Newton Mowry (Cal-lie's cousin), comic singer; Ed and Caroline DeHass (married), globe rollers; Capt. French, magician, ventriloquist, and banjo specialist; and his wife, Callie, housekeeper, chief cook, and mate. On Sunday, November 3, 1878, they poled the New Sensation away from the bank, to start the long journey down the rivers south.

Certainly no time was to be lost. The current was their sole dependence for motive power, for the Sensation could boast no towboat and had no engine. The big sweeps had been designed only to steer the boat, especially in to the landings and back again into the current. Ice was already appearing and Captain French was anxious to reach the warmer Mississippi before frozen bonds imprisoned them and perhaps crushed them. Furthermore the "crew" was paid by the performance, and they too were nervous at the prospect of weeks of frozen idleness. The current seemed very slow.

The voyage almost ended at Louisville, Kentucky. Here the dangerous rapids of the Ohio barred their way—falls which were hazardous even for steamboats in the hands of experienced rivermen. The frail Sensation, in the hands of actors and showmen, would seem to have little chance. There was a canal around the danger point, it is true, but it was owned by a private company which demanded a prohibitive toll—more money than Captain French possessed. Every pilot in town seemed to be in the employ of the canal company and they only shook their heads and assured Captain French of the danger of the rapids. At last a man who had lately been discharged by the canal company offered to carry the Sensation through for five dollars. It was a desperate chance, but there seemed no other way. Captain French accepted the offer, and the New Sensation, with all on board, headed into the boiling foam. Fifteen minutes later she emerged, slightly scarred but sound, below the rapids. The discharged pilot had made good, and he was paid double his fee and gratefully put ashore.

The first performance was given at Elizabethtown, Illinois, on Christmas night of 1878, almost two months after the showboat had started from Cincinnati. There the big rocks at the landing provided ample protection from the fast following ice, and French knew that he could safely pause to replenish his diminishing funds. There were no printed handbills and therefore no record of the program. But if we may judge from the list of actors and from subsequent performances, this was a modest little variety show of music and dancing, singing, a stump speech, globe-rolling, sleight-of-hand, and ventriloquism, with a finale of banjo and chorus. It set the pattern for many a later night, for plays were seldom performed on French's boats.

Farther down the river the ice floes became more and more threatening, until finally near Cairo progress was completely blocked. The Sensation was again miraculously saved, this time from the imminent danger of being ground to splinters, by a persistent little steam tug. After repeated efforts it succeeded in snaking the showboat to safety at the Cairo landing. It is small wonder that here Mr. and Mrs. DeHass deserted the boat, in favor of a less perilous life on shore, to leave Mrs. French the only woman on board. It was through the happy accident of a chance meeting on the Cairo wharf between Capt. French and Frank Herbert, an old circus friend, that the show could perform. Herbert's two sons, whom he was training as acrobatic artists, joined the cast, with their "Aerial Suspension," or "Sleeping in the Air" act.

Somehow the little company struggled on. Now they were on the broad Mississippi, with sand bars, sawyers, fog, and always the cold. When the head wind was stronger than the current, or when fog settled over the water too thick, they tied up at the bank, sometimes for days, and they counted themselves lucky if there was wood enough for fires. More than once, if the river fell rapidly when they were tied to the bank, the Sensation was left half-stranded, the bow on land, the stern afloat. But the river always rose again and carried them on their way.

As often as they could work in to a landing, they put on their show. Since their progress was unpredictable, being entirely dependent upon current, weather, and accident, advance advertising was out of the question. As soon as they arrived at one of the settlements dotting the river banks, they beat a drum and two of the men went up the bank to post hand-printed signs. That evening the show was repeated, and if twenty-five or more spectators sat in the auditorium the stand was starred on the log-map. Normal seating capacity was eighty-nine, with a maximum of one hundred if stools were placed in the aisle. Sometimes when luck ran right, successive shows could be given for five or six nights, and then again weeks separated performances. One of the disturbing facts about every showboat was that the weather was always more important than the show. Sometimes it followed that a good boatman was more important than a good actor, but this was not true of the Sensation.

It was an exhausted but hilarious troupe on board a battered Sensation that finally reached New Orleans in the spring. As Captain French tied up below Canal Street, his must have been a double satisfaction. First of all, he had won out over the river and all it could offer. Contrary to the dire predictions of every onlooker and passerby, here were he, his wife, his troupe of entertainers, and his boat, built with his own hands, all safe at their goal, in spite of storm and fog and all the terrors that lurk in the river. In the second place his idea had triumphed, an idea he had nursed ever since the days on board the Spaulding and Rogers FLOATING CIRCUS PALACE. For once he had been successful. The daring trip had been made not only with safety, but with profit as well, for he had a tidy sum in his pocket, far more than he needed for a tow upstream. He had proved, too, that self-supporting river entertainment could be kept wholesome and clean, a fact that held rich promise for him and his family. During the two weeks' rest, when his little troupe saw the sights and ate the food of the strange city, his head was seething with plans for the future. Certainly the trip next season could be less arduous and even more successful than the first. Captain McClure of the coaler SMOKY CITY agreed to tow them back to the Ohio for twenty-five dollars. The big steamer tied the little SENSATION alongside, with two other boats that desired the same service, and started the long trip upstream. It was on that lazy journey, when French and his wife had nothing to do except watch the sluggish current slip past, that they planned for Callie to add to her duties next season the role of performer in the show. She had tired of being merely cook and housekeeper, and the Captain willingly offered to put her into any act she might choose. In later years Mrs. French insisted that they made their decision chiefly because her biscuits were always "burnt offerings" and her housekeeping was cluttered with cobwebs.

One morning they found themselves being cut loose from the SMOKY CITY, and were informed that on account of low water the big boat could go no farther. The locality seemed a strange coincidence, for they were at Elizabethtown, Illinois, where the NEW SENSATION had put on its first show. Again they tied up behind the protecting rocks, and there they remained the rest of the summer of 1879.

It was to be a very busy three months for all hands. Callie at once began work on the plan on which she and her husband had agreed. She was determined to learn an "act," and thus become a real partner in the showboat venture.

She had been brought up in Waterloo, Ohio, a village too small to get on a map, and far from navigable water. She therefore knew very little about either shows or boats. But even before her marriage,

French had told her about the breath-taking tightrope feats of Madame Olinza on board Spaulding's FLOATING PALACE, and always with evident admiration. This then would be her act, she resolved.

She stretched a rope tight between two cottonwood trees well up on the bank, and industriously began her practice. For two weeks she performed one foot above the ground, carrying either a balance pole or a parasol. Each week thereafter she moved the rope one foot higher on the trees and cut the balance pole a little shorter each day. By the end of August her husband assured her that she was every bit as good as the celebrated Olinza herself. At night on board the SENSATION she was preparing also a sentimental song act, with "The Blue Alsatian Mountains" and "By Killarney's Lakes and Hills." She planned and made a costume that would fit both her acts. It was a brown flannel swallow-tailed coat and knee breeches, red vest, green stockings, black Tam O'Shanter hat, and black soft-soled shoes. Callie may have been an eighteen-year-old country girl, but she knew her colors.

In the meantime Captain French had not been idle. During the day he was at work on the boat—improving the steering gear, installing new footlights, repainting the hull and cabin, replacing the window shutters that had been raked off when the SENSATION had been swept too close to overhanging willows. At night, when Callie was practicing her sentimental song act, he wisely climbed the bluff to the Rose Hotel, to enjoy the genial talk as much as the fine view up and down the Ohio. French was a peculiarly social individual, especially in the company of men, and he always had around him an interested group to listen to his tales of shows and the river. Though he had had little formal education, he had enjoyed a rich experience, and he possessed in fine measure that genial honesty of heart that invites friendly talk.

But the half-busy days and pleasant evenings ended in October, when the NEW SENSATION cast off her lines from the Elizabethtown bank to begin her second trip down the rivers. Only two performers from the year before had remained with the Frenches, their two cousins. Maurice Dolen still did his blackface minstrel act and stump speech, and now he added a burlesque on French's sleight-of-hand act. Newton Mowry's comic songs made excellent contrast with Callie's sentimental ballads. She had learned to play the dulcimer to accompany French's banjo, and she was also his assistant in the magic act.

A fifth member, Sidney Allen, an acrobat and contortionist, joined the company at Cairo, Illinois. Later, he wrote concerning the second trip of the NEW SENSATION:

Each day and night at the mercy of wind and current we went waltzing and floating down the river. Every run we were in danger of wrecking the showboat, we were continually fighting sandbars, wind, and current, caving banks and overhanging trees in bends of the river. Most every day some carpenter work had to be done on the guards surrounding the boat, repairing broken windows and shutters. When we were caught in such places our large oars or sweeps, our only motive power, were of no avail.

Such descriptions lead one to believe that the hardships of that second cruise equaled those of the first. Certainly its programs, honest and wholesome attempts to offer to the river people what they would enjoy, represent substantial improvements over earlier efforts. Here is a typical evening's entertainment on board the NEW SENSATION in 1880:

Legerdemain (sleight-of-hand and magic)—By Mr. French, assisted by Mrs. French.
Comic Songs—By Newton Mowry.
Comedy Farce, "Mr. and Mrs. Brown"—By the Frenches and M. Dolen.
Acrobat and Contortionist—Sidney Allen.
Stump Speech ("My Platform") and Burlesque (on French's magic act)—By Maurice Dolen.
The Aerial Suspension Act—Mr. and Mrs. French.
Comedy Farce, "Razor Jim"—By the Entire Company.[3]

[3] Principal Sources: Numerous newspaper files, letters, handbills, logbooks, and manuscripts.
Other Sources: Items listed in the bibliography under Maurice Elfer, Edward Eustace, Meigs Frost, Corinne Hardesty, Alvin F. Harlow, Pete Martin, Sidney Snook, Wesley Stout, and G. Harry Wright.

VI

THE LAST NIGHT
OF THE FIRST "SENSATION"

The Saga of the Frenches

THOSE NINE annual cruises of the SENSATION, the first in 1878 and the last in 1886, reeled themselves off so fast that most of the adventures were never recorded in the logbook. Every year there were new towns, new associates and friends, new acts. New power had come with the purchase in 1885 of a tiny towboat, the MARTIN P. MURPHY, and the next year this had been replaced by the more efficient SENTINEL. This new power, with resulting new territory, had brought a new high in door receipts. The river people were developing, too, a new confidence in showboat entertainment. Certainly a new prosperity had come to the Frenches. Everything was new, it seems, except the river and the showboat, and these had battled one another for nine years. The river with its ice, sand bars, sawyers, rapids, battering winds, and grasping willow branches; the NEW SENSATION, with the vigilant Captain French on board to repair, repaint, and replace. The boat had rendered a valiant service, but at last her seams had begun to spring, she was leaking badly, and half her hull was watersoaked. It was time for a new boat. So when the 1887 season ended at Augusta, Kentucky, her captain headed her toward Cincinnati, where he planned to build a new boat at the very wharf where he had built the first.

The old showboat tied up at the foot of Lawrence Street at noon, July 16, 1887, and at once the Captain went ashore to employ workmen and sign contracts. He did even more, for by sundown old friends began dropping over to the SENSATION and after supper the group had grown so large that they moved from Mr. and Mrs. French's room back of the stage up to the deck over the auditorium, where the elaborate steering gear had once been before they had acquired the gallant little SENTINEL to do the pushing. And up there at night the blue sky and the stars had a way, Callie French always said, of cupping down over them, shutting out everything except the river below, and of course the night wind.

John McNair, with his wife beside him, was there. Two years before he had joined the Frenches and since that time he had been like a member of the family. Now he was acrobat and musician on board the showboat and engineer on board the tow. Ida Fitch had been Callie's best friend in the old days; a year before she had come aboard the SENSATION for a visit, and had remained as Mrs. McNair. Her father, Hiram Fitch, a short stubby quiet man who never shaved, sat over against the rail where he could see the ripples far up the river. He and his son-in-law were to be chief builders of the next SENSATION. The suave Tony Lavely had come down for a visit, and also the stalwart Charlie Breidenbaugh, both of them later to manage showboats. Captain Jack Summers, who had commanded a number of palatial steamers on the Mississippi, was there too, and with him half a dozen other friends of the Frenches.

On this particular night a certain excitement was in the air, and talk was running fast.

"And so you are going to junk the old boat," said Captain Jack. "You know, French, these showboats are such flimsy things that I can't tell the difference when they're new and when they're old."

"This one has stayed with us nine long years—at least part of her has—and she's taken everything the river could hand out," replied Captain French. "She's gettin' a little waterlogged now, a little leaky too, I guess, especially round the bow. That's the sand bars."

"What do you mean, Cap'n, by *part of her?*" asked Charlie Breidenbaugh, who was anxious to learn everything about showboats. "Seems to me she's all here now, even the rotten part."

"Yes, she's all here now, but you see what's here now ain't all the same as what we started out with nine years ago," replied French. "This barge she's on now is just seven years old." He turned his chair around so he could straddle it and rest his hands and chin on the top of the back, his favorite position when talking.

"It was at Vidalia, wasn't it, Mr. French?" said Callie. (Through a quarter of a century of happy married life, she always called her husband "Mr. French.") "I remember it like it was yesterday."

"Yes, it was at Vidalia, Louisiana, just across from Natchez, on our second trip down," French continued. "We didn't have any tow-boat then, and so we'd drifted down from Pine Ridge, where we'd showed the night before. We'd started about four o'clock that morning, as we generally do, but the wind had come up earlier than usual, and it was ten before we began pulling in toward Vidalia. We were swinging in a little below the landing, nice as you please, when all of a sudden we stopped with a jerk and the boat shivered all over. We had struck a check post under the waterline, and a stream as big as your leg was spurtin' halfway across the hold down below."

"And do you know what Mr. French did?" interrupted Callie. "He was that excited he began throwing Irish potatoes out of a barrel on the stage, through the window, toward the bank, one at a time! It was awful! He never once thought of our clothes or my new quilts or anything else! Just potatoes! Thank goodness, what little money we had and his watch he had on him."

"Yes, business hadn't been good coming down," French resumed; "too many towns wouldn't let us land, and we were just about broke. I thought the SENSATION was sure a goner that time. Her bow was under two feet and her stern nearly six. As soon as we all got out on the bank and dried out a little—there were only six of us on board that trip—I went uptown to see what I could do. Luck was with me. I ran into two merchants—I'll never forget them, Jim Rollins and Ricky Ward—who had seen my show the year before down at Baton Rouge. Jim said he'd loan me thirty dollars if Ricky would, and with that sixty I bought a new barge over at Natchez, just down from Pittsburgh. We tied big floats to the sides of the SENSATION's cabin, sawed her loose at the middle and the corners, and she bobbed to the surface like a fishing cork. We mounted her on soaped skids and in less than two days we had her all fitted on the new barge—the same old SENSATION on a new hull, and that's what's under her now.

"The only real trouble we had was that the new barge was two feet wider than the old one, but we spread the side walls out a little and let them slant. And it has been good that way," he added, "stronger, more room for us inside and less hold for the wind outside.[1] By skipping a town or two, we reached New Orleans that year—I think it was 1880—as early as usual. But that was the hardest and the wettest two days' work I ever did. Tony," he concluded, "did you ever try sawing under water?"

[1] These slanted cabin side-walls, constructed by Captain French to meet an emergency, became the standard showboat pattern for the next generation.

The immaculate Tony Lavely had never tried sawing anywhere, but he had a question to ask. "Captain French," he said, "you mentioned something about people not letting you land at some places. What did you mean?"

"I meant just that," the Captain replied. "It's not like that any more, because all the people on the rivers know us now. But in the old days at many a landing the sheriff and half the men of the town met us at the bank, shaking their fists and their guns at us, and pointing down stream. You see too many whiskey boats, and medicine boats, and gambling dives had come by, all pretending to be a show, and they naturally thought we were one of them. People didn't know the difference and you couldn't blame 'em. It was mighty hard to cure them of that idea, but they know us now."

"And I'll tell you why they know us," Callie interrupted, "because I know Mr. French won't tell you. My blood boils when I just think about it. That was the first time I ever saw my husband good an' mad.

"It was the first year that I was giving an act—mostly rope-walking —so it must have been our second trip down. Two towns had already refused to let us land that week, so we were happy to find a good crowd gathering when we tied up to a little landing in Missouri, or maybe it was Arkansas, I've forgotten which. I was selling tickets that night and I noticed that not a single woman had passed in. Too many of the men had winked at me as they paid their money. Curtain time came, and a good crowd was in, but still not a single woman. I knew Mr. French was getting madder and madder, because he was red clear down to his collar. Instead of pulling the curtain, he walked out in front of it, and said something like this (Callie lowered her pitch an octave to imitate her husband's voice):

" 'Men, there is not a woman in the audience. Not a wife, mother, daughter, or sweetheart. This is not a show for men only. If you thought it was, you never made a bigger mistake in your life. My wife is a member of our troupe, and I respect her as much as any of you respect your wife. Now go, and as you pass out, get your money at the ticket office.'

"At first the men thought it was just a gag, a clever way to open a dirty show. Mr. French had to tell them a second time that it was not a men-only show, that if they would bring their women we would give them the show, but it would be a good clean show, the only kind they'd ever see on French's NEW SENSATION.

Courtesy Capt. Ralph Emerson

Edwin Price's Second Showboat

Olive Ulrich, Singing Soubrette

"When those men saw that he was in earnest, they shuffled out like whipped puppies, and not a one of them stopped at the ticket office to get his money back. When they were gone, we all went to bed. We felt blue because things seemed to be getting a little rough.

"Hours later we heard a ruckus on the bank, and a man called, 'We've got our women, and now we want our show.' Mr. French lighted up, collected the extra money, and seated them, still in his night shirt, while the rest of us got ready. It was after midnight before the show was over, and after that Mr. French made them a friendly speech, telling them what kind of a show they could always expect from the SENSATION. And that's the kind they've always got," she added.

"Yes, we never had any more trouble after that," said Captain French. "The story of that night traveled all up and down the rivers, and we are still asked about it almost everywhere we go. It's been retold so many times that half the landings on the Mississippi think it happened at their place. But there's one thing certain—no showboat will ever again have the trouble we had with the sheriffs—not as long as their shows stay clean."

For a minute the little group fell silent. A steamer, twice as long as the showboat and many times as high, was churning up the river, with all her lights ablaze. They could hear her waves lapping against their sides below, and the SENSATION began a peculiar motion, as if she started to sway and then each time changed it to a jerky little jump. The sound of the big boat's low-pitched whistle came over the water.

"That would be good on a showboat to get them in with." John McNair seemed to be half talking to himself. "We got a whistle over there on the SENTINEL, but it's mighty puny by the side of that big fellow. The folks can't hear ours half a mile away. We're goin' to have a *cal*-li-ope—some call them steam pianos—on the new boat.[2] They say that will get them from ten miles back in the brush. I've already drawn the plans. That is, we'll have it," he added, "if Aunt Callie there can play it."

It would be hard to say whether Mrs. French bridled a little because of his seeming doubt of her ability or because of the *Aunt* prefixed to her name. (After all, she was only twenty-five.) "If it's got a keyboard," she answered, "I'll play you 'The Blue Alsatian Mountains,' the same as I used to sing it."

[2] River people of the last century invariably mispronounced *calliope*, probably because they saw the name in print before they heard it pronounced.

"Yes," Captain French agreed, "we're sure goin' to have a *cal*-li-ope. We're goin' to have some church windows, too, wine-colored and blue, at each end of the stage, so at night they'll show up fine with a good light shinin' through. Too bad, Ida," he continued, turning to Mrs. McNair, "we didn't have those windows when you and John there got married on the boat that night down at Darrowville, Louisiana. It was so stormy that we couldn't do anything else, so we got you two married right down there on the stage. It was as good as having our show, except of course no money comin' in," he chuckled.

"Won't you tell us about the first time you ever saw John?" Ida had been married exactly a year, and she was very much interested in her husband's past.

"Well, it was back in '84, when Price and me were still working together," Captain French began. "We laid the Sensation here up at Paducah, and just the two of us took his little picture boat, the Sylvan Glen, on down the rivers. We were making tintypes at almost every landing, and we aimed to reach New Orleans in time for the Cotton Exposition. When we were tied up at Vidalia, we heard there was a circus over at Natchez that night, and we crossed the river to see it. It was a Robinson Show, and John McNair here was their acrobat and chief musician. The minute I saw him turning that double back flip of his without a springboard, I knew he had the stuff, and when I heard him play the tuba I punched Price and I said, 'That boy would do mighty well on a showboat.' So after the show we hunted him up and told him all about our business, and when we left him, he promised to join the Sensation the next spring. He did, and I reckon he ain't regrettin' his choice," with a wink at Ida. "I guess there ain't anything on a boat or in a show that John McNair can't handle."

"No, I ain't regrettin' my choice," John answered, "but I'll say I had a devil of a time gettin' up to Pittsburgh to join up with you. My partner and his wife were with me right here in old Cinci, and the three of us wanted to get to Pittsburgh. The fare was five dollars apiece, and together we had twelve dollars. We drew to see which one of us would get the short portion, and I got it. They went on, and I hunted up a steamboat captain to make some kind of deal. First I offered him my watch, worth seventy-five," tapping his vest pocket, "if it's worth a cent, for passage to Pitt. He said he had a watch, and he guessed he'd have to have the cash if I wanted to go on his boat. Then I offered him a suit of clothes, almost brand new, but he said he already had a good suit too. I was puttin' my stuff back in the valise, when he happened to see a clown suit. It wasn't much better than a union suit except it was green-and-tan striped with a fancy band around the middle. I'd paid six dollars for them tights, new. But he liked 'em and said I could ride with him as far as I liked. That's how I got to Pittsburgh to join up with the SENSATION."

"You've been a good partner ever since, even if I do keep you on a salary," Captain French said.

"Cap'n," asked Charlie Breidenbaugh—Callie in her own mind had already accused him of wanting to *buy in*—"Cap'n, have you ever had a real partner, one that got his share of the take?"

"Well, yes," French replied, "I guess I've had several. Of course my first partner was Callie here. She still is, and she'll be my last one, too, except she's no ordinary partner—she gets *all* the take. I've had two ordinary partners, and both of 'em seemed to have peculiar ways. I guess they'd say the same about me." The Captain was always fair-minded.

"The first one," he continued, "was Titzman—Muley Titzman, we called him, because of that little blind dun mule of his. After the SENSATION's second trip down—it must have been about 1880—the OAKLAND towed us back up to St. Louis, where we thought we'd like to take in the Fair. Titzman was on the Grounds, running a merry-go-round with that little dun-colored mule. When I first saw him, he had his seats full and his mule had balked. Wouldn't budge an inch in spite of everything they could do. I offered to get him started. I just set fire to a newspaper under that mule, and he started with a jump—almost broke the flying jinny. After that Titzman and me got to be good friends. I bought half interest in his little outfit, and we ran it together the rest of the summer. When the Fair closed, we loaded the merry-go-round and the mule on the SENSATION, and Titzman went along, too. At each stop we'd set up the thing on the shore as an added attraction, and did a pretty good business at ten cents a ride.

"On that same trip down, that mule came in mighty handy. Thirty miles below St. Louis, about halfway to St. Genevieve, we came to a big island, with the channel and the government light on the Illinois side. But we were traveling on the Missouri side, and we took a chance on the chute there rather than maneuvering across. About three miles down we came to a dead end, a dike all the way from Missouri to the island. There we were, in a pocket, no current, no power. We got that mule ashore, hitched him to the showboat and we had a tow back up to the place where we had gone wrong. Whenever that brute would stop, all we needed to do was strike a match and he'd get goin' again. It's funny how long he remembered that fire I'd built under him. It took us two days to make the three miles to the head of the island, and by the time it was over everybody had frozen feet, except that little mule."

The spirit of reminiscence was taking hold of the little group, and they spoke that night of near-wrecks and starving periods as most men speak of a slight cold or missing a meal. Even Callie, often very reserved, was talking more than usual.

"I always said that mule brought us bad luck," she said. "On that same trip we almost starved to death. I remember the ice began drifting down on us fast, and the water near the shore was frozen too hard for us to break through and land. We had to drift with the floe for several days, and at last we had to punch it out of the way in front before we could make any progress at all, with the ice battering us on both sides. It seemed to close in on us like a pack of cold wolves. At last just below Commerce, Missouri, we managed to get into a stretch of open water below an island. We tied up behind a big tree that had toppled into the river on account of a cave-in, but its roots still held. We barricaded ourselves there against the ice with saplings and brush the men cut from the island, and they hung logs, end up, over the guards of the SENSATION to break the force of the ice that got through to us. We felt safe for the first time in almost a week, and then we began to get hungry. For days we hadn't been able to pull in to shore for groceries and the supply was low. The men shot a rabbit or two that wasn't much for twelve hungry people. After five days of it three of the men got our little yawl into the river, half rowed it and half skidded it over the ice, to the town of Commerce. They were gone almost all day, and the whole distance, there and back, wasn't much over four miles. They didn't have too good luck, because the town was in just about the same fix as us. The ice had closed the river for them too, and their land roads weren't much. So food was scarce. Our men did bring back, I remember though, a hog's head, a sack of meal, some canned stuff, and a bushel of potatoes.

"That was one time when Mr. French was glad to take over the cooking. And you should have seen what a mixture he concocted. He dumped all the food on the boat, including the hog's head, into the biggest pot we had, with plenty of salt and pepper, and stirred it with an oar from the life boat. Before it was done cooking we could hardly fight those hungry people away from the pot. We dished it up in bowls and ate it with spoons like thick soup. My, it was good! The very best food they ever ate everybody said. They called it *Sensation Stew Français.* That one pot kept us going for four days, and then the ice left us as suddenly as it had come. We didn't lose any time about casting off and getting on down the river. At the first town we played we bought groceries and cooked a good meal right after the show."

"When we got off on that starvation story," said Captain French, "I was startin' to tell you about the other partner I had. That was Ed Price. He was always doin' some of the funniest things you ever heard of, and yet he had a lot of sense. I'll never forget the night I met him. It was in '82, I think, and we had started that year from Pittsburgh. As we were floating down past St. Mary's, West Virginia, a storm hit us, a real whirler. When that wind got hold of us, we didn't have any more control at all, and it slapped us right into a little shanty boat that had tied up below the landing. It was too dark to see what we had done to it, but when I managed to get the Sensation over to the shore a hundred yards down, I walked back to see what had happened. I found a little man, no bigger than Ida there, in his underwear, standing on the roof of his shanty, shaking his fist at us. He was so mad and excited he couldn't even cuss—he was just sputtering. His boat, he called it the Sylvan Glen, wasn't hurt much, and before long we got to talking business. He was making pictures of people, tintypes he called them, at two bits apiece. He thought maybe he could get some good business out of the crowds that we drummed up for the show, and so he decided to come along with us. We lashed his photograph boat to our side and started on. We did pretty well together. He took pictures in the daytime and we showed at night. We drew a crowd for him and he helped boost our show. Before long we decided we ought to be partners. So I bought half the Sylvan Glen and he bought half the Sensation, and we agreed to split the expenses and the take. Business was good on the lower River, and both of us was making more than either would have made separately. But when we started back up the river, and a little picture-making on his boat was all we could do, he sold his half of the show back to me, and, because he asked me to, I sold my half of the Glen back to him. You see the expenses on the SENSATION were a lot more than on his little outfit. When we started out from Pitt in June, though, doing fine business, he wanted to buy in again, and then when business fell off as we were coming back up the next spring, he wanted to sell back again. It went on that way for three years—when business was good he bought in, and when things went hard he sold back to me. Two years ago I told Price I wouldn't sell to him any more. At first he thought I was joshin' him, and when he found out I meant it, he got that mad he couldn't talk. We were standing right up here where we are sittin' tonight, and Price began pullin' his mutton-chop whiskers with one hand and scratching the side of his leg with the other, the way he does when he gets excited. Said he'd build his own showboat, by God, he'd name it PRICE'S NEW SENSATION, and he'd drive us from the rivers. He took off after that, and I heard the other day that he was down at Paducah outfittin' a boat."

"The river's a mile wide"—it was John McNair talking—"and I guess there's plenty of room for him. But he'll have to hustle if he gets a showboat as good as this one we're gona build. By the way, Cap'n, what'll you name her?"

"Well, John," French answered, "I've never run any show except the 'New Sensation' even when it was on a wagon. So I guess this second boat will be the NEW SENSATION too. Eh, Callie?"

"That's right," Callie answered. "FRENCH'S NEW SENSATION. If it was named anything else, I'd think I'd got on the wrong boat."

"Yes, I hope it will always be the same good show, no matter if you do have to change the boat under you, and I know it will." Charlie Breidenbaugh couldn't realize that he was speaking a prophecy. In reality there were to be four more boats and always the same name, the NEW SENSATION.

There was a lull in the talk as the group watched a stern-wheeler approaching closer and closer. As she rounded the bend, the moonlight turned the spray behind her into a moving snowbank, with her mounting decks towering in front of it. The dignified tones of her great whistle reached them at exactly the same moment that the SENSATION under them began bobbing up and down on the waves the steamer made. Captain Jack leaned forward in his chair as if he were watching the finish of a race. "They're faster than they used to be and maybe a little fancier, but not so good. A steamboat nowadays is nothing but a fifty-dollar barge with twelve thousand dollars' worth of gingerbread and smoke stacks on her. Still dangerous too.

I've been on six that went down: one blowed up, two burned, and three snagged. And I ain't through yet."

"Sounds like a dangerous business," said dapper Tony Lavely. "From what Captain French has just been saying, showboating isn't exactly what you'd call safe. Captain, what would you say is the worst spot the New Sensation has ever been in?"

Captain French had to think a minute. "Well," he said, "after that business at Vidalia that I was tellin' you about, when we lost the hull from under us, I guess the next worst happened to us at Tiptonville, Tennessee, it must have been on our third or fourth trip down. Almost a mile above the town we were trying to pull over to make the landing on the darkest night I ever tried to see through. The first thing I knew the bow began rearing up, with a sound like sandpaper on the back of your hand, except louder. And sure enough, there we were more than halfway up on a gravel bar. The boys worked until midnight, but we couldn't do a thing. There just wasn't enough water there to float her. We were all tired out, and at last we decided to go to bed and do the job next day. During the night the river kept on falling, and by morning we were a way up on dry land, and by the end of the week the Sensation was a hundred yards from the river. Things looked bad. No food, no money, no salaries for anybody!

"Four of our people quit us right there. They sacked up their clothes, and set out on foot through the snow and woods for Cairo, eighty miles away. I heard later that they made it all right, the folks on the way givin' them grub and shelter.

"We had been late gettin' started that year, and that was the coldest winter I can remember. Somebody over at Tiptonville had seen what a fix we were in, and some of 'em over there invited us to give our show in their courthouse, no rent and no license fee. Our job was to get over there with enough stuff to put on the show. We still had that blind mule with us then, and so we built a sleigh out of green saplings, loaded our trunks on and started out. We had one bad creek to cross, but it was pretty well frozen over. We had almost made it over, when the ice broke and all our costumes and equipment got good and wet. We fished them out, and later had to dry them all by the courthouse stove. We played three nights in the District Court Room to good crowds, and we gave them the best we had. Magic and songs, acrobatics, a stump speech, that Aerial Suspension Act we learned from the Herbert boys, and some kind of comedy-farce for all of us. They appreciated our efforts, too, and we got enough money to stock up and start all over again when a rise in the river floated the SENSATION clear the next month. I'll never forget the good people of Tiptonville."

"Showboating seems a pretty rough game," said Tony Lavely.

"Yes, it's been a little rocky at times," answered French, "but I wouldn't trade it for any other business in the world. Somehow it gets hold of you. When you take a good show to a landing where a show ain't never been before, or even a place that ain't had a show for a year, and you watch their faces, you get paid for a lot of trouble. Most of 'em haven't done anything but work all their lives and that's all livin' has meant. For a little while anyway they *feel* something, and they like it. It's like releasin' the safety valve before she blows up.

"And then, too, there's good money in showboatin', and we're gona get it with this new outfit. The roughest days are over, because things'll be different now. With that tow of ours back there," pointing to the SENTINEL, "we can go where we please and stay out of the bad spots."

"I sure hope you're right," said Captain Jack, as he got up and shoved back his chair. It was eleven o'clock, late for old people, as the Captain remarked, and the other visitors were also getting ready to go ashore. As each one shook Captain French's hand, he wished him luck in the building of the new boat.

"And don't forget the cathedral windows," said Tony Lavely.

"And the *cal*-li-ope," said Charlie Breidenbaugh. "That seems a mighty good idea to me."

"And twice as many seats as you've got on this one," added Captain Jack.

Ten minutes later lights in the cabin below had been blown out, and the dark boat rested.[3]

---

[3] The incidents related in this chapter are an authentic though informal summary of what happened to the Frenches from 1800 to 1887.

Principal Sources: Logbooks, manuscripts, albums, newspaper files, and interviews.

Other Sources: Items listed in the bibliography under Maurice Elfer, Meigs Frost, Corinne Hardesty, Rose Knox, Sidney Snook, Wesley Stout.

VII

SHOWBOATING: A BUSINESS

Two Captains Courageous

WITH HIS second boat Captain French adopted as his motto, "Always Good—Now Better than Ever," which appears on many of his later handbills. Certainly the new boat lived up to the new slogan. John McNair and his father-in-law Hiram Fitch built her during the summer of 1887, with Captain French rather fussily directing operations. She was twenty feet wide and one hundred and ten feet long. She had, like the original boat, only one deck, but above the main cabin she boasted a texas, where most of the company had quarters, and on top of this an ornate little pilot house shaped like a church steeple. An ingeniously rigged gear enabled a pilot here to steer both the showboat and the tug behind.

The auditorium was roomy, fitted with two hundred opera chairs instead of the rough benches of the first boat. The stage, proportionately larger than the old one, was equipped with a canvas drop, painted with an Italian water scene and rolled from backstage. Painted wing flats furnished scenery. The windows were bordered with cathedral glass, as Captain French had promised, wine-colored and blue, and between them frolicked the same circus freaks. The outside window trim was changed to a harmonizing maroon and the outside cabin walls were the same gleaming white as the original. The innovation of which all on board were proudest was the calliope, the second ever to be installed on a showboat. It had been designed by John McNair and the graduated brass pipes poured by the foundry in Cincinnati. Mounted on the roof of the texas, just behind the pilot house, and fed by steam piped from the SENTINEL behind, it added much to the general decorative appearance of the boat. True to her word, Callie French did the playing, always donning asbestos gloves. For almost a year her repertoire was limited to "Cricket on the Hearth" and "The Blue Alsatian Mountains." [1]

The expansion of Captain French's business in the 1880's was much broader, however, than merely the matter of a new boat and a calliope. Real prosperity began for him with the purchase, in 1885 at Louisville, of the little steam tug, the MARTIN P. MURPHY, which he bought for his gold watch and ten dollars. McNair, who had recently joined the company, added to his duties of acrobat and tuba player those of engineer. Although the little boat proved not strong enough to push the SENSATION upstream, she could handle her at the landings, in and out, and at the crossings, and could increase her speed downstream. After a year French traded the MURPHY (and $350 to boot), down at Donaldsonville, Louisiana, for the SENTINEL, a more powerful tow-boat with a steel hull. The acquisition of this boat gave to the NEW SENSATION for the first time complete freedom of the rivers. It made showboating not only immensely safer, but it made it predictable, a business with a schedule. Showboating was no longer to be the victim of weather and current and accident. With the SENTINEL behind him, Captain French not only knew that he would reach a given landing five hundred miles away, but he knew exactly at what hour he would arrive. That certainty meant advance advertising, and that in turn meant crowds and prosperity, and those made possible a bigger and better show. Now, instead of hiring a tow from Port Allen or New Orleans back up the river, the showboat could do business going up the river as well as going down, and it could even hurry first to the starred landings to skim off the cream in advance of competition— for there were soon to be other showboats—and turn back at leisure to play the less desirable stands. Captain French in his later days always insisted that he could never decide which of the three was most responsible for his success—his wife, the steam tow, or John McNair.

Even before the purchase of the steamer, Captain French had begun to expand his original territory of the lower Ohio and the lower Mississippi. At the beginning of his fourth season he had the SENSA-TION towed up to Pittsburgh, four hundred fifty miles above any former starting point. He stopped here only long enough to employ new actors, rehearse new acts, and outfit the boat, and then got an-

[1] A legend on the river insists that French's first calliope was later installed on Menke's GOLDENROD, and from there transferred to The Mariners' Museum at Newport News, Virginia, where a calliope is now on exhibition.

other tow well up the Monongahela River, where he opened with a fourteen-feature specialty show on April 15, 1882, at Rice's Landing. The opening marked an innovation in schedule as well as in territory. From that time on, instead of beginning his season in the fall, he was to start in early spring in the North, where the mining people were ready for entertainment after a long winter, and then reach the South in late fall and winter, when the sugar cane and cotton money was flowing freely. He thus set the pattern for showboat schedules for a generation.

When he arrived in the South that same cruise, he left the Mississippi to venture a short ways into Bayou La Fourche, the heart of the sugar cane section. He found here people—boatloads of them—almost isolated from the outside world. They were eager to spend money for good entertainment, for the cane crop had been good and no show had ever before penetrated to this "region of sugar and gold." But the bayous are slow sluggish streams, without perceptible current, choked with vegetation and overhanging branches. They take their source from a river with a low spot in its bank, ooze out over the adjacent low territory, and finally drain themselves either into a river farther south or into the Gulf. French sometimes found that water lilies piled up in front of the showboat so deep that they would bear the weight of a man. Not infrequently snakes dropped on the deck from overhanging branches. The only way for the NEW SENSATION to travel such a stream was to use her sweeps, day and night, with a man stationed on the bow to cut away obstructions. It was a big price to pay, even for the eager crowd that greeted them at every landing, and the SENSATION was soon back in the free-flowing Mississippi. But Captain French had discovered the finest showboat territory in the whole country.

So it was that the new boat, the second SENSATION, pushed by the gallant SENTINEL, four years later worked not only the La Fourche region but penetrated deep into the Bayou Teche country as well, a veritable gold coast for the showboat. Every night—and the stands were often not over five miles apart—the auditorium was filled to capacity with a strange people. Of French descent, they spoke a language that varied all the way from pure Parisian to a mixture called cajun. Performers on the stage began complaining that excessive talking in the audience was interfering with their acts. Spectators persisted in grouping themselves in excited little knots instead of remaining seated in the new opera chairs. Captain French employed special ushers to secure quiet and order. Then it was discovered that each of the noisy little groups had its interpreter, who was translating the words spoken in English on the stage into the *cajun* of his fellows. They were watching the action on the stage and getting the words through their more gifted brother. The speaking parts in the program were promptly heavily cut, and the action and music emphasized—an excellent example of Captain French's willingness always to adapt his show to his audience.

The same year that French broke into the rich Teche country he added in the North the Big Kanawha River with its rough but ready-spending West Virginia mining elements. Here at the historic village of Poca the SENSATION loaded on a record crowd of more than three hundred paid admissions. One wonders where the Captain put the hundred who did not have chairs! He tried with almost equal success the Monongahela (the "Mon" to French), and this time he ventured up its little tributary, the scenic Youghiogheny, with its show-eager iron and steel workers. Surely the industrious little steam tow was writing new attendance figures into the SENSATION's logbook, and adding many miles to her map.

Along with new territory French had added also new methods, especially in the matter of drawing his crowds. In the early years no advance advertising had been possible because wind and current rendered his schedule wholly unpredictable. He had to devise methods, therefore, of letting the inhabitants of a region know of his presence after his arrival. On the first trip he beat a drum to attract people to the landing, spoke through a megaphone, and tacked up handmade posters on convenient trees and prominent village corners. Two years later he was able to have a fife-and-drum corps, which not only performed from the deck of the showboat but paraded the village streets as well. He also acquired a small cannon, which he fired immediately after tying up. On the rivers the story is still told of how Sid Allen, who had the privilege of firing the cannon, on one occasion accidentally pointed it in the wrong direction and blew a hole in the SENTINEL's smoke stack.

By 1883 an outdoor free show had been instituted on the SENSATION. Just before curtain time, after the cannon and the band had co-operated to assemble a crowd at the bank, Mrs. French, dressed as an old lady, would teeter along a tightrope stretched above deck, carelessly singing a song as she minced forward, to the mixed alarm and

delight of all onlookers. Then Sid Allen, acrobatic artist, would perform daring feats in the air and on the trapeze. The light of torches
added a weird effect to the acts.

When the second NEW SENSATION left Cincinnati on December 6,
1887, she was able, with the assistance of the SENTINEL, to dispense
with most of her former advertising methods. Now, as she approached
a landing, the calliope announced her presence for miles in all directions. She was expected, for an advance man, traveling in a speed
launch, days before had pasted up dated posters and distributed handbills. He had also mailed postal cards to rural box holders and had
made arrangements for a license and, in the larger places, a wharfage
fee. Thirty minutes before the performance the calliope played again,
and then followed a free concert by a slick ten-piece band, the members of which went below well before curtain time to double either
in the orchestra or on the stage. In the meantime patrons had been
buying tickets at the booth near the bow, and were being ushered
to seats. If the auditorium filled before the concert above was ended,
the music was "cut" and the performance began early. It was over
by ten o'clock and the boat was clear fifteen minutes later. The showboat usually cast off her lines before four o'clock next morning because the later wind, with its easy hold on the clumsy superstructure,
seriously impeded progress, even down the river. Again Captain
French's procedure set a pattern destined to continue for generations
in the showboat business.

The trim new boat carried a program as up-to-date as her crowd-
getting technique. It remained a specialty show, a type that became
characteristic of the NEW SENSATION. In addition to a generous sprinkling of orchestral numbers, a total of twenty-three "acts" appear on
the handbills of this date, usually about fourteen of these constituting
a single program. The show opened with blackface minstrelsy, featuring dancing and joke-telling. Captain French still headlined the bill
with his magic act, though he had dropped his banjo exhibition. Musical numbers, with the exception of sentimental songs and fiddlers'
contests, did not seem so popular as acrobatic acts, minstrel features,
comic monologues, and stump speeches. The show always closed with
a comedy-farce, such as "The Lying Valet," in which most of the
cast on board took part.

Much of the credit for the marked improvement in the SENSATION's
offerings during this period should go to Mrs. Ida Fitch McNair. She

had come on board in 1884, when she was thirteen, to visit her friend Mrs. French. The next year she was married to John McNair on board the boat when it was wind-bound at Darrowville, Louisiana. She first took minor roles in the closing comedy, and then in the minstrel opening, and later tried a juggling act of her own. In the meantime she was understudying all the female roles, even Mrs. French's part in assisting the Captain in the magic act. Before long she was designing and making costumes for most of the specialty acts and planning the whole show. At last she became stage manager and director, with the duties of trying out new acts and new actors, of creating song and dance patterns, and of conducting rehearsals—though the last were few in number after the first week of the season. Her greatest responsibility was to see that the acts chosen for a given program moved steadily forward to an orderly conclusion. Her work on the show was twice temporarily interrupted by the birth of her daughters, Frenchie and Clarkie, who, like their parents, soon became performers in the show.

The years 1884–1889 were important not only to the Frenches and McNairs but also to the growing institution of showboating. In expanding his territory, Captain French had discovered a fundamental principle of the business—that it was best adapted, both in service and in returns, to regions lying near the outskirts of civilization. With his new boat, his steam-tow, his advertising technique, and his general show procedure he had set a pattern for showboating for years to come. Best of all, by the wholesomeness of his programs, coupled with their attractive variety, he had restored confidence in river entertainment and in showboats.

In April, 1894, Captain and Mrs. French found themselves the proud owners and operators of two showboats, both of them the finest that had ever floated on the Mississippi. The usual pressing question, this time doubly acute, was what to name them. Already French's trade name, NEW SENSATION, had come to stand for something on the rivers, as Callie French expressed it. No other name, for both sentimental and practical reasons, seemed possible. One of the new boats, therefore, was named FRENCH'S NEW SENSATION No. 1 (the third boat to bear the name), and the other was called FRENCH'S NEW SENSATION No. 2 (the fourth to bear the name). The former SENSATION they sold to Orke, McNair, and Armstrong, all of whom were already associated with the boat. Orke was a juggler, J. E. McNair a pilot, acrobat, and musician, and Armstrong a band leader. The three, with the assistance of Wiley Preston McNair, operated the boat for the next two years as the VOYAGEUR.[2]

The Frenches' new and exciting acquisitions had come about in this way. The NEW SENSATION, with its towboat methods, its expanded territory, its improved ways of advertising, and its attractive vaudeville offerings, had proved so successful that competition had appeared. C. F. Breidenbaugh—the same Charlie Breidenbaugh who had been present at the birth of the second NEW SENSATION in 1887—had launched the THEATORIUM in 1889. He had built it, with the help of Jim Hennen, at Hawesville, Kentucky, on the Ohio, a hundred miles below Louisville. They had built well, profiting from Captain French's experience, for this was not only the largest, but also the finest showboat to date. Tony Lavely, who had been operating a dog-and-pony show, was made the manager, Breidenbaugh the captain, and the new palace started down the rivers on its first cruise. It had reached Donaldsonville, Louisiana, when it encountered French with his NEW SENSATION in 1890. Business had been bad up the river, and Tony apparently did not realize that he was on the edge of showboaters' paradise. The owners were therefore happy to sell the new showboat to Captain French for a cash price that represented only a small loss to the builders. This THEATORIUM, destined to bear eight successive names through a long and varied career, became FRENCH'S NEW SENSATION NO. 1.[3]

The other boat came into French's possession in a somewhat similar fashion. Early in 1893 Eugene Robinson had built, at Jeffersonville, Indiana, with New Orleans capital, two magnificent boats, one a freak museum and menagerie, the other a showboat. Both he called FLOATING PALACE. For two years the two plied the river towns with entertainment, but financial difficulties followed close after them. Prospective stands seemed to have a disconcerting habit of asking Robinson if his boats were the NEW SENSATION, and, upon a negative answer, they usually furnished meager audiences. In the spring of 1894 Captain French on Bayou La Fourche received a telegram that the Robinson boats would be sold at auction next day in front of the Federal Court-

[2] In 1894 the boat was purchased by Troni Bros., and tied up at New Iberia, La., as a dance hall. It was later converted into a cane barge.
[3] It was successively labeled THEATORIUM, FRENCH'S NEW SENSATION NO. 1, NEW OLYMPIA, WATER QUEEN, GREATER PITTSBURGH, WATER QUEEN, COTTON BLOSSOM NO. 2, WATER QUEEN.

house in Louisville, Kentucky. The Captain got there—via a gasoline speedboat—in time to bid in the larger FLOATING PALACE at a figure far below what it had cost the builders.[4] This became FRENCH'S NEW SENSATION NO. 2.

And so it was that Captain and Mrs. French, early in 1894, found themselves in possession of the two finest showboats on the rivers. Either could properly be termed a Floating Palace, and from this date the phrase became synonymous with *showboat*. The SENSATION NO. 1 (formerly the Breidenbaugh boat), with a hull one hundred and thirty-two by twenty-eight feet, was the first showboat with two full decks throughout. She had an octagonal pilot house, highly ornate but nevertheless possessing a certain restrained dignity in keeping with the fine lines of the boat. The auditorium, with a normal seating capacity of six hundred and twenty-four, extended through both decks, with a gently sloping floor, a tier of boxes, and a balcony. The stage, provided with two drop curtains and ample scenery flats, was twelve feet deep, with a proscenium fourteen by nine. Oil-burning footlights gleamed above an orchestra pit big enough for ten musicians. Dressing rooms and generous living quarters were provided with running water, in the West always a mark of luxury during the nineteenth century.

The SENSATION NO. 2 (formerly the Robinson PALACE), boasting all the features of the other boat, was even larger and more palatial. Its hull, one hundred and fifty by thirty feet, carried two lofty decks, with a texas and pilot house above. Its double-decked auditorium, with twelve plush-lined boxes and two balconies, seated seven hundred and fifty-nine patrons, with the double aisles free. Both inside and out it was well covered with wooden lace and other decorative designs, and the dressing rooms were paneled with mirrors. Evidently the showboat was feeling the influence of the gingerbread-adorned palatial river steamers of the preceding decades. The footlights, the last touch of modernity, were fueled with acetylene gas pumped from under the stage. The flat wing and back scenes were ample for settings in the forest, in the street, and indoors. No wonder Captain French could not resist bidding her in at the Louisville auction, even though he already possessed an ample boat!

Fortunately the McNairs, after an absence of two years on the

---

[4] The museum boat was bid in by a sugar company and converted into a cane barge.

Courtesy Donald T. Wright

The AMERICAN

Lightner's FLOATING PALACE

VOYAGEUR, had returned, in response to Captain French's urgent invitation. The Captain had facetiously written in his very best style:

By the high priest of Jericho and Jehoshaphat you are ordered to appear on or before the 15th of April . . . on board the NEW SENSATION to show cause why you hold a license as engineer and to receive in good and lawful money the sum of forty dollars per month and your grub for such services as you are able to render to your humble and obedient servant,

A. B. French

With the McNairs available, the problem of managing the two boats was considerably simplified, especially since Mrs. French, who had already been granted a pilot's license in 1888, now applied for and received a captain's license. She became captain and pilot of the SENSATION No. 1, and her husband took charge of SENSATION No. 2. The McNairs were divided about equally between the two boats, though there was always much visiting back and forth. Usually Capt. Callie French, J. E. McNair, and his daughter Frenchie were on SENSATION No. 1, and Capt. A. B. French, Mrs. J. E. McNair, her daughter Clarkie, and Wiley Preston McNair were on SENSATION No. 2. The rivers do not record two families, living constantly together, happier than the Frenches and the McNairs. This wholesome relationship proved so binding that even their later retirement from the business was not to change it.

Mrs. French was ready for her new responsibilities. As early as 1888 she had been granted her first pilot's license for the Mississippi River, and upon each renewal thereafter it had covered more and more of the western waterways, until by 1895 it was good for "the Ohio, the Mississippi (both Upper and Lower), and all tributaries and bayous flowing into or out of said rivers."

Callie herself, in a reminiscent mood during her last visit to New Orleans, left a whimsical account of applying for her licenses:

I remember it like yesterday, I was proud—the first woman pilot, the second woman captain on the rivers. I put in my application for examination in New Orleans in 1888.

It needed three river pilot endorsers. I got seven: Captain George Clark, Captain Henry Partee, Captain J. D. Hegler, Captain Oscar Whitten, Captain Wes Conner, Captain Tom Good, Captain Jim Baldwin. . . . Captain O'Reilly and Captain Youngblood were the examiners.

Captain O'Reilly said, gruffly: "Well, I don't see anything in the regulations says a woman can't be a river pilot."

Captain Youngblood said: "If I didn't know your name, young lady, I know those seven who endorsed you. They're good enough to pass any-body."

And I captained and piloted steamboats on the rivers from 1888 to 1907 and never lost a boat or had an accident.

The Frenches soon found that the operation of the two showboats brought decided advantages. In the first place the two outfits could get over more territory in one season than any SENSATION had before been able to cover. In general the earlier pattern was retained. They started as soon in the spring as ice permitted at a point well up the Ohio, and played the Upper Ohio, Allegheny, Kanawha, Mononga-hela, and Green when the steel mills were running full force. During the late summer they reached the Lower Ohio and its tributaries and the Upper Mississippi, as far north as Prairie du Chien. During the fall and early winter when cotton money was plentiful, they visited the Lower Mississippi and its tributaries, adding the Atchafalaya and Yazoo regions as new territory. Of the sixty navigable streams whose waters flow either into or out of the Mississippi, thirty-nine were entered by one of French's SENSATIONS during the season of 1897. During the same year these boats visited fifteen states. Each boat was efficiently chaperoned by a steamer-tow: No. 1 was pushed by the MARY STEWART, and No. 2 first by the RUTH and later by the CLYDE.

Another advantage of operating the two boats simultaneously was in the matter of program. The Frenches were now able to offer an unusual number of acts, and an interchange of actors between the boats added even more variety. Handbills and logbooks of these years list a total of forty-two items, all of them in the category of vaudeville. The usual performance included a skit or short play (often "Irish Justice"), sentimental songs (on board SENSATION No. 2 these were illustrated by lantern slides lighted with acetylene gas), at least three musical numbers, an acrobatic act, several novelty acts, a blackface minstrel session, a dance number, a magic act, with an afterpiece or grand ensemble for the finale. One or more numbers featured "the Singing Soubrette" with her short full skirt, bespangled bodice and tight waist, low neck, and very short sleeves. That was the nearest approach to the risqué that Captain French would permit. Even so, more than once when the boat was playing the Monongahela or the Kanawha River, the little songstress had to be rescued from those who would have had a closer view than the stage allowed. Immediately before the final act Captain French usually made a "thank you" speech in which he extolled the beauties of the particular town where the boat happened to be playing. "I hope," he would repeat at each town, "when I retire, to make this place my home." If door receipts had been unusually good, he closed with the lines, "When I am called to that undiscovered country, I hope my friends will bring this body right here for its final resting place." His wife was constantly reminding him that someday she was going to have to bury him all up and down the Mississippi.

During 1897 the NEW SENSATION No. 2 staged "Uncle Tom's Cabin" on the Northern rivers, the only instance of one of French's boats ever offering a full length drama.[5] The play was discontinued, for obvious reasons, on the cruise South when the boat reached Kentucky. Meanwhile the NEW SENSATION No. 1 was also trying an innovation. The handbills announced an old fiddlers' contest as the finale on the program, when "Randy Bill"—no other name has survived— would defend the musical reputation of the SENSATION against all challengers. The next year both boats reverted to straight vaudeville.

Whatever the bill happened to be, the Frenches always had the cleanest and the best shows on the rivers, as any old-timer would tell you. The spirit of family life permeated the whole performance. The arrival of the NEW SENSATION at many landings became an occasion of social as well as entertainment significance. Families came in buggies and surreys and boats and on horseback from ten or twenty miles away, as much to greet old friends, including "Aunt Callie" and "Old Man French," as to enjoy the show. The mine owner sat between the collier and the foundry worker, the master of a plantation rubbed elbows with the poor white. Men and women who many years before had loved the dramas of old Boston or aristocratic Charleston now enjoyed the showboat's rich variety programs with as keen a relish as those families who had never before witnessed footlight entertainment. Here was appeal to all ages, all classes, all tastes, and all purses. The genuine showboat was the most democratic institution which the frontier produced.

As French's reputation for good entertainment spread up the rivers and down the bayous, he was able to attract more and more of the real talent of the vaudeville stage. It was no longer necessary for everybody on board "to double in brass," as in the old days. Specialists were often responsible for no part of the show except their own act.

[5] Corinne Hardesty (New Orleans *Item-Tribune*, August 25, 1929) insists that "French essayed Shakespearean roles," but evidence seems lacking.

At last the entertainment had become more important than the battle with the rivers, and consequently some real artists were developed. J. A. Coburn and Lew Baldwin, later called Coburn's Greater Minstrels, were with French two seasons. There also were Ed Renard, celebrated ventriloquist; the team of Cunningham and Curran, billed on the SENSATION as "A Knockout Song and Dance," later on the Keith Circuit; Smith and Fuller, a musical team on the boat, afterward internationally famous on the stage; Jerry Cohan, father of George M. Cohan, featured in a song number on the SENSATION; Charles Grapewin, comedian supreme, of later fame in "The Awakening of Mr. Pipp"; and many another who walked from the SENSATION's footlights to the nation's vaudeville stage. Even Nellie McCoy made her professional debut on the SENSATION. Both variety show and legitimate theatre began scouting French's showboat each season to glean the best of its talent.

It was Ida McNair's duty to hold tryouts and advise French about applicants. One of the Captain's favorite stories concerned a song-and-dance act, a father and four daughters. Mrs. McNair had approved, but Captain French hesitated, because the girls were unmarried, and, as he phrased it, "the river moon seemed to have a queer power with such people."

"These girls just ain't the marryin' kind," the father insisted. The contract was finally signed, with the agreement that for each daughter who married during the season one-fourth of the act's pay was to be deducted. That was in April. When the showboat docked at New Orleans in December, all four daughters had married and the father was doing a guitar-solo act for board only! Cupid's toll had been heavy, for showboat romances had a way of ending in weddings.

The showboat, especially Captain French's, proved attractive to actors despite low salaries. It offered far more, too, than an opportunity to live leisurely. It represented a rare combination of river life, stage life, and domestic life. The logbooks reveal intimately all three sides of what must have been a peculiarly satisfying, and at the same time interesting, way of living. While some entries record only the name of the town, the "take," and the weather, others add revealing details:

At Elizabethtown, Illinois, "Old friends McAfees boarded to go with us as far as Rosio [probably Rosiclare, Illinois].

At Vanceburg, Kentucky, "Stopped to get Sam and Rosie married— high wind."

At Friar's Point, Mississippi, "John [McNair] caught cat[fish] wt. 20½ pds."

At Wellsville, Ohio, "Tooker bros. [acrobats] joined us here."

At Cairo, Illinois, "Caro too big for us only $86.45. Wharfage $5.00. license $10.50 but got off for $5.00. Rain."

At Ravenswood, in West Virginia's mining section, "No use to stop hereafter—town no good almost held by toughs and our folks threw a bucket of slop on people on flat and they cut two new lines for us."

At Vidalia, Louisiana, "Town presented Mrs. F[rench] with lapfull of roses."

After twenty-two years on the rivers, in 1900 Captain and Mrs. French decided to visit Europe. They had accumulated a comfortable fortune, the Captain's health was not good, and they were feeling that characteristically American urge "to get culture," as Sam Dodsworth would say. The NEW SENSATION No. 1 with the tow MARY STEWART, they sold to E. A. Price, once their partner and friend, recently their bitter rival. Since the name was reserved from the sale, Price re-christened the boat the NEW OLYMPIA, after Dewey's flagship.[6] The NEW SENSATION No. 2, their favorite, they leased to John McNair.

Upon their return to America, six months later, they were greeted with the news that No. 2 had burned, at Elmwood Landing, Louisiana, on the Atchafalaya. The acetylene gas, stored for the footlights in a tank under the stage, had exploded, and the flames had enveloped the boat quickly. Fortunately the fire had occurred well after the audience had gone ashore, and all employees, including both crew and actors, escaped safely over the gangplank, most of them in sleeping garb. The boat, scenery, wardrobes, and properties, as well as $7,700 in cash in the safe,[7] were a total loss. As soon as proper clothing could be secured, the entire cast and crew, with Captain McNair, went over to Smoke Bend, just above Donaldsonville, where E. A. Price's former boat the FLOATING OPERA had been tied up for years. Though the seats had long before been removed, McNair bought the boat and tried to put it into operation again. It was so rotten, however, that it was adjudged unsafe, and it was finally sold as a houseboat to the Levee Board at Thibodeaux, Louisiana.

One boat sold to his rival on the rivers, one boat burned, and a substitute adjudged too rotten for safety! For the first time in twenty-

[6] Before the year was out the NEW OLYMPIA was washed onto a stump at North Bend, Ohio, by the waves from the big steamer CITY OF LOUISVILLE, and sank, to be later raised and renamed the WATER QUEEN, Price's best known boat.

[7] The U.S. Treasury later redeemed $3,000 of this amount.

three years Captain French found himself without a showboat. He was sixty-six years old, and the river hardships of the earlier days were beginning to tell on him. For some years he had talked of retiring to his plantation in Alabama, for he was financially independent. But it was one thing to retire with a showboat on the river, and it was an entirely different thing to retire with nothing on the river, nothing for his heart to follow. The old Captain was a little sensitive on the matter, and when asked what he intended to do, he would only say, certainly wholly unconscious of punning, "I can't retire without a SENSATION on the rivers."

The four of them, Captains A. B. and Callie French, John McNair and his brother Wiley Preston McNair, spent most of New Year's Day of 1901 making plans for the new boat. This—their fifth and last NEW SENSATION—was to be the biggest and best boat of them all. Into this one they planned to put all the knowledge gleaned from their twenty-three years in the business, and into it, too, they intended to put the money needed. A contract embodying the most minute specifications was signed with the Robert Taylor Shipyards at Higginsport, Ohio, and by June the work was underway. Much of the material was secured from Cincinnati, one suspects for sentimental reasons, since French had constructed his first two boats there. All of the actual building, however, took place at Higginsport. After a heart attack, Captain French was forced to return to the plantation in Alabama, accompanied by his wife. His last words to the McNairs, who were left in charge, were, "John, you and Wiley make this one even better than the Robinson boat." He meant the NEW SENSATION No. 2, which had burned the year before at Elmwood.

The boat was completed by fall—one builder recalls that news of President McKinley's assassination arrived while they were at work —and John McNair got it out ahead of the ice, in time for the tail end of a short season. It was, as Captain French had instructed, both bigger and better than any of the former SENSATIONS. The cost had been twenty-five thousand, and every dollar had been carefully spent by the thrifty McNairs.

One hundred and forty feet long by forty-two feet wide, the new boat was two-decked with a texas and pilot house above. It had a capacity of nine hundred and sixty people, seated in folding, cushioned opera chairs, most of them on the gently sloping floor of the auditorium. The narrow but ornate balcony, which looked like a fringe suspended above three sides of the main floor, ended in a double tier of cushioned boxes that flanked the generously proportioned stage. The back section of the balcony was labeled, "For Colored." The ticket office and the Captain's suite were at the bow, partly under the rear of the auditorium. The rooms at the stern, back of the stage, served both as dressing rooms and as living quarters for married couples and single women. Bedrooms for unmarried men, kitchen, and dining room were on the steam towboat. Outside, the colors were white and maroon, with glittering gold on the calliope; inside, red, gold, and green, with blue in the drops. Two conveniences new to showboats appeared: on each side was a derrick for raising and lowering the gangplank; and the entire boat, inside and out, was illuminated with incandescent electric lights, with especially brilliant effects on the stage.[8] Evidently the builders were remembering the tragedy of gas-started fire that overtook their former boat.

Captain French did not live to see this finest expression of all his plans and dreams. In the spring of 1902, accompanied by his wife, he set out from Columbia, Alabama, to join the NEW SENSATION somewhere on the Ohio. In the meantime John McNair had taken tow to Pittsburgh, organized a new show, and then had proceeded up the Monongahela. On May 8, at Charleroi, Pennsylvania, immediately after the first show of the season, he received the news that French had died of a heart attack in a hotel room in Cincinnati. The old Captain was buried at Glendale, Ohio, the home of his people.

Callie French, captain, pilot, and owner, immediately took charge of the NEW SENSATION. Speaking in later years of her arrangements at this time, she said, "John McNair managed the crew, Ida McNair managed the programs, and I managed the boat."

During the next five years she continued in general the policies that had characterized the four former French boats. The performances were restricted to high-class vaudeville, first of all clean, but also vibrantly entertaining, and carefully adapted to the varying needs of the audiences in different regions.[9] With a lengthened season, from April to March, the big boat extended its range, reaching as far east

[8] Although showboats did not use electric lights until 1901, steamboats installed them as early as 1882. These early lights were open arcs, used mainly as searchlights and cargo lights. Since at that time dynamos generated only enough power for one light at a time, the current was turned to the one arc in use. Incandescent lights came into use on steamboats in 1895.

[9] Lyle Saxon (*Father Mississippi*, p. 22) insists that at least on one occasion the boat played "Triss, or Beyond the Rockies," but handbills or logbooks do not substantiate his statement.

as little Charleroi on the Monongahela; as far north as Hastings, Minnesota, only twenty-eight miles below St. Paul; as far west as Forsyth, on the White in Missouri; and as far south as Evangeline's Oak, near St. Martinville, Louisiana. During a good season gross receipts totaled forty thousand dollars, about half of which became net profit.

By 1907 both Callie French and John McNair were ready to retire. Callie was forty-six and McNair slightly older, but both had spent most of those years on the five boats called FRENCH'S NEW SENSATION, and both had accumulated fortunes sufficient for their needs. Perhaps these two far-seeing operators had observed, too, that picture shows on land were fast growing more numerous and cheaper, and that better roads and improved conveyances were daily carrying larger crowds away from the rivers to land-centers of entertainment.

The final decision came rather suddenly early one night when their old rival E. A. Price tied up his WATER QUEEN (formerly the third SENSATION) beside them at Naples on the Illinois River. Captain Price, still determined to put the Frenches out of the showboat business, offered a figure representing a neat profit over the original investment five years before, and the papers were soon signed conveying FRENCH'S NEW SENSATION, this time including the name, to Price. Then the WATER QUEEN canceled her bill for the evening's performance and everybody boarded the SENSATION for the Frenches' last show.[10]

Late that night before she went to bed, Callie French wrote in her logbook, "Our showboat has become an institution instead of an experience."

A very true and wisdom-filled entry, certainly, but at the same time a very surprising one to come from Callie French's pen. She had been born November 20, 1861, at the little village of Jackson, Ohio. Sixteen years later, as a high school junior in the neighboring town of Washington Court House, she had married Captain French, then almost three times her age. Together they had removed the stigma from river entertainment, and had brought a new world of happiness to thousands of overworked, underprivileged frontier people. They had fought all the forces of the rivers, both natural and human, to make the showboat an institution, as she now rightly

[10] Price later sold FRENCH'S NEW SENSATION to J. W. Menke, who operated it until it was disabled in 1930 by a windstorm at Mound City, Illinois. She was pulled into the old Navy Yard there, and later sold by Federal Court order for $1,500 to pay storage costs.

termed it, something fine, worthy of record. They had made it a symbol of wholesome joy, and, incidentally, a thing of profit. Through it all Callie French was the most energetic, the most efficient, and the best loved woman on the rivers. "Aunt Callie" could manage an obstreperous audience or a rough crew as easily and as gracefully as she handled the big boat in the treacherous river currents. And now she was retiring, to manage Calumet Plantation at Columbia, Alabama, without the Captain, it is true, but carrying with her that same energetic and enduring joy of living that had brought happiness to her and to him and to thousands of others along the rivers. She took with her from the boat only one souvenir—the signal bell which her husband had molded twenty years before from eighty-five silver dollars.[11]

No one will ever know in what mood this amazing woman wrote that cryptic sentence across the last page of her last logbook: "Our showboat has become an institution instead of an experience." Was she giving her reason for leaving showboating, which had now lost for her much of its old-time charm? Or was she congratulating herself upon her own part in developing, from the haphazard show-life on the rivers, an institution of service? [12]

[11] On Calumet, Callie French, Mr. and Mrs. John McNair, and their daughters Clarkie and Frenchie built up an interesting stationary circus. In 1914 Callie married C. H. Tomlinson, a planter and merchant of Columbia. She died in 1935, and was buried with the McNairs near Columbia. Much of the circus paraphernalia is now rotting on the plantation, where the same silver bell still calls the farm hands from the fields, but the menagerie and the prancing circus horses have long ago died of old age. Frenchie McNair married E. E. Hammond of Dothan, Alabama.

[12] Principal Sources: Numerous newspaper files, scrapbooks, logbooks, letters, and manuscripts.

Other Sources: Items listed in the bibliography under Maurice Elfer, Edward J. Eustace, Meigs Frost, Corinne Hardesty, Rose Knox, Paul B. Pettit, Herbert Quick, Lyle Saxon, Wesley Stout, Albert S. Tousley, G. H. Wright.

VIII

The Calliope

An Interlude

WHEN THE showboat calliope opened up, the effect was inescapable, for its steamy music spread for miles in all directions. Its great undulating masses of sound billowed over neighboring villages and inshore farms exactly as the clouds of steam from its pipes rolled over the player at the keyboard. No better announcer of the showboat's arrival could be imagined. When its piercing tones proclaimed the glad tidings that a show was at the landing—and that was the meaning of this music to village ears—the result was instantaneous. Dogs barked and children laughed hysterically, and all began a mad race to the river. Many grownups held their breath with excitement, and more than one man closed his little place of business and grinned broadly as he went home to prepare his family for the evening's entertainment.

The noisy instrument made its formal debut on July 4, 1856, at Worcester, Massachusetts. Joshua C. Stoddard, the same man who had dreamed up the horse-drawn hayrake, had invented it the year before. He organized the Steam Music Company (after 1857, the American Steam Music Company) for its manufacture, and secured the patent in October, 1855. His instrument consisted of a series of graduated whistles with double balanced poppet valves, pitched to produce the notes of the scale. These were inserted at spaced intervals in the top of a four-inch main feed pipe, V-shaped, laid flat on a substantial frame, and the valves connected with a keyboard, about two feet wide, at the open side of the V. When a given key was pressed by the player, the connected valve released steam into the appropriate whistle to produce the desired note. The number of whistles varied from thirteen or fifteen to as many as fifty-eight. Most of the cheaper instruments had only twenty, and most of the better ones thirty-two. Stoddard named his raucous instrument cal-*li*-o-pe, after the Greek muse of the same name, meaning *sweet-voiced*, or *magnificent-voiced*. The river people of the nineteenth century either mispronounced it *cal*-li-ope, or called it a steam piano.

The American Steam Music Company continued to manufacture calliopes until the Civil War. During the next quarter century few of the instruments were built, though a man named Kirkup and the Van Dusen bell works of Cincinnati executed a few individual orders. Thomas J. Nichol, who had been Kirkup's bookkeeper, revived the business around 1890, and for three decades thereafter supplied most of the calliopes used by showboats and circuses. He built the simplest and therefore the cheapest calliope obtainable, little more than a combination of iron pipes and brass fittings with a keyboard attached. His instruments, with favorable atmospheric conditions and plenty of steam, easily carried music eight or nine miles. When Nichol died in 1924, his business was continued as The Thomas J. Nichol Company.[1] In the meantime George Kratz of Evansville, Indiana, was pursuing the trade, from 1897 to 1914, when he was accidentally killed. The Kratz instruments were more individualized, both in design and quality, than the Nichol products, and some said, sweeter toned.

Immediately upon the appearance of the calliope, the instrument was proposed for various uses—to furnish city-wide music for towns in lieu of municipal bands, to welcome incoming boats at the larger wharves, to attract notice as an advertising device. During the late 'fifties, most river packets carried either a calliope or a brass band, some of them both, to entertain the passengers and to announce the arrival of the boat. "The Missouri River is now the most musical stream in the world," boasted a local Iowa paper in 1858. From St. Louis to St. Joseph flowed a continual strain of melody. The Union Line of Packets, a dozen boats making weekly trips on this route, all carried full brass bands or calliopes, "that discoursed sweet music as they landed at every place." [2]

After the hiatus of the Civil War, however, the calliope did not resume these rather unusual duties. It became definitely restricted to institutions of amusement, such as the circus, the showboat, and the

[1] Later doing business as a subsidiary of General Devices and Fittings Manufacturing Co., Grand Rapids, Michigan.
[2] Council Bluffs (Iowa) *Bugle,* May 5, 1858.

excursion boat.[3] Spaulding and Rogers' FLOATING CIRCUS PALACE had installed one even as early as 1858, an American Steam Music Company instrument. The first showboat after the War to use a calliope was French's NEW SENSATION, the old Captain's second boat, in 1887. This instrument was manufactured, in accordance with the specifications of John McNair, by the Van Dusen foundry of Cincinnati. After 1890 the calliope became a characteristic and essential feature of showboats. Most of these instruments bore the Thomas J. Nichol label.

The calliope served the showboat well. It was sometimes placed on the towboat, convenient to its source of steam, or often on the top deck of the showboat with its steam piped either from the tow or, in rare instances, its own special boiler. Like other members of the cast, it "doubled," for in its quiet moments its pipes distilled drinking water. Its main duty, however, was to announce the arrival of the show to the whole countryside. The uncertainties of the river made advance advertising both unreliable and expensive. And then, too, in the early days when competition was keenest, showboats sometimes billed landings that they did not expect to play, for the purpose of misleading some energetic rival. Therefore even the best advertising was not trustworthy. But when "Oh Dem Golden Slippers," "Turkey in the Straw," or "Dixie" echoed over the countryside, beyond all doubt a show was at the landing. Patrons always waited for this giant voice before deciding that the boat had actually arrived. It was more than a reminder. Such music had greater power than hundreds of posters, for those merely promised for the future, while the vibrant music somehow demanded immediate action from all who heard. The showboat, no longer mute, had found a mighty voice with which to announce itself to its public.

Some showboats achieved popularity mainly through the skill of their calliope players. In addition to musical knowledge, quick wit and ready ingenuity were also necessary for the playing of these instruments, for most of them lacked a full scale of sharps and flats. And then, too, some of the keys and valves usually stuck in the middle of a tune. Mrs. Norman Thom of the PRINCESS, or Bobbie Wills ("Calliope Red") of the AMERICAN, or L. Ray Choissier ("Crazy Ray") of the NEW ERA could wheedle music from any calliope. Ruth Wil-

[3] The Route Book of Ringling Bros. World's Greatest Show for 1893 labels a photograph "The Inevitable Calliope," suggesting a well-established tradition by that date. Very few steam calliopes were ever used by carnivals.

liams, Joe Baird, Harry Sutton, Charles Tredway, and Clint Cole have charmed thousands, some of them gathered at the river bank, some standing amazed in their fields far inshore, and some bending over washtubs in their own back yards. Their favorite tunes were "My Old Kentucky Home," "Oh Dem Golden Slippers," "Dixie," "I'm a Yankee Doodle Boy," "Goodbye, My Lover, Goodbye," "The Blue Alsatian Mountains," and "Out of the Wilderness." Only one tune, "Home, Sweet Home," was taboo, for superstition said that the calliope playing that melody would rest on the river bottom before the next sunset.

Occasionally tunes became unrecognizable from the awkward hands of such men as the lovable Walter Falkenstein, that calliope player with heart of gold but fingers of putty.[4] Even when the melody did not seem familiar, it echoed from hill to hill down the long river valleys, with a strangely compelling urge. Many versions of the story are still current along the Middle Rivers of the Kentucky mountaineer, who, hearing a calliope for the first time, mistook it for some varmint and hurried down to the landing with his gun and hound-dog to exterminate the animal. No wonder an early writer on the showboat warned that when the calliope, the chimes, and the brass band united to rouse the night, "mothers should have a care for their little ones." Whether the music was always pleasing or not, certainly the giant organ performed well its duty of announcer.

More than any other object, the calliope became the symbol of the showboat, its reverberating echoes inseparable from the glamor of the stage and the beauty of lighted rivers. Even now when its strains float over river water, the old spirit lives again for anyone who has ever seen a showboat performance. Owners seemed as sentimental in this matter as patrons. Many a seasoned veteran at the end has carried away from his boat only the calliope, as best representing to him what his life had been. Norman Thom reserved only the calliope when his PRINCESS was dismantled in 1928, and carried it to his home in Beverly, Ohio. Eugene Eisenbarth was rebuilding and improving his calliope in the basement of his home in Marietta long after he had retired from his FLOATING THEATRE. Ray Choissier bought the WATER QUEEN's corroded calliope in 1938 for $200 when the old boat was stripped. He stored it in his garage in Pinkneyville, Illinois, and steadfastly refused to sell it to a movie corporation for three times that

[4] Falkenstein died at Lowell, Ohio, in 1942, leaving an estate of $15,000 to "the sick and the needy" (Marietta [Ohio] *Times*, December 2, 1949).

sum, much to the bewilderment and disgust of the businesslike repre-
sentative of the film company. Ray merely remarked, in speaking of
the incident to his old friend and employer W. P. McNair, "Ah,
Wiley, we meet some strange people in this world." [5]

[5] Choissier later (1946) sold the instrument for a much larger sum to King
Bros. Circus.

Principal Sources: Letters from Alexander Clark, Curator of Manuscripts,
Princeton University Library; various manuscripts, newspaper files, and interviews.

Other Sources: Items listed in the bibliography under David Buckman, Lucien
Burman, Florence Dorsey, Paul Gilbert, Carl Holliday, N. C. Meeker, Raymond
Spears, and Wesley Stout.

IX

Of Joy and Profit

Captain Price and His Boats

Paducah lies on the Tennessee River at the point of its confluence with the Ohio. Only a few miles above, the Cumberland also empties into the Ohio, and fifty miles below the waters of all three rivers flow into the turbulent Mississippi at Cairo. Situated thus strategically among the rivers, Paducah was for many years a favorite wintering place for showboats. Here in February and March, safe in the celebrated "duck's nest" harbor against the east bank of the warm-flowing Tennessee, they would gather after an early winter on the Southern rivers. New paint, new acts, new jobs, and sometimes even new owners were in order. All energy was bent toward repairing and correcting last year's troubles and also preparing for the new season to open in April or May. It was a happy as well as a busy time.

If you had been on the Paducah wharf in April, 1908, you would have seen the biggest family of showboats ever to operate simultaneously under one man's name. That name was Price—E. A. Price he signed himself, when he could be persuaded to sign at all. Four big showboats lined up at the Paducah wharf bore his name, each worthy to be called a river palace, and each with its nervous little steam tow at its stern. In the past Edwin Price had owned other showboats and in the future he was to acquire still another, but certainly 1908 was his banner year.

At the head of the line floated French's New Sensation, acquired the year before from Mrs. Callie French; next, Price's Greater New York, which only the year before had been Emerson's Grand Floating Palace; next the venerable Water Queen, which at one time had borne the Sensation label; and at the foot of the palatial row, the slightly smaller New Era.

[83]

On board each of the four show palaces Edwin A. Price was owner and captain. When he tied up his entertainment fleet at Paducah that spring in 1908, he had been on the rivers exactly a quarter of a century. For this was the same little chop-whiskered man who had been the eccentric friend of Captain French, and then later his unpredictable rival. The two had met when French's first SENSATION had bumped into Price's SYLVAN GLEN, the little daguerreotype boat. From that rude meeting sprang a friendship that fast ripened into a partnership. For the keen-eyed little Price saw great opportunity in the crowds that the showboat attracted, and soon bought half interest in French's show. The GLEN and the SENSATION were lashed together, and did a thriving business down the river. Price was a valuable addition to the show, for he was a popular and competent piano player. Furthermore, he was almost a sideshow in himself. The quick-motioned, bowlegged little man, always wearing a black alpaca coat, regardless of season, scampering down the aisle to the orchestra pit, clutching at his mutton-chop whiskers with his right hand and scratching his left leg with the other (as he always did when he got a little nervous), was doubtless the best unbilled act of the show. River people had begun calling him "Old Man Price" long before he was middle-aged, because this quaint little figure with the shining round face invariably gave one the impression of having somehow escaped from the album covers of the past.

Price was as unusual in his business dealing as in his other habits. Whenever showboat business fell off, especially when it ceased altogether during the tour upstream, he insisted on selling his half-interest back to Captain French. The nervous little man could not bear the sight of expense money going out when nothing was coming in. Next season, as soon as profits began flowing toward the ticket office, Price would buy back his half-interest in the boat. He repeated this performance of buying and selling back for almost three years.

The climax came in 1885. As the NEW SENSATION approached New Orleans, Price sold back his interest as usual. He left his baggage on the slow-moving showboat, and took a faster conveyance to New Orleans, where he had business to transact. Two days later Captain French happened to tie up at Port Allen (Baton Rouge), next to a big steamer docked for the night. The entire load of passengers became patrons of the SENSATION for the night performance. During the show, when the auditorium was crowded to its very windows, Price returned to get his belongings. Witnesses testify that instantly

The Eisenbarth-Henderson
FLOATING THEATRE.

E. E. EISENBARTH, Manager.

PRODUCING——
Goethe's Literary Masterpiece "FAUST"

Captain Eisenbarth's Favorite Poster

(Above) Mrs. Thom and the Calliope of the PRINCESS; (below) Ray Choissier Removing the WATER QUEEN's Calliope

one hand began plucking nervously at his whiskers while the other frantically fumbled for his wallet. He had sold too soon this year! He demanded immediately to buy back his interest in the SENSATION. But Captain French said *no*, and continued to repeat *no* in spite of the wiry little man's near-hysteria.

That incident put Edwin Price in the showboat business for the next forty-three years. He went immediately to Paducah, Kentucky, where he built a boat modeled closely after Captain French's. In fact he called it PRICE'S NEW SENSATION until he was informed that French would probably object to the theft of his trade name and that the resulting publicity might stamp him as an imitator. Thereupon he called it PRICE'S FLOATING OPERA, probably borrowing his phrasing from the Spaulding Circus of pre-war fame. Exactly therein lay the key to the difference between these two men. Captain French would have been a pioneer in any business in any region. Till the day of his death he was leading the way in every improvement that came to showboating, a fine example of vigorous but cautious courage. On the other hand Captain Price was never the first to try anything. Throughout his life everything he did he had seen someone else do successfully, whether it was mixing a new kind of paste or launching a showboat. He always waited to profit from the other man's trial. So it was that his first FLOATING OPERA was as much like the original SENSATION as he could build it; like French's boat it also was a "floater" —without a tow. Like French's, it displayed circus scenes in gaudy paint between the auditorium windows. Like French, Price restricted his program to vaudeville, and he covered almost exactly the same rivers that French had played. He had learned not only French's methods and advertising technique, but he had also become acquainted with the old Captain's friends—and friends were vastly important to the operator of a showboat.

Again following Captain French's example, he replaced his first boat after a few years with a better one, which he powered with a steam tow. In no other way could he have competed with the rival SENSATION. During the next eight years these two showboats shadowed and dodged each other on the rivers like over-cautious boxers. Captain Price acquired the disagreeable habit of tying up beside the NEW SENSATION, and offering a very similar show at a slightly lower price. In order to elude him, Captain French resorted to the extreme measure of advance-billing three or four towns for the same night, and then dashing quickly, just before curtain time, to the one where he was actually to show. Price tried the same device, insisting that French was following him, with the confusing result that many landings found themselves billed by both boats for the same night, but never knew whether both boats, or indeed either of them, would appear.

And so the gay game of competition continued up and down the rivers. It was generally conceded that the Price performance was as wholesomely clean as French's but it invariably gave the impression of cheapness. As one patron recorded, even the piano "sounded a little tinny." It is certain that Price paid his actors rather scantily. At one time he became so over-suspicious that he refused to put his name to any contracts at all, and he even took care not to write his name or the name of his boat on his logbook. He never granted interviews to the press and never permitted an employee to talk to reporters. Economy became his watchword. It is said that he could tell the day of the week by the condition of his pockets—how much twine and how many rusty nails they contained. On Sunday he carefully wound the string into balls and treated the nails with kerosene. When he passed out a handbill, he gave the reader only a minute, and then snatched back the circular for future use. A small amount of printed matter was thus sufficient for a whole season. Old-timers used to say that Captain Price's exhibitions of economy were the best acts of his show.

In spite of the strange eccentricities of this man, his business thrived, and his showboat became the only really successful competitor of the NEW SENSATION. When Captain and Mrs. French decided in 1900 to sell their SENSATION No. 1, preparatory to touring Europe, Captain Price became an eager purchaser. His reasons for buying French's boat are obvious: his own boat (his second FLOATING OPERA), never too well built and in service since 1891, was in bad condition and must soon be replaced; by purchasing from French, rather than building, he not only acquired an excellent boat, but he also cut in half his rival's potential business. Heretofore French, with his two boats, seemed to have an unfair advantage over him with only one. Now he intended to even the score. He wanted not only the boat but also the trade name—the NEW SENSATION. But Captain French steadfastly refused, inasmuch as he still owned the SENSATION No. 2, which was being leased to John McNair. Price was finally persuaded, in spite of his superstition that a change of name brought bad luck, to rename

the boat PRICE'S NEW OLYMPIA, after Admiral Dewey's flagship, at
the time much in the public notice.[1]

Price's new acquisition was the old THEATORIUM sold by Breidenbaugh in 1890 to French and at that time rechristened NEW SENSA-
TION. Now with its label changed to NEW OLYMPIA, Price hurriedly
transferred to it his program, crew, and band, and finished a short
season in the South. He then started North, and was evidently intend-
ing to winter at some point well up the Ohio. He got only as far as
North Bend, Ohio, when the disaster which his superstitions had been
predicting overtook him on September 8, 1900. Waves from two passing steamers—one of them the big CITY OF LOUISVILLE—washed the
little showboat against a stump, and sank it, with a great hole amidships. The imagination fails when one tries to picture the excitable
and nervous little Captain in the throes of such an emergency!

But Captain Price was not lacking in ingenuity. He raised the
OLYMPIA, had her towed to Leavenworth, Indiana, and rebuilt almost
completely. He followed an old river custom: a boat once sunk, then
raised, must always be renamed. And so she now became the WATER
QUEEN, destined to see more years of service than any other showboat
that ever floated on American rivers.

On board the resurrected boat economy was still the motto. According to Billy Bryant, who with his parents and sister came on
board as actors at Augusta, Kentucky, the living quarters for actors
were bare and small, but clean. In each tiny room a dry-goods box,
with shelves nailed in it and a small mirror above it, served as both
washstand and dresser. Beside it was a bucket with rope attached for
the drawing up of river water. A bunk with a straw mattress, a stool,
and a small oil stove completed the furnishings. The stage was
equipped with oil-burning footlights with sliding frosted glass screens
for dimmers. The scenery was painted on both sides for double duty.
No upholstery softened either the straight little folding chairs in
the auditorium or the narrow boxes that flanked the stage.

The spirit of economy also prompted an emphasis on the WATER
QUEEN's band, for music could be used in the pre-show advertising,
it furnished the featured opening number of the program, and it could

---

[1] The second FLOATING OPERA was later bought by J. E. McNair when the
NEW SENSATION No. 2 burned. The old boat, tied up at Smoke Bend, La., was
being used as a dance hall. McNair found it too rotten for use as a showboat,
and sold it to the Levee Board at Thibodeaux, La., who used it as an office boat.

be conveniently sandwiched in between the various acts throughout the evening. Price uniformed his musicians in white sailor suits (*once white*, Billy Bryant assures us) and round sailor hats with ribbons at the back. For purposes of an imposing parade, Captain Price required that all actors "double in brass." Sometimes a corked or muted instrument had to be given a person who had no musical ability, but he nevertheless suited up and marched with the band. Such was the predicament that Billy Bryant's father found himself in soon after the "Four Bryants" joined the show. The band leader was thoughtful enough to give Sam Bryant an alto horn with a cork in it so that, although he marched with the parade and went through all the motions, he just could not blow any sour notes.

As soon as the WATER QUEEN tied up at a landing, the calliope, the same that had been on the original Breidenbaugh boat, played a spirited concert with such numbers as "Turkey in the Straw," "Old Kentucky Home," and "Oh Dem Golden Slippers." Then the rather suspicious-looking eight-piece brass band, consisting of six musicians, a plugged alto horn and a bass drum (strapped to little Billy Bryant), would line up impressively on deck, all in uniform, and march ashore. It paraded down the two or three streets at a lively clip, and stopped at a prominent corner for a free concert. The standard, usually carried by a child, read "Price's Great Moral Show." At most small towns "the regulars" were assisted by members of the local band, who were anxious to play with "professional musicians." Needless to say, Price did not object to accepting their services without cost to himself. If many tickets remained unsold by late afternoon, the whole musical procedure was repeated, and this time the band continued to play as it paraded back to the WATER QUEEN, in hopes of luring the crowd after it.

The main program was not any better than the band concert. A typical feature was Sam Bryant's magic act of turning water into wine, and then the wine back to water. The magician sometimes became so enthusiastic at the applause as to drink his own concoction, always with dire results. When Mrs. Violet Bryant, Sam's wife, sang "The Fatal Rose of Red," with lantern slides, we are assured that the audience wept out loud. It recovered its composure somewhat when Daughter Florence did "The Wedding of the Lily and the Rose," and it became hilarious when young Billy Bryant "simply wowed 'em" with his mother-in-law gags, and took ten bows on "The Green Grass Grew All Around."

One secret of the thrifty Captain Price's success in the showboat business was his willingness always to improve the show the moment that profits seemed to justify additional outlay. In 1904 he acquired a new band leader, Harry High, who bettered decidedly the quality of the boat's entertainment. It had formerly been Captain Price's policy to employ an actor or a cabin boy and hope that the individual might be able to "double in brass" for the band. With the advent of Mr. High, the policy apparently was reversed: now the Captain employed a musician and hoped that he would be able to double on the stage. Leader High himself records that he often played the role of the heavy—the villain—on the stage.[2] The result was that the WATER QUEEN boasted one of the best small bands on the rivers. The Captain paid for the additional expense of the superior musicians by offering an occasional paid afternoon concert or an aftershow—"Only 10¢ extra!" the handbills said.

In the meantime Captain Price had become associated with a young man who was to make showboat history. Back in 1900 while his showboat was on the upper reaches of the Ohio, Price employed Ralph Waldo Emerson as pilot.[3] By the time the boat reached Cincinnati, which marked the margin of territory covered by the new pilot's license, Price had taken such a liking for the young Emerson that he continued him on the payroll, employing him as advance agent.

Up to this time Price's advertising had been a simple matter. Ten days before his arrival at a landing, he would send two complimentary tickets to the postmaster, who, out of gratitude, tacked an announcement on his bulletin board and mentioned the coming event to his

[2] Harry High recalls his introduction to showboats. When he joined the WATER QUEEN, Captain Price met him at the railway station and escorted him to the boat. As they started down the river bank, the little Captain suddenly began shouting and running to the showboat as fast as his short legs could carry him, where they were astonished to see a fight in progress. Steve, the Captain's son, was chastising a bandman for an impertinent remark to Mrs. Price. After serving as band leader on Price's WATER QUEEN, Emerson's GRAND FLOATING PALACE, and the EISENBARTH-HENDERSON FLOATING THEATRE, Mr. High is now (1950) bandmaster in Evansville, Indiana.

[3] Christened Ralph Waldo Emerson Gaches, he soon shortened his name to Ralph Emerson. He was born at Pittsburgh in 1878, but at the age of ten he moved with his father and step-mother to Letart Falls, Ohio, where his attention was inevitably drawn to the river. Three years later he ran away from home to become dishwasher on a small packet. During the next forty years he became successively clerk, head clerk, master, pilot, showboat advance man, and finally, showboat owner and operator. During his long career he owned in all nine different showboats, among them the finest and largest the rivers have known.

customers. This meager preparation was followed up after the boat's arrival by the calliope (the WATER QUEEN's could be heard for eight miles), the band parade and concert, and a few handbills that Price himself usually struck off on the little hand press which he carried along.

Ralph Emerson was soon to change all this. He traveled a week ahead of the show, plastering each town with announcements. To penetrate inland from the landing he used a horse and buggy, a bicycle, or his own power. Farmers owning land adjacent to country crossroads were induced to erect and maintain signboards to receive the brilliant posters, for Emerson emphasized back-country advertising, and designed special placards for these outlying districts. One read: LISTEN FOR SHOWBOAT CALLIOPE NEXT FRIDAY; another head-lined the distance and the direction to the scene of the show; and a third offered a prize for the first family of twelve to arrive on board. Furthermore he mailed a special post card announcement to every resident on the Rural Free Delivery routes. Ralph Emerson was a good advertising man, and his methods paid big dividends. Frequently at a landing whose population was only two hundred the WATER QUEEN would get an audience of five hundred. In fact the young man became so important to Price that he was allowed to buy one-half interest in the WATER QUEEN, rumor said, to enable Price to avoid paying him a big salary. His wife Mrs. Ralph Gaches served as schoolmistress for the children of families on the boat, and at one time had ten pupils in the "country school" which she held five mornings each week on the stage.

The programs continued to be mostly vaudeville because Captain Price believed the river people preferred this kind of entertainment. Each spring, by advertising in the *Billboard*, he recruited an entirely new list of acts at either Paducah or Cincinnati, for a performer seldom remained on a Price boat for the second season. The salary was low, and then too the Captain liked to present a fresh program at the landings where he had played the year before. When the group gathered on the boat for the first rehearsal they selected one of their own number to serve as director for the season. "The Five Pickerts," "The Six Conklins," "The Four Bryants," "The Musical Toys" (Evalyn and Ben Toy), "The Three Suttons," and "Bob Lively et al," as well as others, appeared on this stage. The Captain seldom employed unmarried men or women. Couples and children in group acts, he believed, were more economical in living quarters, and less conducive to social embarrassment. His offerings were of the variety type, with singing, dancing, acrobatics, character and humorous readings, "lectures" and "political" speeches in the Artemus Ward tradition, sleight-of-hand, and other specialty acts. Music and humor dominated the show. Reliable contemporary critics labeled it "cheap but clean, and very copious." Audiences demanded a duration of three hours.

During a performance, when Captain Price was not needed in the orchestra pit to play the piano, he placed himself in the first row of the audience. At the conclusion of each act he would jump to his feet, especially if the show did not seem to be going well, and, clapping noisily, shout out, "Isn't that just splendid!" "The best I ever saw!" "Did you ever see a better show!" or some similar encouragement to the audience. Quite often the onlookers became almost as much interested in their self-appointed applause-prompter as in the performance itself.

With such an advance man as Emerson and such a manager as Price it is little wonder that the WATER QUEEN prospered, and her owners soon launched into a policy of expansion and boat-buying that must have turned even the Title Registry dizzy. They had already bought LIGHTNER'S FLOATING PALACE. They came across this boat down in the La Fourche Bayou in Louisiana, and immediately Captain Price wanted it. In the first place, she was so small—only ninety feet—that she could slip around the sharp curves and glide over the lily pads of the bayous where the big WATER QUEEN had to use devious and slow methods of navigating the sluggish streams. Furthermore the little FLOATING PALACE [4] had on board a negro minstrel program of only five or six performers, and these could sing their songs and tell their jokes in the cajun dialect, with most pleasing results on bayou audiences. As Price phrased his argument, the little boat was "taking in more and spending less than any other concern on the rivers." And so the two partners bought the showboat, changed her name to the NEW ERA, and put one of the McNair boys in charge of her.

Then Ralph Emerson found another PALACE—this time a real one —that he wanted as much as his partner had wanted the little one. It was Swallow and Markle's NEW GRAND FLOATING PALACE, one of

[4] The similarity between this name and Price's two early boats called FLOATING OPERA has misled some into believing that Price had three boats by that name. After selling his boat to Price and Emerson, Lightner settled at Thebes, Illinois, where he dealt in real estate.

the several big and very elaborate showboats built by the Pope Dock Company at Parkersburg, West Virginia, during 1900–1910. With her tow, she had cost the builders $40,000, and the cautious Captain Price could not be persuaded to make such an investment. "One stump, and that beautiful thing," he argued, "would be at the bottom of the river like any other showboat." But Emerson was determined to have the "beautiful thing." When his partner steadfastly refused to co-operate with him, he sold his half of the WATER QUEEN to Price, and then his half of the NEW ERA to Wiley Preston McNair, and with his augmented capital purchased the magnificent boat.

From the opening night Emerson's NEW GRAND FLOATING PALACE was remarkably successful. The new owner's efficient advertising methods and his generous salary policy to first-class performers kept the big auditorium crowded—and it held nearly a thousand people. Its name became synonymous with the best in the entertainment world, and its brilliant young captain, with an enormous blue diamond sparkling on his immaculate shirt front, became the envy of all the River. Here at last was proof of what everybody had always wanted to believe: a showboat captain was rich.

In the meantime Captain Price was seriously considering retiring —that is, if he could sell advantageously his WATER QUEEN and his half of the NEW ERA. He was nearing sixty, he was getting a little tired of the constant bustle of life on the boat, and he had accumulated a modest fortune. Just as he was contemplating these comfortable possibilities he happened to tie up one April night in 1907 by the side of French's NEW SENSATION at Naples on the Illinois River. The big, well-equipped craft, the fifth of French's boats, reminded him of that "beautiful thing" which by this time he realized he should have bought with Emerson. Suddenly his river-worn WATER QUEEN, which had been the third of French's boats, seemed very meager by the side of this new palace. He remembered, too, the long years of bitter rivalry when the SENSATION always seemed to get the crowds that he should have had—years when he used to say to Captain French, "You waste more than I take in." In a moment half his sixty years had slipped away and with them all idea of retiring. Before he knew it he had bought FRENCH's NEW SENSATION, boat, program, name, and all.

Strangely enough Captain Price still wanted Emerson's NEW GRAND FLOATING PALACE, which certainly had proved itself a money-maker. In less than a month he had purchased it from Emerson. He changed its name to PRICE's GREATER NEW YORK, and took personal

charge of the big establishment. He employed his son Steven to manage the WATER QUEEN and J. W. Menke, his new advance man, to
look after FRENCH'S NEW SENSATION.

And so it was that the fidgety little Captain that spring morning
in 1908 looked with understandable pride upon his showboat world
floating before him in the "Duck's Nest" in Paducah: the two big
boats—the SENSATION and the GREATER NEW YORK, and the venerable
WATER QUEEN and the smaller NEW ERA, each with a ready little
guardian tow behind her.

Ironically enough for Captain Price, in 1908 the showboat business
began a gradual but sure decline. The road show and the picture
theatre, combined with improved land transportation, were beginning to cut into the dividends of river entertainment. Captain Price
with his keen perception of business trends was quick to sense the
change. Always expecting disaster, he feared that he had invested too
heavily in his fleet of boats, and took prompt steps to correct the
blunder. He first sold his half interest in the NEW ERA to Wiley Preston McNair, who already in 1910 owned half the boat. Then he leased
the faithful WATER QUEEN to Otto Hitner, who operated her three
seasons under the name COTTON BLOSSOM [No. 2].[5] Upon her return
to him, he sold half-interest to Jim Bonnelli and Bill Paden, who
managed her one year under the name GREATER PITTSBURGH. After
her sale to Roy Hyatt, her name was changed back to WATER QUEEN,
which she remained.[6]

Captain Price continued to operate his remaining two showboats
for the next ten years, relying on the help of his son Steve and
J. W. Menke. The NEW SENSATION continued to offer a variety show,
with frequent short skits and dramatic and humorous readings, just
as in the days of the Frenches. The GREATER NEW YORK, however,
began running more and more full-length drama, with a rich inter-
larding of music. During his first season on the new boat, Price offered
"Humpty Dumpty," which on account of its possibilities of clean
humor and grotesque characterization fitted very well into the Price
tradition. During 1912, his most successful season, he played "Ten
Nights in a Bar Room" to capacity audiences at almost every stop.
As one member of the cast expressed it, Captain Price played "Ten

[5] Sometimes known as "the little COTTON BLOSSOM," this boat had no relation
to the big original COTTON BLOSSOM with the recessed head.
[6] After the longest life of any showboat on the rivers, she was finally demolished by ice near the mouth of the Big Kanawha River in 1936.

Nights . . ." for ten months with ten actors and made ten mints of money. With its moralizing possibilities, its appeal to the fast-growing prohibition and church elements, and its satisfying melodramatic emotional effects, the drama was especially well adapted to the socially-starved region. It was played "straight"—that is, sincerely and earnestly, with no hint of burlesque either on the stage or in the audience.

In his use of legitimate drama, the cautious little Captain was following proven precedent, for he had already heard of the remarkable and unexpected success of the Eisenbarth-Henderson boat, which played only legitimate drama. In fact Price had been one of those who had warned Eisenbarth that only a program of vaudeville and specialty acts could succeed on the River. Now that his own advice had proved bad, Price was quick to follow the successful lead of Eisenbarth. But only on *one* of his boats! He was still the cautious little Captain.

The Price boats became known as far as the rivers were deep enough to float them, and wherever they went their eccentric Captain became a favorite year-round topic of conversation. Innumerable stories were told about him until he became a legend, and people who had never seen him waited expectantly for his next visit; those who knew him waited also, for they were anxious to renew their friendship with this wiry little figure out of the past, who, with all his queer ways, seemed not to have a single enemy in all the river world.

Prosperity did not make him less frugal. Though he could write a sight-draft for $50,000, he still stuffed his pockets with rusty nails and twine. When eggs were scarce, he loaded his showboat at New Orleans with oranges, at six cents a dozen. On the voyage up the river he exchanged them, "an orange for an egg," and at St. Louis his cargo was worth ten times what it had cost him.

Upon occasion there was never a more imperious captain than Price. Once at Friar's Point, Mississippi, during a violent blow the WATER QUEEN broke her lines and was rapidly swinging into the current. In the emergency, a deck hand was trying to tie a line to a spare anchor that was kept by the ticket office for appearances. When Captain Price shouted, "Cast it over!" the man hastened to answer that he hadn't finished tying it, but the impatient Captain, by this time beside himself with excitement, shouted back, "Damn it, throw it over anyway!" The man did. The anchor was never recovered, but the Captain had had his way.

Though Price could not swim a stroke, he had a bad habit of falling into the river. When the showboat was about to dock, in his excitement, the Captain always got out on the top deck and began giving orders to the pilot, minute and thoroughly confused instructions. In his nervousness he would pull at his square-cut whiskers with his right hand, scratch his left leg with the other, all the while manipulating his body in the direction he wanted the boat to go. He invariably ended up in the water. According to his pilot, on one such occasion he fell into the icy Ohio wearing a straw hat (he always dressed out of season) which he had bought on sale for a quarter, and yet his instructions were, "Don't worry about me, get my hat!" He insisted on personally buying all groceries used on the showboat because he believed he could shop more economically than anyone else.

He collected a pile of rocks on deck, and whenever he was uncertain as to the sounding, he would throw one overboard, a trick he is said to have learned on the tortuous upper reaches of the Allegheny. He kept a little black book in which he wrote the names of people whom he knew he would never employ. Yet he always paid his debts and salaries promptly. Men found him sociable and talkative when he was not busy, though he never smoked or drank. Women found him unapproachable and tart, though they invariably spoke of him as "that cute little Captain!" It would be difficult to find in any region at any time a man more filled with the strange contradictions of a scheming economy and a generous heart than Edwin A. Price.

On his seventieth birthday he announced to his friends that he was ready to retire, that he had no desire to *work* "on borrowed time." (The Captain knew his Bible.) His next move, contradictorily enough, was to buy a showboat rather than to sell one. This time it was the COLUMBIA, originally built for Walter Needham at Cincinnati as the AMERICAN. With a seating capacity of six hundred and fifty, besides the small balcony, it was not large—one hundred and twenty by thirty-two feet—but it was exquisitely outfitted and furnished. It boasted hot and cold water, a heating plant, an electric system fed by two large dynamos, electric fans, and a huge calliope. On the upper deck it flaunted an American flag formed of seven hundred and fifty colored electric lights. Under its stage the well equipped print shop put out a three-sheet daily *Herald*, in addition to handbills for the boat and window placards for the celebrated Bloomer Girl Baseball Team, also under Needham's management. It would seem that contemporaries had reason to point to this boat as probably representing the acme of elaborateness in the outfitting of floating theatres.

Because of financial difficulties Needham sold the AMERICAN to the five Thompson brothers, who were pilots on the Missouri River. In their hands it sank at Bonnett's Mill, Missouri, in 1917. They raised it, and, discouraged by its condition, sold it to Emerson for a thousand dollars, who in turn offered it to Price.

The Captain could never resist a bargain, whether in a straw hat or a showboat, and he promptly bought it. In fact, he had been wanting for some time a boat smaller than either his NEW SENSATION or his GREATER NEW YORK to put into the hands of his son.

Steven E. Price had been one of his father's showboat managers, and in 1910 he had married a girl employed at the time as actress on board the WATER QUEEN. He had never tried acting, but he had tried real estate, and now he was sure he preferred the showboat business. His father therefore made him and his wife a present of the AMERICAN, now renamed the COLUMBIA.

The old Captain had not forgotten his resolution to retire. As soon as he settled the matter of the COLUMBIA, he sold the GREATER NEW YORK in 1917 to J. W. Menke,[7] and the next year he transferred to the same man FRENCH'S NEW SENSATION. Then with his wife he retired to his home in Newport, Kentucky. It was an undramatic but comfortable exit for the man who had owned eight different showboats—four of them simultaneously—during a third of a century in the showboat business.

Steven Price continued to operate the COLUMBIA during the next ten years, mostly on the Missouri River. Mrs. Price became his efficient program director. She nearly always selected a melodrama which particularly emphasized a female role, such as "Nellie the Sewing Machine Girl." Generous specialty numbers were offered between acts. Always more interested than her husband in the showboat, she was left in charge in 1928 while he took a tow of coal down the Mississippi. He contracted pneumonia and died before he could reach home. His father sold the COLUMBIA to J. W. Menke, who had ten years before bought two of Price's other boats. The old Captain himself died two years later, and the name of Price passed forever from the showboat world.[8]

[7] The GREATER NEW YORK sank, a total loss, five days after Menke bought it, in the Ohio, near Newburgh, Indiana.
[8] Principal Sources: Letters, scrapbooks, logbooks, manuscripts, and newspaper files.
Other Sources: Items listed in the bibliography under Billy Bryant, Kyle Crichton, Carl Holliday, Ethel C. Leahy, Sidney Snook, and Wesley Stout.

X

Broadway on the Rivers

The Big Boats and Captain Emerson

A NEW ERA for the showboat business began with the dawn of the twentieth century. It was to be a period of daring investments, giant voluptuous boats, immense luxury-loving crowds, extravagant and exotic shows, and flamboyant advertising. Captain Emerson's slogan, "After the minnows comes the whale," characterizes the era. Owners of these river queens were forced into financial speculation beyond their means, and at the end of the period, about 1915, losses and heartbreak were even bigger than investments and profits had been.

One boat construction company and one man were mainly responsible for this strange chapter of showboat history, the company with a large capital, the man with a big dream of what a showboat could be. The builder was the Pope Dock Company of Parkersburg, West Virginia, which after 1900 became chief showboat designer to the nation; the man was W. R. Markle of Steubenville, Ohio.

Since boyhood Markle had lived on the Ohio, but he had never become a riverman. He had known both Captain French and Captain Price, but he was not a theatre man. By nature he was a promoter. His ideas of the river and of the theatre somehow came together to form this glorious dream of his. He would build the biggest showboat with the finest show and the greatest profits that the river had ever seen. Through him the showboat would enter the world of big business.

He tried to interest capitalist after capitalist, to no avail. To these men it was not enough that he should furnish the idea and put it into execution, while they were to put up the money. In his disappointment and discouragement, he turned to card-playing and gambling as a last means of amassing sufficient capital to turn his dream into reality. His friends began calling him "Double R" Markle, a name that stuck to him the rest of his life.

By 1900 he had saved from his card-playing enough to persuade the Pope Dock Company to begin construction of a showboat according to his specifications, with the promise of additional thousands to be paid in as the building progressed. By August, when scarcely more than the frame of the long, graceful boat had been laid down, all his investment had been used, and the Pope Dock Company was refusing to go further until additional funds should be forthcoming.

And so it was that on the night of August 10, 1900, "Double-R" Markle sat at a gaming table in the parlors of the Stagg Refreshment Hall in Parkersburg, with Matthew O. Swallow of St. Marys, West Virginia, opposite him. By midnight Markle had raked in $1200. He could have won more, but he was playing him "soft." He had found out that Swallow had plenty of money, and he preferred a possible partnership to an extra thousand or two. After their "friendly game" they retired to Markle's room to talk showboats and the fortune that surely awaited the man who modernized the business. Daybreak found them at the dock inspecting the unfinished giant hull, and by lunch time Mat Swallow had turned over to the Pope Dock Company enough money for the completion of the first of the super-built, ultra-modern showboats. Markle and Swallow were to be equal-sharing partners.

The new boat was ready by the spring of 1901, and because the partners could not agree on a more individual name it was christened SWALLOW AND MARKLE'S GRAND FLOATING PALACE. She was one hundred and fifty-two by forty feet, yet drew only eighteen inches of water—trim, well-built, and graceful. Her whole exterior gave one the impression of combined sturdiness and slender grace, without any of the boxlike awkwardness of the earlier showboats. The wooden lace was so well subordinated to the general design as to be noticeable only as detail. The single color effect, glistening white, tended to exaggerate the size of the boat, especially her length. Her auditorium, resplendent in white and gold, seated almost a thousand people in comfortable armed opera chairs. It was brilliantly illuminated by electric lights clustered in interesting designs, and it was cooled by huge electric fans. The roomy aisles and the twenty-foot stage were covered with Brussels carpet in scarlet and gold. The whole design, suggestive of strength and efficiency combined with luxury, furnished a pattern for all the larger showboats that were to follow, and almost overnight set the Pope Dock Company up in a specialty, without competition for the next ten years.

Markle, remarkable for his courage and his ingenious ways and means, quickly assembled a crew and cast from Parkersburg and vicinity, chartered the steam towboat CRICKETT, hurried his less gifted partner off the scene, and was ready for the rivers.

On that first trip the NEW GRAND FLOATING PALACE played all the way down the Ohio, dipping into the Kanawha for three weeks, and then down the Mississippi to Baton Rouge. She was carrying a show, modeled after the French and Price performances, of sensational specialty acts spaced with music. The afterpiece featured a musical team and trained dogs. The second year musical comedy was added, and in 1904, ironically enough, half the show was devoted to moving pictures, their first appearance on a major showboat. Little did Captain Markle dream that he was introducing the octopus that was eventually to put the showboats out of business.

The venture prospered even beyond the predictions of the enthusiastic Markle. One factor contributing to this unusual measure of success was the GRAND FLOATING PALACE's advertising, which was copied after Ralph Emerson's for the Price boats. The gay handbills and mammoth gaudy posters, almost a show within themselves, captured the imagination of the public through claims of size and superiority of the new boat: *Represents More Capital, Brains, and Energy Than All Other Shows of its Kind; Largest Showboat In the World; $60,000 Invested*, the posters howled. Prospective customers were assured that *By a Special System of Ventilation and Countless Electric Fans, The Theatre Is Kept Unusually Cool and Refreshing* and that the program represented *The High-Water Mark of Mirth, Melody, and Minstrelsy*. The boat challenged competition with: *Placed before the Public Without Fear of Competition . . . Asking No Favors.* "The $10,000 Challenge Marine Band" on board was composed of "the best musicians in America," under the direction of James Hagen.

What Markle did not know about theatrical matters was supplied by Norman Thom, who planned and directed the programs, and also doubled in the band. He emphasized a mixture of music, specialty acts (sleight-of-hand, minstrelsy, humorous readings, acrobatics), and short plays. A brief intermission in the middle of the performance, devoted to candy selling, became a raucous interlude, itself a free sideshow. The master of ceremonies, resembling a circus ringmaster, announced from a front corner of the stage the virtues of the boxed gumdrops and candy hearts, and assured the audience of "a prize in every box, and all for just 10¢." Coatless young men galloped up and down the aisles to supply the demand, while the stage was littered with gaudy blankets, fancy lamps, and assorted gew-gaws, the prizes for the lucky numbers.

The first evidence of financial prosperity was the purchase by the partners, in 1902, of the tow boat CRICKETT, which had up to this time been leased by them. The next year Markle bought Swallow's interest, to become sole owner of the business. The boat became popularly known as Markle's QUEEN, and its reputation for magnificence, both in appearance and in program, approached the exaggeration of a fairy tale. Wherever it stopped, it was crowded to capacity. Its owner bragged that for three months he did not have an empty seat in his auditorium for a single night. The boat began making three-night stands in some of the larger towns.

Certainly "Double R" Markle had realized his dream. But in a most tantalizing fashion, the more generous door receipts became, the bigger the dream grew. The constantly crowded auditorium suggested a bigger and finer showboat, and in 1905 the Pope Dock Company built the SUNNY SOUTH for Markle.

The new boat was higher and bigger than the PALACE, with a seating capacity of twelve hundred. Her exterior gave the impression of extreme trimness and dignity, contrasting vividly with the ornate interior decorated richly in light green, crimson, and gold. Unlike the FLOATING PALACE, the SUNNY SOUTH was to specialize in musical comedy and full-length drama, in keeping with the general sophistication of the establishment.[1] Such elaborate costumes were provided that some editors nicknamed it Markle's "Fashion Plate." It seemed in many ways to cater to the wealthier class, and yet its general admission price, like that of the PALACE, remained seventy-five cents.

The first performance, July 4, 1905, at Gallipolis, Ohio, featured the musical comedy "Trip Around the World," starring Joe K. Kelley. The set was a ship's deck, with Kelley watching for possible shore lines through binoculars. His announcement of the vessel's approach to a foreign shore was the cue for the chorus to enter properly costumed to represent the country observed, by song, dress, and manners.   *314822*

---

[1] By this date the popularity of such programs had been well proven by the success of the Eisenbarth-Henderson boat (See pp. 106–7).

Courtesy Donald T. Wright

Reynolds' MAJESTIC

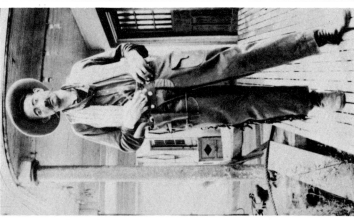

Courtesy Tommy Windsor

(Left) Willard Cole of the PRINCESS; (center) Dave Batchelor of the COTTON BLOSSOM; (right) Bruce Rinaldo and Tommy Windsor (in black face) of the PRINCESS

The boat's advertising, on gaily illustrated handbills, was in keeping with the general atmosphere of refinement: *A Clean Performance— No Coarse Jokes, No Double Entendres, Nothing the Most Perfect Lady Will Object To—A Good Show, A Big Show, A Moral Show*—were among the most frequently repeated promises. Programs were described by such phrases as *The Best Actors of the Nation, Musical Artists Galore, An Evening of Dramatic Surprises*. Across the bottom of most handbills ran the line: *An Eclipse of all Former Floating Theatres*. Bill Menke was the advance man. After Markle sold his GRAND FLOATING PALACE to Emerson,[2] for the next four years he devoted all his talents—and they were many and varied—to the SUNNY SOUTH. He deliberately pointed the boat's personality and reputation toward a brilliant and sophisticated gaiety.

At many towns patrons rowed out to buy tickets before the boat reached the landing, and often all the reserved seats had been sold before she tied up. With heavy door receipts and a fast-expanding popularity, Markle's dream continued to grow. Perhaps his own extravagant advertising hypnotized "Double R" into the belief that there was no limit to what a showboat could be. He became once more primarily the promoter and the gambler, and carefully planned a boat that he believed could never be surpassed.

In September, 1909, his dream came off the ways of the Pope Dock Company to startle the showboat world. "Biggest" and "finest" had been used too often to be adequate to describe this new palace theatre. She was two hundred feet long and forty-five feet wide, with twenty-one boxes on two levels clustered about the stage and all around the front of the balcony. Her capacity was fourteen hundred.[3] On the outside she was plain, almost to the point of severity, the least ornate of all the big showboats. But on the inside she was the most highly decorated of them all. The stage and auditorium seemed to be modeled after the Majestic Theatre in Denver, Colorado. Ceilings and walls were studded with twenty-five hundred lights clustered in intricate designs. Gilt friezes and highly wrought brass decorated balcony and box railings. Draperies and upholstery were of red velour, and the floor was richly carpeted. Full-length wall-mirrors exaggerated the size of the spacious auditorium. The stage, large and elaborately

[2] This was the same "beautiful thing" which, when sold by Emerson to Price, caused that grizzled old Captain to enter upon his "second spring" of showboating (See p. 92).

[3] The seating capacity of the GOLDENROD has since been cut down under a thousand to avoid certain additional taxes.

decorated in frieze and gilt, was well equipped with three drops and eight sets. Markle's unlimited credit had been used to install every convenience known to the river.

At first the proud owner called his unusual craft simply W. R. MARKLE'S NEW SHOWBOAT, for he could not find a name suited to this climax of boats. When his sister visited him on board, however, she suggested the name GOLDENROD, and GOLDENROD she was promptly dubbed and still remains.[4] A special steamboat was built to do the towing, and christened the W. R. MARKLE.

Markle became so engrossed in his new marvel that he sold the SUNNY SOUTH to Coleman and Menke,[5] to devote all his time to the GOLDENROD. A change was coming in river entertainment, a definite swing toward melodrama, which he failed in part to recognize. He was still taking in more money than any other showboat captain on the rivers, but he was also spending more. He carried on board a Ford motor car, in which he made frequent excursions. He insisted on an expensive program, a combination of musical comedy, music, and specialty acts. He was so proud of his boat that he spent most of his profits in keeping her in tiptop condition. Moreover, he seemed constantly to be the victim of bad luck. In 1910 a storm cost him $21,000, for it sank his towboat CONNIE NEVILLE, and blew his show-boat four miles upstream onto a sand bar. The next year, in backing out of a small landing in Illinois one morning he sank a swank river yacht, and that cost him $15,000. In 1913 he began playing the races in an effort to recoup his fortunes, and the next year he lost the GOLDENROD by foreclosure. A United States Marshall sold her at auction to Ralph Emerson for $11,000, less than a fourth of her original cost.

Markle's dream had been realized, it had grown like an immense bubble, and then it had disappeared, leaving him nothing except the misty memory of a brilliant success. This man who had set a new goal for the showboat world got a job in Pittsburgh as night watch-man on the waterfront at ten dollars a week. When not at work he was to be found in Steubenville where his sister lived. Several times he attempted a "comeback." Once his idea was to erect a circus on

[4] This boat, still doing a good business, is now (1950) tied up in St. Louis, at the foot of Locus Street, where she has been since 1937.
[5] For the later history of the SUNNY SOUTH, for a time called the HIPPODROME, see p. 170. This boat should not be confused with the smaller SUNNY SOUTH, named for it, operating 1929–1934.

several barges lashed together; friends in Pittsburgh agreed to back him, but just before he was to begin operations, they suddenly withdrew their support and foreclosed on him. At the end of the First World War he made arrangements once more to take charge of the SUNNY SOUTH, but again his financial backing deserted him. On another occasion he thought he had repurchased the GOLDENROD, but at the last moment Captain Emerson refused to make delivery.

Measured in terms of money, Markle failed. Measured in terms of showboating, his dream can never die. His "Big Three"—the GRAND FLOATING PALACE, the SUNNY SOUTH, and the GOLDENROD—will always lead the historic showboat fleet, and without them the river legend would be only a meager part of what it is. It is true that the big boat was not the best expression of the showboat's mission. Yet if the West, in its growing realization of its own vastness, demanded immense showboats, Markle's boats were the best version of this desire. For more than a decade he pushed the standards of river entertainment steadily upward, and forced all would-be competitors to improve their shows. His boats brought wholesome entertainment to thousands of people along the rivers.

The Pope Dock Company built other giant showboats besides those for W. R. Markle, among them the WONDERLAND. This new big boat was the result of careful planning by men familiar with the showboat business.

In 1905 the SUNNY SOUTH was carrying an unusual array of showboat talent. Norman Thom, aged twenty-three, who had risen from general handy man to director of the show and cashier and bookkeeper for the boat; James Hagen, officially "Professor Hagen of the Challenge Band," formerly connected with the Wallace Hagenbeck Circus, but now band and orchestra leader, and ticket seller; Joe Robinson, once part-owner of the Robinson Wagon Shows, but now band leader and bass-player; and Walter Pell, pilot, were all on board. On almost any morning this group could be seen earnestly conversing, sometimes on deck, sometimes up in the pilot house. The subject was always the same—they wanted a showboat of their own.

Hagen was the only one of the friends who had any money, and he had saved only one thousand dollars. After prolonged discussion with the group and much plan-drawing, he sent this amount—along with some promissory notes—to the Pope Dock Company of Parkersburg, with full instructions. The new boat was to be plain, large, and very substantial, built entirely of Oregon fir. Fortunately for the progress of the project, Hagen remembered a friend of his, John W. Cooley, a hotel proprietor at Newcomerstown, Ohio, who had both money and interest in showboats. A few visits and Hagen had necessary financial backing and also a partner.

Markle's boat closed the season at Sunshine Landing, Louisiana, and immediately Hagen set out for Parkersburg, where Cooley, who had leased his hotel, soon joined him. Pell and Thom, as soon as the SUNNY SOUTH had been safely tied up at Memphis for the winter, arrived to assist with the work, and by April of 1906 Cooley-Hagen's WONDERLAND, though not entirely completed, was ready to open her show in her home port, Parkersburg.

That season she played the Ohio, Monongahela, Big Kanawha, Illinois, Wabash, Upper and Lower Mississippi, and last, Bayou Teche, that picturesque region where only a few showboats had dared venture. At that time the route was up the Mississippi to Red River Landing, up Red River seven miles, down the raging Atchafalaya and across Grand Lake to Morgan City on Bayou Teche. Here eager audiences soon paid for the dangerous three-day journey. The next year, and each year thereafter, with one of the Thompson brothers as special pilot, she journeyed up the turbulent Missouri, forbidden territory to the other big boats. For the WONDERLAND had been especially reinforced with rods and chains and oak stanchions, not only to withstand the stamping of nine hundred pairs of applauding feet— the capacity of her auditorium—but also to defy the dangers of just such rivers as the shallow and tortuous Teche and the boiling, flood-choked Missouri. She was pushed by the valiant little steamer VERNIE MACK.

A congenial group formed the personnel. Cooley was cashier and ticket seller, Hagen became band leader, Thom was stage director, actor, and scene-painter, Pell did the piloting, Bert Banks was in the engine room, and Bill Menke was advance agent. John Cooley, a giant of a man, more than six feet tall and heavy-set, was easy-going and fun-loving; somehow one got the impression that a joke or a good story was always in the offing. His genial good nature pervaded the whole boat. Unlike most of his competitors, he ignored melodrama to specialize in comedy, with vaudeville and specialties between the acts of the play. A typical handbill promised a play, "A Foxy Bachelor," a comedy of domestic life, to be presented, we are assured, "for laughing purposes only." The cast included, besides Mr. Thom, six actors and six actresses. The four vaudeville acts were described as "Edwin H. and Kathryn Deagon in a New Idea in Comedy and Singing," "The Sisters Nogaed, two Clever Girls in New Song-Dances," "Merrihew and Rainey, Musical Experts, Performing on a Number of Novel and Legitimate Instruments," and "The Prentice Trio, Comedy Acrobats."

During her later years, the WONDERLAND added to her repertoire of comedies the happy variety of nature-western, such as the "Call of the Woods." Manager Cooley defended such offerings with one of his favorite sayings: "I like to laugh and most folks are like me." His policy of mirth seemed to pay well, for the boat usually had almost a thousand in her auditorium each night, even at landings where the total population was far less. The average intake for the season was about $400 per day, and the average expense was $100 a day, with a capital investment of $40,000. The WONDERLAND played towns also on the return trip up the rivers. She added the afternoon matinee with considerable profit, especially up the Missouri, where the populace often demanded two shows.

In 1908 Cooley bought Hagen's share in the WONDERLAND, and two years later sold a half-interest to Norman Thom, who in turn sold to Walter Pell in 1915. Thom remained on the boat as program director and leading man, however, after he ceased to be part-owner, for he always seemed to feel an unusual loyalty to the WONDERLAND, partly because he had helped to plan and actually to build her, partly because for eleven years she was his home. His name had become so identified with the boat that even the silk pillow tops sold on board were gaudily stamped with his likeness. Once the WONDERLAND grounded at Ironton, Ohio, but was floated again. In 1918 she struck a rock, then collided with a steamboat, and sank at Belleville, West Virginia, a total loss. Norman Thom was the last man to leave her. The current of the Ohio wrenched her cabin from the submerged hull, floated it downstream, and finally smashed it on the concrete docks at Ravenswood, West Virginia.

John W. Cooley, after his showboat interlude of a dozen years, returned to his hotel business at Newcomerstown, Ohio, and Norman Thom went in search of a showboat that needed a program director and actor.

No account of the big boats would be complete without some mention of the COTTON BLOSSOM, the original of a whole bouquet of later boats bearing that name. At first she bore another name.

At the beginning of the century, a trim-built but small young man was "working" the Ohio valley with a medicine show. His wagon was labeled, "E. E. Eisenbarth—Healer and Entertainer." Business was good, and he soon got possession of a river show, which he called EISENBARTH'S NEW WILD WEST AND FLOATING OPERA. The boat exhibited an Indian or two, some Western weapons and costumes, and presented roping and shooting contests. While the show was on tour, Eisenbarth met Susan Henderson, an attractive and wealthy girl, whom he married a year later.

Susan, it seems, had ideas as well as money. She did not approve of Wild West shows, and she strongly objected to the vaudeville offered by most of the showboats. She believed that "culture" should be carried to the people along the rivers, and to her that meant the legitimate drama. She agreed to furnish the money for the building of a first-class showboat provided it should present only programs she approved. Her husband agreed to her terms; in fact, Eisenbarth became as enthusiastic about the revival of drama as his wife. Both insisted that the people wanted to see plays and both considered themselves missionaries of better entertainment.

A glassware barge was purchased, and rebuilt at New Martinsville, West Virginia, into a double-decked showboat, probably patterned after Captain French's NEW SENSATION No. 2, which Eisenbarth had seen. She was comparatively small, with a capacity of only six hundred, but she was substantially built and arranged to ensure economical upkeep. She was elaborately christened THE EISENBARTH-HENDERSON FLOATING THEATRE—TEMPLE OF AMUSEMENT, and a little steamer purchased to do the pushing was renamed SUSAN, in honor of Mrs. Eisenbarth.

Those experienced in the business, including Captain Price, warned that no showboat that presented drama instead of the current vaudeville could be successful. The advisors predicted that it would be a fatal mistake to attempt plays for river audiences. But Eugene Eisenbarth had made up his mind, and no amount of advice or ridicule could turn him from his purpose. He was a small man, not much over five feet in height, his sandy hair and full mustache and goatee slightly lighted with gray. Honest eyes, a straight nose, and fine features gave the impression of resolute sensitiveness. The ringmaster of a circus would not have been ashamed of the immaculate pin-striped gray suit, high cornered collar, black bow tie, and diamond stud which he wore. His favorite maxim was that a man's outward appearance indicated the condition of his mind. If that is true, certainly there could have been no confusion in the mind of this man as to what he wanted to do. He intended to give the rivers drama.

During its first season the TEMPLE OF AMUSEMENT presented two plays, "Musical Toys" and "The Little Wild Cat," the first scarcely more than an act. Music—good music—filled the periods between acts. Even the calliope occasionally attempted an overture from the classics. Contrary to all predictions, the little auditorium was filled every night to overflowing. The second season "The Merchant of Venice" and "Hamlet" were added, and still the crowds came. The privileged saw in this new river entertainment much to remind them pleasantly of other times and other places; the underprivileged, who undoubtedly found some of the lines a little difficult, felt immensely complimented that they were being offered "the best in drama." All agreed that they liked what the new show offered. Within six months, every boat on the rivers had added to its program a full-length play, in most cases a melodrama, in order to meet the competition. Susan Eisenbarth's faith in "the better entertainment" was fully justified and her husband's missionary zeal grew even faster than his bank account.

Early in 1903 the TEMPLE OF AMUSEMENT was tied up at Grand Tower, Illinois, preparing for the evening show. The SPRAGUE, the largest towboat ever on the Mississippi, then just completed at Dubuque, was being given her first tryout. Through an error in the signals, she headed straight into the showboat, rammed her into the bank, and cut her in two amidships. In five minutes the halves had settled to the bottom, though no lives were lost.

Eisenbarth recovered full damages for his boat, and salvaged much of his equipment. He then employed the Pope Dock Company of Parkersburg to build him another showboat. In general design it was a replica of the first, but considerably larger, and the old name was elaborated into THE EISENBARTH-HENDERSON FLOATING THEATRE— THE NEW GREAT MODERN TEMPLE OF AMUSEMENT. Posters, head-lined *The Great Moral Theatre*, assure us of "the largest seating capacity of any floating theatre in the world," the "most thorough ventilation," and "complete electrical equipment." The stage was fitted with two sets of wood-wings, and a back-drop displaying a remarkably real garden scene. The auditorium contained boxes for the *elite* and a pit for the orchestra. Sleeping quarters for both actors and deckhands were provided on the main showboat, with only the kitchen and dining room on the steamer-tow, for the purpose, some suspected, of bringing all occupants under the watchful eye of the Manager. The whole atmosphere of the boat was one of restrained but prosperous refinement.[6]

The programs continued to be complete dramatic productions, with a rich setting of good music. The climax came in 1904 when Eisenbarth devoted the entire season to "Faust." The beautifully sedate poster for that year carried a large photograph of Eisenbarth, above it the name of the boat, and below it the simple announcement, "Producing Goethe's Literary Masterpiece FAUST." The poster as sharply contrasted with the flamboyant advertising of the other showboats as did the play itself with their former vaudeville programs. Eisenbarth's cultural ideal was Goethe, exactly as his wife's had been Shakespeare.

But Eisenbarth became a little bitter. His trouble was not with the river audiences, or with Goethe or Shakespeare, but with his actors. He complained that he could not find men or women capable of portraying the great characters of the classics. River folk did not seem to agree, however, for door receipts averaged over four hundred dollars for each performance. After the death of his wife Susan, gradually he began turning more and more to melodramas. Thousands in the Ohio Valley still associate the name of his boat with "Human Hearts" and "Uncle Tom's Cabin."

Eisenbarth, though carefully frugal in most matters, was willing to pay for a good band, and insisted that his band play good music— "cultural music" he called it. By 1908 he had developed one of the best bands in the Middle West, under the efficient direction of Harry High, himself a gifted cornetist. Earlier High had been band leader on both Price's WATER QUEEN and Emerson's GRAND FLOATING PALACE. With him were Norman Hanley, baritone and euphonium player; Dick Mitchell, trombonist; Howard Tozier, cornetist; Raymond Sillito, drummer; and Bert Potter, bass player.[7] At each landing the band gave, as a public service, a free open-air concert of good music, lasting well over an hour, immediately preceding the evening

[6] The big boat was pushed successively by the COLUMBIA (not to be confused with the showboat of the same name), the GONDOLA, and the MOUNTAIN STATE. After she became the COTTON BLOSSOM (1909), she was towed by the WALTER P. NEEDHAM (the MOUNTAIN STATE re-christened), the SOPHIA M. GARDNER, the ECLIPSE, and the JEWEL.

[7] Hanley, an English-born musician, was the composer of the spirited march "Salute to High," honoring his band leader. He doubled on the stage as the "heavy" or villain. His present address (1950) is Raleigh, N.C. Raymond Sillito is at Akron, Ohio.

performance. The program for such a concert, played at Havana, Illinois, on July 4, 1908, follows:

1. March—Salute to High .... Hanley
2. Reverie—The Wayside Chapel .... Wilson
3. Overture—Fackeltanz .... Meyerbeer
4. Bass Solo—At the Bottom of the Deep Blue Sea .... Arr. by High
   By Mr. Dick Mitchell, with band acc'p't.
5. Cornet solo—Three Star Polka .... Bagley
   By Mr. Howard D. Tozier
6. Selection—The Time, Place and the Girl .... Howard
7. Chillian Dance—Mañana .... Missud
8. Trombone Solo—Leona Polka .... Arr. by High
   By Mr. Dick Mitchell
9. Selection—Il Trovatore .... Verdi
10. Euphonium Solo—Tramp, Tramp, Tramp .... Rollinson
    By Mr. Norman Hanley
11. Overture—William Tell .... Rossini
12. March—Port Arthur .... Seitz

In many respects the management of the TEMPLE OF AMUSEMENT suggested dignified thrift. The repertoire usually consisted of one play, never more than two. All musicians doubled as actors. The TEMPLE avoided the towns, where fees were high, to play the small landings, most of them marked only by a light; even the owners themselves were often puzzled to know where all the people came from who crowded into their auditorium. She shortened her route after 1906 to exclude all points south of Cairo. She employed no advance man and used no handbills and very few posters. As one member of the cast later remarked, "We didn't need them; as soon as the folks heard the calliope, they knew we were in town." For the TEMPLE OF AMUSEMENT had an "approach" all her own. When the boat was five miles from the site of the evening's performance, the calliope would strike up its liveliest tunes, easily heard seven miles distant, and continue playing until a few minutes before the boat was to touch. At a signal the calliope left off in the middle of a tune and the band took up the same air. The effect was to cause the hearers to believe they had been hearing the band all the time. The show never performed on Sunday, and often rested two other days during the week. It began its season later than other boats, and closed a little earlier. And yet the TEMPLE cleared more money than most of the other boats—a tribute both to its program and to its management.

Eisenbarth's complete triumph over his critics and the prophets

of failure not only forced other showboats to revive the legitimate
drama; it also had a marked effect on Eisenbarth himself. He became
opinionated, crochety, always sure he was right, impatient with
others. During the season of 1908 he happened to hear a young man
standing on the deck express some objection to the program. Eisenbarth seized him by the arm, rushed him over to the rail, and heaved
him over the side into the soft river mud below. He became much concerned about the conduct of the cast. He forbade both smoking and
fishing, the last because an actor had become entangled in some tackle
carelessly left on deck. He printed his rules on cards which he tacked
up in all cabins, and even back of the stage. At the bottom of the little
card was the assurance, "May the Supreme Being bless you all; but
this show *can* get along without you." That saying became a "gag"
among the performers, especially in the summer of 1908, when malaria
swept the boat. Half the cast were ill and the other half were doubling
in their parts. At last Norman Hanley, who at the time was carrying
three principal roles in "Human Hearts," became too ill to act, and
the boat had to discontinue performances for two weeks. Some wag
collected all the cards and tacked them on Hanley's cabin door. Eisenbarth was so alert in detecting violations of his rules that the crew
secretly called him "Double-Eye Eisenbarth," probably punning on
Captain Markle's well known river name "Double R."

Eisenbarth realized that the time had come for him to retire. The
death of his Susan, followed by his marriage to a second wife,
who had nursed him through an attack of typhoid fever, had largely
taken away the old zeal for bringing "culture" to the river people.
On his posters, along with the usual promise, "Complete Dramatic
Productions," there appeared now a new phrase—"and Polite Vaudeville"—which must have irked the old apostle of culture. Without the
missionary spirit, showboating had no goal for him except the further
accumulation of money, and his fortune was already sufficient for
future needs.

Early in 1909, therefore, he sold the TEMPLE to Walter Needham
and Harry Steiner, an Amusement Company of Chicago, Illinois.[8]
The last glimpse which the records reveal of Eugene Eisenbarth [9]
shows him in the basement of his home at Marietta, building a master

[8] Needham and Steiner owned a Cowboy Baseball Team that toured on the
river steamer NELLIE, and also a Bloomer Girl Baseball Team that traveled by rail.
[9] Captain Eugene Eisenbarth died in 1925 at 432 Front Street, Marietta, Ohio.

calliope which he hoped would be suitable for playing both classical and popular music.

Needham's first move was to change the name of the NEW GREAT MODERN TEMPLE to the COTTON BLOSSOM. As the result of a collision, the bow was damaged, and in making repairs the new owners built in a concave or recessed head, sometimes called a "dishpan front." This cavity was filled with electric lights, and became the identifying feature of the boat. All the simplicity of the former missionary spirit was obliterated. New white and gold paint, an abundance of red velour for the auditorium, new scenery and drops for the stage, and an elaborate system of lighting, inside and out, competed with the luxury of the finest of the Markle boats. A cast and crew of forty were employed, the band was uniformed in red and gold, the programs were shifted away from the classics to a mixture of melodrama (always a complete play) and vaudeville, and the COTTON BLOSSOM entered the big-time circuit on the rivers.

After only one season Walter Needham, realizing that his best talents lay in the direction of the Bloomer Girl Baseball Team, sold his rejuvenated boat to Ralph Emerson, one of the best liked men on the rivers. This efficient "gentleman captain" had already made a reputation as the "Showboat King" when he was managing the NEW GRAND FLOATING PALACE five years earlier. At that time he had employed Bill Menke as his advance man. Now when he acquired the COTTON BLOSSOM, he sent ahead that veteran agent Ray Lambert familiarly called the Wildcat, whose reputation collected as many stories as the boat he represented. At one crossroads in a region known for its violence Ray was once vigorously wielding his paste brush, putting up a road-side poster. Suddenly a rifle bullet whizzed by his ear, and entered the flipping bristles. Three times he started that fast-moving brush, and three times a bullet hit it. He got a little nervous and was hurriedly gathering up his materials for a quick getaway when a mountaineer stepped out of the bushes, with the reassurance:

"Don't mind me, Mister. I ain't gona hurt you. They sez a carnival's a-comin' next month with a shootin' gall'ry what gives you five bucks ever' time you hit six o' them tin ducks a-movin', like the one last year. That there brush goin' up and down's the nearest thing to them ducks. So I wuz just a-practicin' a little." On another occasion when Ray was working a whiskey-still district, he was a little startled when a native, who had evidently mistaken Lambert for a revenue officer, significantly asked him what to do with his horse and buggy "just in case you don't come back."

Ray at last fired himself from his job with Captain Emerson. It happened in this way. The Wildcat was of course supposed to travel *ahead* of the COTTON BLOSSOM to do the advertising. But his gas-boat was constantly breaking down, and finally he found himself trailing the big boat. In spite of all he could do, this condition continued for a week. Finally with the aid of wind and current, he caught up with the COTTON BLOSSOM at Paducah. In his best apologetic manner, he said,

"Captain, I'm plumb sorry I couldn't post any bills. But I can tell you something! The folks in those towns sure did like your show. I talked to all of them right after you left!"

"That's fine," Emerson answered. "But I never heard of any showboat before that paid an advance agent to trail along behind to find out how the people liked the show!"

Emerson himself was an excellent advertising man. He inaugurated a publicity campaign, aimed chiefly at creating good will, that launched the COTTON BLOSSOM on a constantly mounting wave of prosperity for the next four years. He installed powerful search lights that wrote across the sky, *Show at the River Landing Tonight.* His "paper" was neither so voluminous nor so extravagant as Markle's, but its phrasing captured the imagination of the people. They could not forget such a slogan as "After the minnows comes the whale," and they always waited for Emerson.

Now with the COTTON BLOSSOM, and after 1914 when he acquired the big GOLDENROD, he followed some of Barnum's advertising techniques. His boat carried "Gay the Handcuff King," who broke out of the town jail at each stop. On board also was a baseball team, organized with members of the cast and crew, which played town clubs. Captain Emerson himself played first base. Recently he wrote, in reminiscent mood:

I spent about $200 those days to outfit my boys, and they were good ball players, above the average, and played about two games a week. It paid a big dividend. I gave the boys $1.00 each game, and the town club got a ticket each, about twelve. Well, you know all the boys brought someone else . . . It was laughable to sit down in the audience that night and hear some gal say, "The villain was third baseman," or "the hero played short," or "the owner played first."

Naturally a very generous man, Emerson was past master of public relations. Frequently he would take a whole church congregation for a free ride on Sunday afternoon, and more than once, on a promise of one-fourth the door receipts, a grateful minister led his flock to the box office, to the profit of the Church and also of Captain Emerson. At one town in the Bible Belt, the minister let it be known that he envied "the wicked show" its crowd; thereupon Emerson proffered his auditorium—calliope, band, and all—for the Sunday service, and the good parson to his great delight spoke to the largest congregation of his career.

But the Captain was a showman as well as an advertiser. He refused to accept the traditional patterns of entertainment, and insisted on keeping his stage abreast of the times. He knew that audiences were tiring of musical comedy, and he tried to give them what they wanted. Furthermore he was willing to pay for plays that suited his taste and also for good acting. When other managers were presenting their shows as relics of the past and playing inexpensive non-royalty productions, Emerson was turning vigorously to his own time, and each season purchasing some of New York's most popular hits, such as "Peg o' My Heart," "Brewster's Millions," "East Is West," and "Johnny Get Your Gun." His elaborate production of "Remember the Maine" amazed all who saw it, and even his "Trail of the Lonesome Pine" became the most popular melodrama in the Middle West. A line on his posters, *We Show You the Present, Others Only the Past,* was not idle talk. His actors were the most competent since the Chapmans, and his full cast enabled him to reduce doubling to a minimum. His stage scenery and costuming were matters of wonder to his audiences.

In vaudeville Emerson loved the spectacular, and for season after season he featured on his boat such specialists as that master magician Harry Blackstone and that band master supreme Merle Evans.[10] His between-acts tended toward the sensational and the bizarre. His exotic women who swallowed electric light bulbs, his Hindu princes with all their trappings, his supermen who discharged rifles down their throats or sawed their wives in two delighted an age that reveled in fakery. He kept his patrons in a constant state of suspense between trips by promising to reveal on his next visit the secret of his tricks. But when he came again he brought so much new magic that there

[10] Blackstone, recently characterized in the national press as "the world's greatest magician," played an extended engagement in 1949 at the Erlanger Theatre, Chicago. Evans since 1931 has been bandmaster for Ringling Bros.

was never any time for revelations concerning the old. The true secret of the "Showboat King" himself was his understanding of human beings, especially his almost uncanny knowledge of what they liked.

By 1914 the COTTON BLOSSOM was getting a little rickety at the seams, for it had never been so well built as Eisenbarth's first TEMPLE. In that year Emerson, who always seemed to know exactly when to sell out, sold a half-interest in the boat to Daniel Otto Hitner. The new owner scarcely had opportunity to show what he could do when in 1917 the COTTON BLOSSOM, while she was playing "Uncle Tom's Cabin" at Mt. Vernon, Indiana, was crushed by ice along with her tow-steamer JEWEL. To the last, she never played any program that did not include a "complete dramatic production," as Captain Eisenbarth had phrased it.

Hitner was not content, however, to allow the celebrated name to remain at the bottom of the Ohio. He salvaged a few opera chairs and other equipment, hurriedly placed them on a grain barge, and called it the COTTON BLOSSOM PAVILLION. The next season at Mound City, Illinois, he rebuilt the barge PRINCESS (formerly the MISSISSIPPI) into a large two-decked showboat, one hundred and eighty-two by forty-five feet, seating twelve hundred. (Its identifying feature was the absence of a pilot house.) This he christened COTTON BLOSSOM No. 1 because during the same period he chartered the WATER QUEEN from Roy Hyatt and temporarily changed her name to COTTON BLOSSOM No. 2. No. 2 proved a bad venture and she was soon restored to her owner and her former name. But the COTTON BLOSSOM No. 1 Captain Hitner operated quite successfully.

It would be more accurate to say that Mrs. Hitner operated the showboat successfully, for Hitner was a better riverman than showman, and wisely turned all stage matters over to his wife. She employed a cast of more than thirty, twelve of whom doubled in an excellent band and orchestra, uniformed in white; she selected and rewrote or adapted the plays; she directed the productions and coached the vaudeville acts; and she herself was the featured comedienne for year after year. Daughter Hope played the part of the little ingénue quite fetchingly, and occasionally a lead role. It was Mrs. Hitner's practice to adapt for dramatic production one of the best sellers of the day, such as *The Little Shepherd of Kingdom-Come* or *Mrs. Wiggs of the Cabbage Patch*. Most of the cast doubled either in the orchestra or in the vaudeville between-acts. Tommy Windsor, formerly sleight-of-hand specialist and actor on the WATER QUEEN, during one season was a most attractive leading man. The director was fortunate in being able to secure other competent artists, most of whom were more interested in a vacation than in salary, for the relaxed comfort of life on the COTTON BLOSSOM had already become proverbial among entertainers. Her program always featured several well-known vaudeville artists, for whom of course there was no doubling assignment. The evening's entertainment, skillfully keyed to a great variety of people in all walks of life, included music, a complete play, and vaudeville. The whole performance lasted a minimum of three hours, a standard that the Emerson boats had set.

Prosperity blessed the COTTON BLOSSOM until 1928. That year the season was shortened to nine weeks, and for the next three years the boat descended by rapid diminuendo in cast, in program, in door receipts, in general reputation. Not all the deterioration can be charged to Captain Hitner, for nobody short of a genius could have kept the big showboat afloat in the fast thickening gloom of the depression, to say nothing of the matured movie-talkie competition. And Hitner was not a genius. In spite of the most unfavorable conditions he did manage to operate her irregularly until 1931, when she was sold for debt.[11]

Each of the big-boat operators has left the distinct impress of his personality and his achievement as an inheritance to the rivers. "Double R" Markle, with the instincts of a gambler, loved the daring financing of the luxurious palaces that astounded spectators. The genial Cooley loved the humor of comedy and the fun of rollicky entertainment. The rather austere Eisenbarth brought a message of culture that was surprisingly well received. The stolid Hitner, through his more discerning wife, spread sentimentality over the waters like a thick syrup.

But there was one man among these big-time operators who seemed to have the qualities of them all and to perform the offices of them all. He was Ralph W. Emerson. His name weaves itself in and out of the story of almost every important showboat of the era. He was part-owner of the WATER QUEEN with Captain Price; he shared the

---

[11] At least four smaller showboats have plied the rivers under the historic name COTTON BLOSSOM. One (Emerson's) burned on the Chicago River, 1933; the WATER QUEEN used the name when Hyatt leased it to Hitner for a short period; another was dismantled in New Orleans, 1936; the last, built by Jim Bonnelli in 1939, was lost at Louisville, Kentucky, by forced sale to Oscar Bloom of the Gold Medal Shows (Pittsburgh), 1941, and burned the next year.

NEW ERA with both Wiley McNair and Price; he bought the GRAND FLOATING PALACE from Markle and sold her to Price; he owned the AMERICAN long enough to transfer her also to Price; he operated the original COTTON BLOSSOM during her proudest period of success; he bought the GOLDENROD, the queen of the showboat world, at an opportune moment and sold her to Bill Menke at another opportune moment. In addition there were the MANITOU at Pittsburgh and the little COTTON BLOSSOM at Chicago. He was boat-financier and riverman supreme. He never built a single one of the big boats, and never lost one; he preferred to buy and sell.

He excelled most, however, as a showman. His programs were rare mixtures of laughter and tears and foolishness and sense. Comedy, melodrama, the past, the classics, the present all belonged equally to his boat. He alone of all the showboat operators refused to bow to tradition, and was constantly readjusting his programs to compete with the best land entertainment.

After the sale of the GOLDENROD to Captain Menke, Emerson remained on the rivers in the steamboat business until 1931. At that time he moved to Chicago, expecting to retire. But the lure of the old life still called him, and he built and operated a small showboat, sentimentally named the COTTON BLOSSOM, on the Chicago River. When this boat burned,[12] he directed the building of a larger one, the DIXIANA, up in Sturgeon's Bay, Wisconsin, which he operated for the Century of Progress Exposition in Chicago.

As long as the showboat legend survives, Emerson will be remembered on the rivers by both his titles, the "Gentleman Captain," and the "Showboat King." [13]

[12] In this fire Emerson's scrapbooks were destroyed, probably a more serious loss for posterity than the boat itself. The Captain, now retired, resides at 1924 Ogden Avenue, Chicago.
[13] Principal Sources: Numerous manuscripts, personal interviews, letters, scrapbooks, logbooks, and newspaper files.
Other Sources: Items listed in the bibliography under Bert Banks, Billy Bryant, Lucien Burman, Maurice Elfer, Ethel Leahy, Frank Madison, W. Frank M'Clure, Sidney Snook, Raymond Spears, and Wesley Stout.

Robinson's Floating Palace

Courtesy Donald T. Wright

Markle's Sunny South

XI

DRAMA PLAYED STRAIGHT

Family Boats

THE SHOWBOAT early became associated with the family. This intimate relationship existed in a double sense. In the first place the showboat, as long as it performed its function of bringing otherwise inaccessible entertainment to the frontier, looked to families—fathers, mothers, children, babies—to fill its auditorium. The moment showboats began skipping the landings in favor of the cities, a practice inaugurated by the big boats with large capacities, they ceased to depend on family attendance. At the same time, they placed themselves in competition with city-made land entertainment, which they could not for long survive. The smaller boats continued to play the outlying regions where geographical conditions encouraged and often necessitated attendance in family groups.

In a second sense these smaller showboats bore an intimate relationship to families: Most of them were owned and operated by family groups, for they were floating homes as well as floating shows. The family on the stage was often very similar to the families in the auditorium. A strong bond of sympathetic understanding therefore existed between the showboat and its clientele. It was true of the Chapman boat back in the 1830's and it was equally true of Captain French's boats at the end of the century.

A long line of "family boats" followed French, each operated by such groups as the McNairs with the NEW ERA, the Roy Hyatts with the WATER QUEEN, the Norman Thoms with the PRINCESS, the Frank Rice Kruses with the TWENTIETH CENTURY, the T. J. Reynoldses with the AMERICA and the MAJESTIC.

The McNairs learned their showboating with Captain and Mrs. French. On board the NEW SENSATION John E. McNair met and married Ida Fitch, and both their daughters, Clarkie Anne and Frenchie, later became child-actors on that boat. John's brother, Wiley Preston McNair,[1] in 1894 joined the show as engineer, trombonist, and actor, and married one of the chorus girls. Her real name was Leo May Dowd, but up and down the rivers she was always "Cousin Annie." McNair acquired the NEW ERA (the former LIGHTNER'S FLOATING PALACE) and the tow steamer MARY STEWART from Emerson and Price in 1906 and 1910 respectively.[2] His wife remained chorus girl and ticket seller until he sold the boat in 1917. She has testified in quite spirited fashion that she never smoked a cigarette, never tasted alcohol, never heard a naughty story, and that no stage-door Johnny ever tried to make a date with her, nor did any of the hot sports of the river towns ever invite her to supper. Most showboat girls were like her.

As soon as McNair acquired the NEW ERA, he rebuilt her at Paducah, adding twenty feet to each end, thus increasing her capacity from three hundred to four hundred and fifty. For years she made the complete showboat circuit, starting each year at Pittsburgh or even up the Monongahela, and ending at New Orleans. During her last years she spent most of the season in the bayou and canal districts of Mississippi and Louisiana, always her richest territory. Often in this region the ticket seller would direct to the main floor a patron, apparently white, who nevertheless went up to the balcony, reserved for Negroes. Segregation in these sections was left entirely to local knowledge. In the North the program consisted of a melodrama, usually "Uncle Tom's Cabin," with specialty acts interspersed. In the South it was vaudeville and music, with emphasis on minstrel numbers, much of it in *cajun*.

The pattern of operations for the NEW ERA was simple. For a while Bill and Ben Menke with their gasoline boat CINCY worked as advance agents, but not for long. Such services were expensive, and furthermore not necessary, since most of the prospective patrons in the bayou districts did not read English. Most of the time, therefore, the boat was "wild-catting," without paper. A well-timed concert by that master of the calliope L. Ray Choissier was all the advertising needed. As soon as the boat touched, everybody "doubled in brass"

[1] In a number of sources the name is erroneously recorded as Wiley Patterson McNair.

[2] The MARY STEWART, 77 tons, built in 1893 at Spottsville, Kentucky, by Captain James Stewart and named for his wife; sold to French to tow his third SENSATION and passed with that boat to Price in 1900. After a sale and repurchase Price sold her with the NEW ERA.

for the parade; even the owner of the boat himself played the slide trombone, and the genial cook Charlie McNickles carried a muted instrument. Sometimes, especially in Catholic communities, McNair would promise a small per cent of the "take" to the church, a device learned from Ralph Emerson, which often enabled him to show two or even three nights in one village. When a storm blew the steeple off the church at Smoke Bend (not far from Donaldsonville, Louisiana), the NEW ERA hurried to the scene to give a benefit performance. "We had them stacked three deep on the guard rails all around the NEW ERA for two nights," the Captain later remarked.

The usual pattern for the NEW ERA, however, was the one-night stand. The family wash, therefore, had to be done on board, and a line-full of clothes on the deck as the boat made her morning hop became almost a substitute for a flag. At least on one occasion, however, Mrs. McNair sent out the laundry, much to her husband's discomfit. For it was his practice to carry a thousand-dollar bill in the pocket of his underwear, for emergencies. He had forgotten to remove it, and when he finally found the cabin to which the bundle had been sent, he saw the baby on the floor playing with the big money. The mammy had thought it an advertisement.[3]

With the coming of the First World War, McNair's business began falling off rapidly. Then, too, movies and automobiles and roads were penetrating even the isolated *cajun* districts, and these forces were taking over the main functions of the showboat. Late in the season of 1917 the NEW ERA was sold, to be beached as a movie house at Houma, Louisiana.[4]

During the ten years that the boat had been operated by Captain Wiley P. McNair, it had traveled over eighty thousand miles on the rivers, to stage almost twenty-five hundred performances, and it had entertained more than a million people, most of whom during that period did not have an opportunity to enjoy any other variety of entertainment.

Among the family boats, the WATER QUEEN had the longest and

---

[3] This story has been authenticated by the McNairs themselves. Most of the legends told about their boat, they brand as false, the most absurd being the story of how the Captain's trombone bell was later used as a funnel for the stuffing of sausage into casings (New Orleans *Times-Picayune*, Aug. 19, 1934 and Feb. 27, 1935).

[4] After selling the NEW ERA, Captain Wiley P. McNair built and ran steamboats on the Panuco River, Mexico, for four years, and then retired to his home in New Orleans. After his death in 1943, he was buried in Columbia, Alabama.

the most eventful life. Originally it had been the THEATORIUM, built by C. F. Breidenbaugh and by him sold to Captain Augustus French, to become the third NEW SENSATION. French had sold to Captain E. A. Price, who operated the boat for more than a dozen years, first as the NEW OLYMPIA and then as the WATER QUEEN. Both Jim Bonnelli and Bill Paden had the boat in charge for a season while Price was busy elsewhere, and then she passed to Roy Hyatt, under whose ownership she played the remaining twenty years of her career.

Hyatt had served both as musician and as engineer on the Price boats. Here he had come to know Mrs. Josie Ikeberg and her husband, who had come on board at Cape Girardeau as cooks. It seems that Josie's husband went home for a month's visit. When he got ready to return to the boat he wrote to his wife for travel money, which she promptly sent. But he was never heard of again. Two years later Josie married Roy Hyatt, and together they purchased the WATER QUEEN, which remained both their home and their business for the next twenty years. They worked on the boat even during the period it was leased to Hitner, Roy as engineer, Josie as cook.

Captain Hyatt, like Hitner, knew the river, advertising, and the ticket office because he had learned these from Price. But he knew very little about the stage or what should go on it. Fortunately he acquired Norman Thom as director and leading man.[5] With Grace Neill as leading lady, he produced such melodramas as "The Unwanted Baby," "The Rosary," and "Lena Rivers." He employed a few well-chosen vaudeville numbers between acts. But Thom left the WATER QUEEN in 1922 when he bought a boat of his own.

After that date the programs appear to have deteriorated rapidly. Tommy Windsor was on board a few weeks in 1928 as leading man and cartoonist, but he soon transferred to the big COTTON BLOSSOM. Captain Hyatt resorted to various means of securing income for his boat. He chartered her for almost three years (1928–1930) to Otto Hitner. He leased her also to a movie corporation for the filming of Gloria Swanson's "Stage Struck," when the name temporarily became THE GLORIA SWANSON.[6] He brought a $50,000 suit against the magazine publishers of Edna Ferber's *Showboat* for the unauthorized use of his boat's name (that was during the period when she was tem-

[5] After the wreck of the WONDERLAND Thom worked one year for the Thompsons on the AMERICAN (later the COLUMBIA), and then joined the WATER QUEEN.

[6] Hitner the year before had refused an offer, by the same company, of $1,000 a week for the use of the boat, because he was not to be allowed the privilege of censoring the picture (See the Evansville [Indiana] *Courier*, October 24, 1926).

porarily called the Cotton Blossom.) He again leased the boat, this time to the producers of the Oscar Hammerstein–Jerome Kern version of Ferber's *Showboat*. In the last years Hyatt was evidently depending more on the sentimental traditions clinging around his boat than on what he could produce on his stage. For a little while he even operated her as a dance boat, giving his performance merely as a floor show.

The spring ice floes of 1936 caught the Water Queen in an unprotected position near the mouth of the Big Kanawha River and sank her. She was raised and two years later dismantled. The Hyatts retired to Lowell, Ohio.

Norman Thom, often called the John Drew of the Rivers, worked as director and leading man on most of the showboats of his day.[7] After youthful experiences in ventriloquism and sleight-of-hand acts, he secured a position as circular alto player and general handy man on Markle's Floating Palace, and quickly advanced to the cashier's desk in the business cabin. The second year he became general manager of the big boat and stage director. In many respects that was a busy season for Thom, for before its end he had not only begun playing lead roles, but he had married. Toots and Warren Leisenring, the child dance team on board, were accompanied by their mother, who soon persuaded her older daughter to join the show as singer of "sentimental hits," as the posters announced. Director Thom fell in love with the new recruit and married her at Thibodeaux, Louisiana.

Succeeding years brought varied experiences. After other work in Denver, Thom returned to Mississippi showboating, a season on Markle's Sunny South, ten years on the Wonderland, a season on the Thompson brothers' American (later the Columbia), and then a long period on Hyatt's Water Queen. It was here that he met and married his second wife, Grace Neill, the leading lady. Together they purchased in 1922 the little Princess, formerly the Bryants' showboat, and operated it for the next six years.[8]

For the first time since William Chapman, a showboat owner was a professional actor. Too many of the captains had been rivermen rather than showmen, as Hitner and Hyatt; and too many of the showmen had been interested exclusively in vaudeville, as French

[7] Thom was born in 1883 at Greenup, Kentucky, but spent his boyhood at Ironton, Ohio. During 1922–1928 he claimed Beverly, Ohio, as his home, and then moved to Hollywood, California.

[8] For the earlier history of the Princess see Chapter XIII. Sam and Billy Bryant transferred the Princess to Ed Darnold and Lew Kinser, and these sold to Thom.

and McNair. Norman Thom, trained from early childhood in dramatic art, was primarily concerned with the drama, both as actor and as director.

On board the Princess his policy was to emphasize full-length plays, usually melodramas, such as "The Tenderfoot," "Heart of Kentucky," "The House of Fear," and "Way Down East." The "refined vaudeville acts" were, for the most part, relegated to the aftershow, for which Thom charged an additional ten cents. He was responsible, almost as much as Eisenbarth, for the dying out of specialty numbers and the supremacy of the sentimental play on the showboat. He accomplished this shift by carefully selecting plays likely to have a strong local interest, such as "Hearts of the Blue Ridge" or "Along the Missouri," and then by exaggerating—or even adding—both comic and sentimental episodes, so as to appeal to people of various tastes. A Norman Thom production on the Princess stage was in effect a complete melodrama plus specialty and musical numbers, all unified into a single focus. The whole was always played "straight," without a trace of burlesque on the stage, and certainly no suggestion of sophistication in the audience. Norman Thom was a good enough director to realize that this simple sincerity was essential for his rural patrons; for them it was a matter both of good taste and of the moral sense. This direct presentation became one of the finest characteristics of the small or "family" showboats, later bringing them and their village patrons into sharp contrast with the larger boats and their urban audiences.

The Princess was in a very real sense a family affair. Thom was owner, captain, leading man, and director; his wife Grace was leading lady and calliope player, ably assisted by her friend Ruth Williams (the fact that Mrs. Thom played from sheet music greatly amused most of her rivals); their daughter Norma Beth played juvenile roles; and Mrs. Thom's grandmother had charge of the boat's kitchen. Every employee was an intimate and trusted friend of the family. All the methods and means were suggestive of a home rather than a commercial establishment. In lieu of an advance agent and posters, Thom depended on the good will of the village postmaster or the town editor (who always received complimentary tickets), and the calliope concert. Occasionally after reaching a stand he would hire a two-horse buggy to drive over the neighboring countryside shouting at everybody he met, "Show at the river landing tonight!" The meager flat scenery—the boat had no drops—was supplemented by greenery and wild flowers gathered each evening from the river bank. Every-day life and stage roles seemed sometimes indistinguishable: One season the rube comedian in "Way Down East" threw away his shoes, refused to comb or cut his hair, and dispensed with all clothing except his underwear and ragged overalls, so that he needed no preparation at all before walking out on the stage. The relation of the boat to its patrons was most intimate and cordial. Captain Thom always had free samples of baking soda or some similar commodity to distribute to his guests. Wherever he happened to be tied up on Sunday afternoon he entertained as many as could get into the auditorium, free of charge, with an orthophonic concert. Vegetables and fruit used on board were gladly received in exchange for tickets. On one occasion as soon as the boat touched at Old Landing, Kentucky, a family of fourteen ("Pa Kinney, Ma Kinney, and 12 young uns," the record reads) immediately came on board seeking admission. They had walked eleven miles to the river, bringing with them seven gallons of huckleberries for their tickets, and had waited five hours on the bank. That night from thirteen balcony seats they saw Norman Thom in "The Parson's Bride." For Pa and Ma it was the first show in twenty-six years, and for the twelve "young uns" the first time in any theatre. Needless to add, the cast ate huckleberry pie, huckleberry cobbler, and plain huckleberries for the rest of the week.

One is not surprised, therefore, that the PRINCESS was immensely popular all along the rivers. Every seat of her three hundred was usually sold long before curtain time. At such a landing as California, Kentucky, one of her favorite stops, the citizens were in the habit of declaring a holiday as soon as she tied up, which culminated in the show that night. Some seat suited everybody's purse, for "shelf" tickets (balcony) sold for thirty-five cents, the first ten rows on the main floor for seventy-five cents, and the seats in the rear, fifty cents. Unlike most of the showboats of the time, the PRINCESS stopped twice each season at each of her ports of call, once going down and again coming up. She always began and ended her season at Beverly, Ohio, where she wintered in the canal, just off the Muskingum River.

Captain Thom was chiefly responsible for the popularity of his boat. The big man—he weighed over two hundred pounds—with his hearty laugh, his generous ways, and his delightful sense of humor, had a crowd of friends about him at every stop. Furthermore, to thousands he was a great actor. On the landings of the Upper Missis-

sippi, in the small towns on the Ohio, in the secluded villages along the
Illinois, the Wabash, the Kentucky, and the Monongahela, in the
mining towns along the Kanawha, and the sleepy settlements border-
ing Bayou Teche and Bayou La Fourche, he brought the best dramatic
art that these regions had known. And they liked it! When Norman
Thom played one of his favorite roles, such as "Harold West, the
rural parson" or "Frank Marvel, the faithful cowboy," there was no
room on his stage for vaudeville, and little desire for it in his audience.

In 1928 the Thoms dismantled the PRINCESS, reserving only the
calliope. The little boat was becoming unsafe, and furthermore her
owners had received an attractive offer which seemed to promise
more money and more opportunity than the PRINCESS stage could
afford. The producers of the screen version of *Showboat* were employing the entire cast, with their calliope, for an appearance at New
York's Belmont Theatre, as a preparation for the opening of the
picture. Thom was to produce the same melodramas that he had been
playing on the rivers. He promptly sent a letter to the editor of the
Times, with two tickets, explaining that he was offering them "in
accordance with the old custom of extending courtesies to the leading newspaper in each town." He promised that the show would be
"clean, moral, and refined."

The opening bill, January 21, 1929, was "The Parson's Bride,"
that perennially beautiful pastoral melodrama, with Norman Thom as
the parson, and his wife as Mary Brown. Specialties appeared between
the acts, such as "Song by Little Kim, five years old and born on a
showboat." A "big-fun after-show" climaxed the evening. The reviewer agreed that "the travesty would have been more effective
if the players had been in dead earnest, but, aware of the audience's
attitude, the players tried to prevent being kidded by indulging in
considerable kidding themselves." For the first time in his career
Norman Thom had burlesqued a drama.[9]

Among the smaller showboats the MAJESTIC holds various records.
In the first place she is the only one of them still afloat and doing

---

[9] The PRINCESS troupe was withdrawn from the Belmont earlier than expected,
probably because of some question concerning copyrights. According to a
story circulated at the time, an author sat three evenings in the audience, trying
to decide whether or not the play was one he had written. When his suspicions
proved correct, the company was withdrawn, to avoid legal troubles. Mr. Thom
never returned to the rivers. He was employed in Hollywood, for minor roles,
until his death ten years later. After 1938 Mrs. Thom resided in Ironton, Ohio,
where she began a book about her husband.

business in 1950, though under rather artificial conditions. She is not only doing business, but she is actively traveling the rivers. As far back as 1939 she was the only floating theatre making one-night stands. Furthermore, her captain and owner, Thomas J. Reynolds, has reared the largest family—nine children—born aboard any showboat. And last, the good boat in all her twenty-seven years has never changed owners or captains. That is an array of records. It might be added that in the past she has turned in some of the worst and some of the best performances of any honest boat on the rivers.

Tom Reynolds, born at Point Pleasant, West Virginia, in 1888, has been on the rivers ever since. First he fished for mussels, and then he ran a junk and produce boat, and finally a glass and tinware barge. One day at noon he tied up by a little moving-picture boat, and before sundown he had moved the outfit on board his own ILLINOIS, and had installed benches enough to accommodate two hundred patrons. At ten cents he filled every seat every night, and during the day he could pursue his usual business of buying and selling. It was the easiest money that Tom Reynolds had ever made.

But in 1916 the ILLINOIS burned at Foster, Kentucky, the fire starting in the projection booth, and the oldest Reynolds son, who had fallen asleep on the front bench, died in the flames. The next year Reynolds built the AMERICA, his first real showboat, with a stage instead of a screen, and live actors instead of the film figures. It was a small boat, only one hundred feet long and twenty feet wide, with a capacity of three hundred. With it Reynolds visited the less accessible landings along the Muskingum, the Monongahela, the Kanawha, the Green, and the Tennessee, playing such melodramas as "Traffic in Souls" and "Tempest and Sunshine." By 1923 he had accumulated enough capital to build, with the help of his brother William and brother-in-law Tom Nichols, the MAJESTIC, which he still operates.[10] Both the showboat and its tow ATTABOY were built at Pittsburgh.

Captain Reynolds with his new boat insisted on keeping his old familiar territory even though he had to compete with the buyers of his former show. He especially liked the tributaries to the south of the Ohio, from the Monongahela in Pennsylvania to the warm

[10] Reynolds sold the AMERICA (not to be confused with the Thompsons' AMERICAN, a much larger boat which later became Price's COLUMBIA and finally Menke's HOLLYWOOD) to his brothers F. M. and William Reynolds, who featured westerns and musical comedy, and finally picture shows. Pushed by a gasoline stern-wheeler, the IDA MAE, the AMERICA operated until 1933, when she was beached as a clubhouse on the Green River near Curdsville.

Tennessee, because along these banks he found inhabitants seldom visited by entertainment of any kind, and therefore eager for the rather humble fare offered by his show. Certainly he encountered a minimum of competition in these faraway places. His favorite of all the rivers was the Green, so narrow that you can throw a rock across it and yet so deep that you can hardly find bottom anywhere. The MAJESTIC was not a big boat, with a seating capacity of only about four hundred and fifty. And yet the Captain will explain that to get around some of those bends in the Green he had "to back and fill" four times. The MAJESTIC with a draft of only twelve inches could float on a mere trickle of water to the very sources of these little-frequented streams. Winter quarters were always at Point Pleasant, West Virginia, where the children attended school.

Captain Reynolds was fortunate, especially during the depression years, in requiring little help outside his immediate family. He himself was captain, pilot, carpenter, and director, and even played a few detective and police roles. Mrs. Reynolds sold tickets, kept books, and superintended candy sales. Since the towboat ATTABOY in those days was powered by kerosene, she was not required by federal law to carry a full crew, and therefore the sons were engineer and crewmen, as well as advance man; in addition, Tommy was also drummer for years in the two-piece orchestra. Daughter Hazel acted the best lead roles the boat ever had, and also danced and played the clarinet in the aftershow. Margaret played the calliope and the piano (the other half of the orchestra), and acted in the show. And then there was Catherine, probably the most gifted and certainly the prettiest of the children, who played the calliope and piano, danced, sang, and played ingénue parts. All the children, when between eight and fourteen, sold candy and ushered. The family lived in quarters on the top deck just above the entrance to the auditorium, both in summer when they were playing the rivers and also in winter when they were tied up at Point Pleasant. The ATTABOY furnished light and heat for the theatre only. Kerosene lamps, oil stoves, and a bucket with a rope attached furnished the utilities for the living quarters. Actors fared in the matter of household conveniences exactly like the family.

As long as the children were "at home," few outside actors were needed. Four or five vaudeville entertainers who could double in the play were sufficient. These the Captain secured each spring by advertising in the *Billboard*. Average pay was twenty dollars a week for each team. Occasionally competent persons signed up, even under such circumstances, for most actors looked upon life on the MAJESTIC as a vacation, when they were forced to rest and forced to save what little they earned because of the simple living conditions, both on board and at the landings where the boat touched. Most actors, for obvious reasons, remained only one season. An exception was Ernest Vevea, who played yokel parts, in his red wig, and who remained so long on the boat that most river people thought his real name was "Toby."

The placidly independent Captain Reynolds selected the plays for his stage and also directed them. He usually chose melodramas. "Ten Nights in a Bar Room" was his favorite, with "Honest Hearts" and "Triss of the Rockies" next.

One suspects that the Captain's choice of melodrama was wise, though he himself might have had trouble in justifying it. His actors were certainly not subtle, most of them not even expert, in matters of the stage. Undoubtedly they were more successful in conveying these greatly simplified versions of life than they could ever have been in handling more intricate treatments. Furthermore the MAJESTIC touched at landings remote from the complex civilization of the outside world, and catered to audiences that would have had trouble in comprehending artistic representations of life involving more than action and emotion. The melodramas pictured life mostly in those terms, with a minimum of intellectual content and with conveniently generalized settings. Always played "straight," without any suggestion of burlesque, they reduced, for artistic presentation, all human existence to the over-simplified formula of good and evil, with the good always clearly triumphant. Otherwise the audiences at Sunshine Landing or Leafy Point either would not have understood or else would have had their moral world sadly disarranged. In either case they would have felt that they had spent their thirty-five cents for a MAJESTIC seat to no good purpose. It is easy to make fun of the older melodrama. It would have been harder to find a substitute to put before the emotionally and socially starved audiences on the river frontiers.

We may be sure, however, that Captain Tom Reynolds did not stop to justify his choice of plays. He presented "Ten Nights in a Bar Room" and "Saintly Hypocrites and Honest Sinners" because his audiences liked them and because he could adapt them to the abilities of his cast and his own skill as director. In 1925 the Captain substituted

an entire program of vaudeville and musical revue for his usual drama.
In addition to various musical numbers he offered a magic act, two
dance features, a female impersonation, a fake mind-reading act, and
two comic monologues. But the new program was not successful,
even though in his effort to make it so Reynolds ventured up the
Big Sandy, where the calliope was seldom heard. Apparently patrons
had come to expect a full-length drama. After that season the Captain
returned to the melodrama, and from then on he relegated vaudeville
to the aftershow. Even such a meager offering must have afforded
most welcome relief to an audience that had just been brought through
the ordeals of good and evil. And it was more than relief. For these
frontier people were more ready to accept the unfamiliar under the
guise of the comic than in any other form. The rube "Toby" could
safely reveal that which the hero or heroine dared not mention.

The procedure followed by the MAJESTIC was almost as simple as
the pattern of life at the landings where it touched. Well before it
hit bank, the calliope on the deck of ATTABOY announced its arrival,
with Hazel or Catherine at the steaming keyboard. Even before the
plank was down, the crowd had begun to gather, though often no
houses were visible from the river. Marion Reynolds, "the advance
man," tacked up a poster or two on the bank and in the village if
there was one, announcing the arrival of "the boat with a spotless
reputation." Then at seven o'clock the calliope again issued its deafen-
ing invitation, and continued its concert until just before eight. Men
and women and children—nearly always in family groups or age
groups—filed into the bright circle of light from the outer darkness,
bought tickets (35 cents and 25 cents) and bags of popcorn, and
settled into their seats as sedately as if they had been entering a church.
Young Tom Reynolds would begin pounding his drums in the tiny
orchestra pit, jumping up and down on his stool in time with the
rhythm like a rider on an ungaited horse, assisted vigorously by one
of his sisters at the piano. Promptly at eight, the curtain was pulled
aside to disclose the first scene of "Honest Hearts." As the play unfolded, act by act, tense faces revealed fascinated emotions. More
than once Captain Reynolds had to leave off-stage business long
enough to convince some stalwart spectator that it was only make-
believe, and that his aid was not needed in bringing the villain to
justice. At the end of the last act, when beauty and virtue had come
safely past all snares of evil, a roar of applause and stamping feet shook
the boat, all the more vigorous because they helped to hide the tears

on many a sun-tanned cheek. There followed a quiet, carefully conducted candy sale, "each package 10¢, and most packages with prizes." During the show Mrs. Reynolds had inserted the proper number of coupons in the packages, and the stage was gaudy with the prizes. The Reynolds children often sold more candy packages than the number in the audience. Then the vaudeville aftershow, for which Reynolds made no extra charge, sent everybody home happy and satisfied. It must have seemed to most of them, as they again walked over the gangplank, that during those two and a half hours they had been visiting strange new worlds far away from their own well-worn and narrow paths of life. By eleven o'clock the boat was dark. The next morning at daybreak she began her hop to the next landing.

In prosperous times the MAJESTIC took in between $110 and $150 per night. During the depression a great change came: often the ticket sales amounted to only three or four dollars. The people would go down to the riverbank, listen to the calliope, and then just fade away when the show was about to begin, because they did not have money enough to buy tickets. Reynolds, like other showboat captains, tried to make adjustments. He used fewer professional actors, with a resulting serious injury to a program that had never been strong. To save time and travel expense he had to omit from his itinerary the remote districts, where he had before been most welcome and where business had been best. He tried adding a ten-cent matinee, but the only result was to cut down the already slim attendance at the night performance. After 1937 Reynolds began playing the larger towns, hoping to show perhaps a week at each stand, even though he got "nervous as a cat" the second night. But here he came squarely in competition with the movie theatres, which were far better equipped for entertaining than the MAJESTIC. Reynolds found that the sophisticated city patrons, even when a few straggled into his show, did not appreciate his performance except to make fun of it. The Captain did not understand the technique of burlesque, and refused to co-operate with them.

And so for the MAJESTIC the depression never ended. During the Second World War she was tied up at Point Pleasant, West Virginia, occasionally operated by local talent for a night show. Beginning with 1948 the old boat, with her captain, was chartered by groups of drama students from Kent State University and Hiram College, and once more took to the rivers, with the co-operation of various local groups in towns along the Kanawha and the Ohio. During these cruises the melodrama "The Drunkard" (first produced in Boston in 1844) was alternated with the modern "John Loves Mary." The "experiment," frankly so called, was like artificial respiration, and could not last long.

Perhaps the happiest of all showboat stories is that of the JAMES ADAMS FLOATING THEATRE, the boat which never had a losing season. But she was not a river boat at all. For thirty years she played the Albemarle and Chesapeake regions along the Atlantic Coast, to full houses and without competition, under the guidance of Mr. and Mrs. James Adams and Mr. and Mrs. Charles Hunter.

Mr. and Mrs. Adams before the First World War were circus performers with an aerial act. He became part-owner of the show and promptly went broke. Then he went into the carnival business with Johnny J. Jones, when he began running a two-car ten-cent vaudeville tent show through the Middle Atlantic Coast States. Vaudeville had never before been shown at so low a price, and Adams made a fortune. In fact his success was so spectacular that many of his company left him every year to start rival ten-cent shows, until competition seemed about to ruin the business.

Adams visited a showboat at Huntington, West Virginia, and the moment he entered the auditorium, the idea of a similar salt-water craft occurred to him. For two years he talked boats with the experts and drew his plans. There would be many differences, to be sure, between his ocean-going vessel and the river showboats, but the principal difference must be in the matter of strength. His should be many times as staunch as the riverboat, which even one playful slap from the Atlantic would have made into kindling wood. So he bought his timber standing in the forests of South Carolina, great beams long enough to run the full length of his hull without splicing. A ship yard at Little Washington, North Carolina built the boat for him of planking four inches thick and thirty-two feet long, drift-bolted every two feet with twenty-seven-inch bolts.[11] The ADAMS was of medium size, measuring one hundred and twenty-two by thirty-four feet, and drew only fourteen inches of water. The auditorium, with its boxes, lower floor, and balcony, comfortably seated seven hundred. The stage was nineteen feet across and fifteen feet deep. Living quarters for the Adamses and Hunters were at the bow,

[11] This construction saved the boat in 1920 in a storm off Tangier Island. For fourteen hours she flew distress signals, with waves breaking over the roof of the theatre, but no help could reach her until the storm had spent its fury.

over the business office and ticket office. The other eight living-dressing-rooms were back of the stage. Dining room, kitchen, and cook's quarters were under the stage, with an entrance through the orchestra pit. The boat was furnished and decorated plainly, almost severely—no gilt and no wooden gingerbread. Technically, to humor the United States Department of Commerce, the JAMES ADAMS was registered as the S. S. PLAYHOUSE, Port of Philadelphia, although it was never in that city, and the name PLAYHOUSE was quickly forgotten by everyone except the inspectors. To the white population she was the FLOATING THEATRE; to the colored, the OPERY BARGE.

Wartime shipping conditions forced Adams to build his tows. Two tugs were necessary for the handling of the awkward showboat in the broad reaches of the rough bay, one in front and one behind. The ELK was a fifty-foot boat with a ninety horse power marine engine; the TROUPER was smaller and less powerful. Each had a draft of five and a half feet, enough to land them often on the shoals as they escorted their bulky charge, with a fourteen-inch draft, in and out the shallow inlets.

During the boat's entire career Charles Hunter, who learned his dramas on the Ohio, was director and leading man, and upon occasion also manager of the boat. Mrs. Hunter, the former Miss Beulah Adams, James Adams' youngest sister, was leading lady for seventeen years, and well earned the title, "Mary Pickford of the Chesapeake." [12] After 1925 Adams spent most of his time in Philadelphia, where he was engaged in real estate; in his absence, his younger brother Selba, with his wife Clara, became the efficient manager.[13] The Ed Faltes Orchestra of ten pieces—on this boat it was never called a band—seemed almost as permanent as the management itself. Actors might change with the seasons, but not so those in the pit. Some of these musicians had been with their employer since the Jones Carnival days and one had worked with Dan Rice, and with Ringling Brothers when they had only "two horses and a buggy." All of them had seen service either on showboats or in circuses. They never left their pit during the performances, for they were not required to double on the stage. Probably their greatest cross was to play the jazz music demanded by the First World War generation, for these old-timers had learned their art under a very different tradition.

[12] An excellent photograph of "Mary Pickford of the Chesapeake" is printed by the *Saturday Evening Post*, Vol. 198 (October 31, 1925), p. 40.
[13] James and Gertrude Adams only rarely visited the showboat, and then in their private yacht.

The ADAMS began with a mixture of vaudeville and drama. But the plays proved so much more successful than the other features that the specialty acts were soon discontinued or relegated to the after-show. Unlike a Broadway producer, Hunter never found it necessary to guess what his audiences wanted, because he knew—melodramas both old and new. "Once you know what is sure fire, you can't possibly miss," he used to say. And he gave them melodramas six nights a week.

Since the boat usually played a week at each stand, she offered six plays, one for each night except Sunday. Here, for example, is the program for 1925, a typical season. On Monday the bill was "The Balloon Girl," in which the heroine, a circus performer, dropped by a parachute trapeze upon the roof of a handsome bachelor clergyman.[14] The embarrassed pastor offered her his robe to cover her exposed legs. She rejected it with this speech, which invariably brought down the house: "Many a high neck and long sleeves cover more filth and indecency than you could scrub off in a week with the Gulf of Mexico as a bath tub." Tuesday night brought "Pollyanna," the little glad girl, always re-enforced by a curtain talk on playing the glad game and looking for the silver lining. On Wednesday night that grand old veteran of the sentimental stage, "Tempest and Sunshine," was a sure shot to every simple and sincere heart. Thursday brought "A Thief in the Night," a mystery play. On Friday night the bill was the exotic "Sooey-San," and the week closed on Saturday in bang-up style with the "Mystic Isle," a melodrama in which two aviators are forced to land upon an island in the Gulf of Mexico, the haunt of bootleggers, Chinese smugglers, and opium runners. By 1931 the program had undergone little change except for the addition of more copyright material: Monday, "Grandmothers and Flappers"; Tuesday, "Gossip"; Wednesday, "Mr. Jim Bailey"; Thursday, "The Girl Who Ran Away"; Friday, "Peg o' My Heart"; and Saturday, "S'manthy."

Such a repertoire must have proved popular, for night after night through year after year the auditorium was full, with tickets selling for fifty, thirty-five, and twenty cents.

Even the aftershow, consisting of two vaudeville acts and an old-

---

[14] It is significant that the girl wore a ballet skirt instead of tights, the traditional costume of parachute jumpers and circus performers. Tights were "frowned upon by the best Tidewater circles," as Wesley Stout puts it, and the Adams' success was grounded upon their standing with the best Tidewater circles.

Emerson's Cotton Blossom

The WONDERLAND

fashioned minstrel number, in which the actors did their only doubling, gave one the impression of having been scrubbed and cleaned, so scrupulously free was it of all suggestion of dirt. On this stage Virtue was always rewarded, Vice always punished. The comedian might occasionally upset the scale of values, but the hero invariably observed the laws of balance. The villain here always conducted his rascality with proper circumspection. Members of the company were as meticulous in their private lives as in their characters and lines, for certainly their generous patrons had a right to expect this much of them.

The ADAMS may be said to have achieved a climax of decorum, practicing far more than mere decency and morality. Edna Ferber in 1924, when she was collecting material, especially setting, for her *Showboat*, visited for a week on the JAMES ADAMS. The Hunters and Adamses entertained their guest most hospitably on board and on excursions over the countryside, for the showboat always carried at least one motorcar on deck. One afternoon on a shopping expedition Mrs. Adams, Mrs. Hunter, and Miss Ferber sat in an ice cream parlor in Eastern Maryland, and the novelist absent-mindedly reached into her handbag for a cigarette. She was about to light it when she noticed the shocked expression on the faces of her hostesses, and she instantly understood. Had that cigarette been lighted, its smoke would have hung thickly along the Eastern Shore for many seasons. On various occasions the boat entertained notables, both foreign and home, always with an extreme degree of formality. Each spring an artist came aboard to paint a new set of scenery; during his four-week stay he was entertained as a guest of honor, almost pompously.

This constant emphasis on decorum and conventionality sometimes had unfortunate results. It was probably responsible for the suspicion that for a long time the Negro population felt for the JAMES ADAMS. According to rumor up and down the coast, the entertainment on the boat was a diabolical bait to lure the blacks aboard, when they would be locked up and transported to Africa. When the Negroes who succumbed to the "lure" found that the only penalty exacted of them was the payment of the fifteen cents admission to the concert and afterpiece, they became enthusiastic patrons of the "opery barge."

Another kind of uneasiness on the boat was not so easily cured. Some of those employed thought they did not enjoy the same privileges as others more favored by the management. A caste system prevailed over much of the boat's territory, and something that closely resembled it appeared on board. Those who had been with the ADAMS for many years were accustomed to the meticulous following of even trivial conventions, and could understand and even sympathize with what appeared to newcomers as social affectation. It seems that the management had the habit of taking along on holiday excursions only the chosen few, and also of admitting only this same select group to the social functions on board. Low salaries for the majority exaggerated this feeling of unrest, for even during the generous 1920's the maximum was twenty dollars per week. A competent young actor concluded a letter to his pal with this advice: "Of all the jobs you better never take this one. Remember, twenty is the limit and no banners or candy to help. Another thing, you don't dare chase [15] any, as they are very particular about that." Lack of harmony on a show-boat was always a serious matter, because living quarters were narrow and the boat confining. There is no evidence on the ADAMS of that willingness to share which made the western showboats object lessons in democratic living.

Charley Hunter and Selba Adams may not have been the best psy-chologists, but they certainly were good managers. Strict business standards governed all procedures. Since there was a surplus of towns available for possible engagements, the boat stopped only at those that consistently furnished large audiences. Two nights of poor busi-ness and the town was dropped from the itinerary. After the ADAMS had defeated three mayors on a higher-license issue, there was no more trouble about fees. Only the plays that produced the highest box-office receipts were repeated. In the earlier years Adams de-veloped a unique advertising technique. He secured lists of car owners and sent to each a complimentary ticket, knowing that the driver would bring with him several paying patrons. In later years he sub-stituted a small announcement in the local newspaper. No advance agents, no parades, no billing of the countryside, and, what would have seemed strangest of all to the Western showboats, no calliope.

And one should add, no competition. Reasons for this fact Adams analyzed quite accurately. He argued that showboating in his terri-tory required too much capital for the amateur, and the experienced showman who had $60,000 was not likely to risk it in the strange salt-water game. Only once did competition rear its ugly head. A secondhand clothier in Elizabeth City, North Carolina, the port where

[15] Escorting local belles to their homes after the show.

the ADAMS always wintered, seeing the rich returns of drama, launched a boat in 1917 to play vaudeville and pictures over the same territory. The newcomer, being neither showman nor seaman nor business man, went broke his third season, and sold his vessel to a logging company.

The real secret of the long success of the JAMES ADAMS lies in a matter more subtle than accounts or advertising. The managers consciously and completely adjusted the boat and everything about it to the ideals of the region where it worked. The ADAMS was unlike the WATER QUEEN or the COTTON BLOSSOM because the Virginia and Carolina Tidewater was unlike the Middle West. The Adams brothers were adept at fitting life on their boat into the traditions and habits of their territory. It is safe to guess that if the JAMES ADAMS FLOATING THEATRE had been playing the lower Ohio, the punctilious conventionality and genteel dignity might have changed to a heartier friendliness and a blunter good humor, for James Adams was a skilled actor both on and off the stage. Even the dignified quarto folder on which the plays for the week were announced, in contrast with the flamboyant posters of the western boats, suggested an atmosphere of sedateness. On the back of each program appeared this significant paragraph: "We feel that we are just as much a part of your community as though we were located there permanently. We have spent a week with you each season . . . Our people have mingled with you socially and patronized your institutions." This harmony between boat and territory was an essential feature of James Adams' success.

In the opposite corner of the page of this same folder appears a suggestion of bitterness: "If the time comes," says Mr. Adams, "that our judgement tells us that our public prefers *mechanical entertainment* we will bring it to you. But until that time comes, we shall continue to bring you our company of thirty people, Flesh and Blood Actors and Musicians, which we believe is of more benefit to your community than *five thousand feet of celluloid* and a phonograph." Evidently the ADAMS, like other showboats, was feeling the competition of the movies.

Each year from November to March the JAMES ADAMS usually wintered at Elizabeth City, North Carolina, in the efficient hands of Eddy and Hazel Paull, friends of the owners. As soon as weather permitted, she would work through the villages of the Dismal Swamp coast, on through the Albemarle and Pamlico regions, and into the

Chesapeake with its hundreds of small coastal towns. Because of depression conditions Adams decided in 1930 to try playing also during the winter months. In December of that year the boat tied up in Washington, D. C., at the Seventh Street Wharf, with a repertoire of three weeks' plays, beginning with "Gossip" and ending with "Mr. Jim Bailey." Members of cast and crew had been requested to remain on board until photographers and newsmen could produce the proper favorable publicity. These gentlemen duly arrived and took their pictures and wrote their stories, but immediately on their heels came also the local fire marshall. After a five-minute inspection, he insisted that the boat either immediately install a steel stage curtain or else leave the city's jurisdiction. Since it was impossible to comply with the first demand, the ADAMS, on the very day that it was to have had its gala opening, ignominiously retreated across the Potomac to Alexandria, Virginia, threw down its landing plank at the Cameron Street Wharf, instituted free bus service from Washington for prospective patrons, and filled the engagement as advertised. The management admitted to being "embarrassed," but it discreetly remained silent on the subject of the highly satisfactory box-office receipts. In less than thirty days the Washington fire marshall had been dismissed, whether because he had sought to protect the local show business or because he had failed to drive the threat far enough away, no one will ever know. In future seasons the ADAMS preferred Alexandria.

Like other showboats the ADAMS suffered during the depression of the 1930's, but unlike most of the others it survived. In 1939 Edna Ferber wrote that the old FLOATING THEATRE had sunk with every scrap of scenery, costumes, papers, and furnishings on board. It was then, she adds, that Charles Hunter cashed the check which she had gratefully sent him years before for the information that had gone into the making of her *Showboat.*

From 1914 to 1918 the Mississippi system carried from fourteen to eighteen showboats each year. Ten or more of these were "family boats," each with a capacity of two hundred to six hundred, for by this time it was clear that the big boats were not to succeed. In addition to the boats already named, others were industriously bringing entertainment to gradually dwindling river audiences. Each has survived, either in history or in legend, stamped with one characteristic or remembered for one dramatic incident.

Doc Bart's FUN BOAT was one of these less-known craft. Though small, she had all the paraphernalia and fanfare of a big showboat—

a band which doubled as orchestra in the tiny pit, a full cast of actors, a minstrel show (colored), a calliope, a towboat, and an advance man. The owner was a licensed physician who preferred the show business. He had appropriately started in a medicine show, then successively worked with a circus, operated a stock company of his own for three seasons, and managed an "Uncle Tom" company in Canada. He felt that he could never be satisfied until he had tried a showboat, and he therefore bought the FUN BOAT, which he operated for the two years of 1927 and 1928 on the Ohio and the Green Rivers.[16]

Doc Bart believed in simplifying program problems. His advance man was instructed to bill "Uncle Tom's Cabin" wherever the people wanted to see it, and at other villages to announce "Girl of the Golden West." In the first, Billy Williams and his wife, the colored cooks, played Uncle Tom and Topsy, with Velma Brewer as Little Eva; in the second, Clair Brewer and his wife Daisy carried the leads. Charles and Dan Payne, saxophone players, worked with "Rastus and Bones," colored acrobats, to put on the between-acts and the minstrel after-show.

Doc admitted that he always had bad luck with his drummers. During 1928 the first one ran into some loose gravel with his motorcycle and landed in a hospital. The next one, who was so temperamental that sometimes he kicked out the head of his drums, had the habit of presenting himself as a prospective buyer to the automobile dealers of every town. The end came at Florence, Indiana, when two men came down to the landing to collect a hundred dollars which the drummer had borrowed, offering the boat as security! The third one, a dreamy-eyed fellow from Louisville, had a mania for playing the calliope, both on and off schedule. Whenever the band played a number that he liked, his own drum rhythms hypnotized him until he went almost berserk. But he was a good drummer, and remained until the end of the season.

The FUN BOAT experienced its most exciting evening at Stephensport, Kentucky, in 1928. The crowd began gathering early, the women with babies in their arms, the men with whiskey bottles and guns sticking out of their pockets. By the end of the first act of "Girl of the Golden West," the audience was paying little attention to the play, the auditorium smelled like a still, and there was much coming and going. Doc could not leave the front unguarded, but he sent his

[16] Bart stated that he bought the boat from Captain Price, but no record of any such transfer has been found.

message backstage: "For God's sake see how fast you can run the rest of this show so we can get these people off before they get any drunker." Forty-five minutes later the boat was cleared, and immediately crossed the Ohio to Rome, Indiana, leaving a rowdy crowd to celebrate in its own way.

A more typical experience occurred when the boat played Mill Landing, far up the Green River. It was a poverty stricken village of six hundred, half white and half black, living in shacks of hand-hewn lumber. The men worked in the chair factory, and the women wove the cane bottoms at home, for ten cents each. The auditorium that night held a capacity crowd—three hundred—though many of the admissions were paid in blackberries or fish. During the whole of "Uncle Tom's Cabin" and even the minstrel show, the audience was so tensely quiet that the Ohio's ripples could be heard lapping against the boat's sides. Asked the next morning if he was not ashamed to take money from these people, Doc Bart rightly replied, "No, we gave them the only pleasure they have had for years, and that for fifty cents or a gallon or two of berries."

After Bart's death in the spring of 1929, the FUN BOAT was converted into a freight barge.

The smallest of this half-legendary fleet of little showboats was Frank Rice's TWENTIETH CENTURY, which bore the ridicule of the other boats on account of her diminutive size. Contemporary with French's first NEW SENSATION, she carried only vaudeville and band, and ceased to operate in 1905 when the drama was being revived on the rivers.[17]

The DIXIE QUEEN enjoyed the unique distinction of being built in 1939 after the depression, during a period when showboats were going out of business. Al Cooper, the lightning cartoonist, and his wife Flo had spent their honeymoon back in 1914 on board McNair's NEW ERA, and, probably because of a nostalgic yearning to recapture the past, twenty-five years later they built this showboat of their own at Kansas City, Missouri. She was a small boat, with a seating capacity of only five hundred and forty, but she was well equipped,

---

[17] Frank Rice Kruse, professionally known as Captain Frank Rice, was born in 1864 in Yazoo City, Mississippi. At the age of eighteen he began operating a showboat, and continued until 1905, when he retired to purchase the Rice Hotel at 137 South Liberty Street, New Orleans. His house became the favorite stopping place for showboaters and actors. The Frenches, the McNairs, the Prices, and many others, signed his register and enjoyed his hospitality. He died at the home of a son in New York in 1947.

especially the stage and the living quarters for the owner. She departed from the older tradition of serving the small landings to go immediately into competition with city entertainment. As soon as completed she played for sixteen weeks in her home port, offering mainly specialty acts. Though her usual territory was Kansas City and surrounding districts, in 1940 she tied up at New Orleans, at South Claiborne Avenue in the New Basin, during the Mardi Gras season. Here the bill was "Putting on Airs," a three-act comedy, with vaudeville numbers between the acts. In 1943 Cooper tied up the DIXIE QUEEN at McGregor, Iowa, while he served as commander of a coast guard patrol boat on the Upper Mississippi. He later sold her to Oscar Bloom, who converted her into an excursion boat.[18]

The DOVE, which specialized in jazz during the 1920's, has become the most legendary of all showboats. During a season of flood on the Tombigbee, her most familiar territory, she was stranded five miles inland, and abandoned. Years later, the waters again rose and took her for a last wild ride on the rivers, and no splinter of her was ever seen afterward. Many of the people of the region—most of them colored —are still confidently expecting her to return, bringing with her the same fascinating rhythms.

Others also have served and sunk. Farnsworth's WATER LILY, built at Pittsburgh, and pushed by the gas boat MARGARET R., presented movies and vaudeville to the smaller landings on the Ohio, Muskingum, Allegheny, and Monongahela rivers during the '30's and '40's. She was the only boat of the era not to show drama. The VALLEY and her gas tow EDNA M., owned and operated by Captain Harry Hart and his family, carried melodrama and vaudeville to the region between Pittsburgh and Cincinnati until she sank, the victim of rats, in 1932.[19] The RIVER MAID (1918–1929), on which Captain Hi was owner, manager, impressario, stage director, and ticket seller, and his wife, chief cook, storekeeper, and sometimes actress, featured such melodramas as "Triss," "Honest Hearts" and "Lena Rivers," with variety turns between the acts. A short humorous curtain talk,

[18] An earlier and smaller DIXIE QUEEN, with seating capacity of 450, operated out of Kansas City, 1922–1933; she sank at Greenville, Mississippi, a total loss. A DIXIE, with a capacity of 300, operated 1911–1916 (See the New Orleans *Times-Picayune*, Feb. 4, 1930, p. 11, and Jan. 20, 1940, p. 12; also the Cincinnati *Enquirer*, June 30, 1916).

[19] Rats gnawed holes in her hull below the waterline when she was tied up at Newport, Ohio, on the Licking River. Captain Hart, his wife, his son William, Jr., and his parents, Mr. and Mrs. William Hart, asleep on board, all got safely to the bank (See the Cincinnati *Post*, Sept. 8, 1932, p. 1).

both a "thank you" and a vaudeville number in itself, probably modeled after Billy Bryant's aftershow speeches, was always delivered by the oldest member of the cast. The MANITOU, owned for a short time by Ralph Emerson, was run aground in 1934 on the Mississippi shore at Guttenberg, Iowa, and two years later she was repaired and converted into a menagerie boat.

The REX, the PEERLESS, the TEMPLE OF HEALTH, Brighton's MEDICINE BOAT, and the IDLEWILD, were all operating in the 1930's. All had either been converted or had sunk before the beginning of the Second World War. The MERMAID belonged to the 1920's and the LONG HORN to the early 1890's.

The family boats, though comparatively small, served more people than the magnificent palace showboats, for two reasons: they were more numerous than the big boats, and they were longer-lived. Certainly the small boats brought entertainment to those who most needed it, those in the outlying regions where the larger boats could not afford to go. The family boats, because of modest investments and small operating expenses, were better able to weather the bleak depression years. As long as there was a river frontier, they brought to it better entertainment than otherwise it could have enjoyed—wholesomely clean and emotionally refreshing.[20]

[20] Principal Sources: Numerous interviews, manuscripts, scrapbooks, personal letters, posters, handbills, and newspaper files.
Other Sources: Items listed in the bibliography under William Aylward, Bert Banks, Kyle Crichton, Meigs Frost, Jan and Cora Gordon, Corinne Hardesty, Ethel Leahy, Paul Pettit, Marion Porter, Sidney Snook, and Wesley Stout.

XII

CALLIOPE MUSIC

An Interlude

THE MEETING between the AMERICAN and the WONDERLAND at Bonnett's Mill on the Missouri in 1915 will live long in show-boat history. Needham and Steiner's trim AMERICAN, headed upriver, was edging in toward the landing about eleven in the morning, pre-paratory to tying up for the evening performance. Calliope Red sat at the steaming keyboard, announcing the showboat's arrival with her favorite, "Oh Dem Golden Slippers."

Suddenly Cooley and Thom's big WONDERLAND rounded the bend just above, on her way down the river, evidently with identical inten-tions as to an evening performance. The calliope player on the WONDERLAND hurled the first insult with "What You Goin' Do When the Rent Comes Round?" Those on board the AMERICAN understood: Their rival was implying that they and their boat were discards, no longer able to make a living. They turned to Calliope Red.

"You ain't gona stand for that, are you, Red, from that bunch of hams?"

Calliope Red, aged twenty-three, with face and hair burnt to the same rich bronze, was surcharged with passionate loyalty for the AMERICAN and all things associated with her. His second love was ragtime music, whether it came from a jug, a saw, the tinny piano in the front of the auditorium, or the iron-lunged monster now before him. He was already rolling up his sleeves for the duel. "I'll make that fake musician jump in the river when I get through with him," he growled. Then he called down to George Emmich, the engineer: "Turn on full steam, Chief. We're gona play calliope music till they're black in the face!"

His reply to the WONDERLAND's insult was "Mornin' Si," which means in calliope language that the persons addressed are clumsy clod-hoppers, antiquated theatrical mistakes, fitted only to be tillers of the soil.

In turn the WONDERLAND fired back with the deliberately chosen indignity, "Goodbye, Little Girl, Goodbye," which freely translated meant, "Your usefulness being passed, it is time for you to leave."

Calliope Red grinned contemptuously and replied with "Sit Down, You're Rocking the Boat."

His antagonist, in desperation, played "I Don't Like Your Family." Red countered with "Silver Threads Among the Gold," a pointed reference to the age of the WONDERLAND.

The calliope man on the WONDERLAND's top deck lost his temper, and his whistles screamed out, "When I Get You Alone Tonight," certainly intended as a threat.

Calliope Red acted instantly to win the day with "Get Out and Get Under." Since getting under a boat meant death, and since, according to Red's conception, death for his enemy would mean eternity in an unpleasant place, by one master stroke he had said, "Go to hell!" Truly a difficult message to send via calliope!

The whistles on the WONDERLAND became silent, and her defender slunk from the upper deck. Red bore his honors modestly, as becomes all heroes.

"I don't brag much as a rule," he said to those around him, "but when it comes to playin' the calliope I don't take nothin' off nobody. I ain't an actor or a box office man, and I don't claim to know how to run the boat better than Colonel Steiner, like some actors I know. But I know my business when it comes to tootin' these pipes. Them actors can play 'Lena Rivers' and 'The Fightin' Parson,' and think they're the ones that's bringin' in the money at the box office. But I'm the one that's really turnin' the trick—and I know.

"Before the boat even ties up at a stand, I sit at this old thing and give 'em a concert they can hear for miles every direction, just to let 'em know we're here. All the people hear the music, which sounds like a big church organ that far away. The men in the fields go to the house to consult their women folks, and the kids begin countin' out the dimes and quarters from the jar on the top shelf of the kitchen safe.

"I whistle it up again along in the afternoon—all good ragtime stuff. Then at 7:30 sharp I turn loose with a grand medley of patriotic airs and march stuff. They can't resist it—nobody could. It brings 'em out like the sunshine brings the flowers. I simply stand up here like a big magnet and draw 'em down to the boat."

The little group around the calliope was already beginning to scatter. "Red, you wouldn't brag, would you?" jibed the cook, who had himself been drawn up to the top deck by the excitement of the combat. But the slightly stoop-shouldered energetic figure at the keyboard, intoxicated with his own music, had already started on his favorite subject.

"This calliope is the best one on the rivers, barrin' none," he announced. "She's got thirty-two whistles, made out of copper and brass, and they hold electricity like a storage battery. They pick it up out of the air after a storm. Many a day I've stood up here playin' when I got a shock every time I touched a key. You got to be crazy about your job when you stick to a thing like that. You hear these actors talking about the specialties they do between acts. Some of 'em *are* good, I'll admit, but sometimes they get the swell-head. Once we had a girl in the show that bragged about singin' with a brass band. Say, if she'd had voice enough to stand up here and sing with this steam baby, she'd been some singer, wouldn't she?"

Red reached over to tinker with some sticking valves. He would have explained to you that any calliope always seemed to have some dead keys, and that half the skill in playing the big monster was the quick ingenuity required to bridge over these vacancies in the melody. His blue cap had slanted to a jaunty angle, and his bandsman's red coat was a little too short to meet the blue trousers. When he had adjusted all to his satisfaction, he turned on the steam again, and struck up, "I Love the Ladies." Some of those on the deck below clapped their palms over their ears, for after the temporary lull the new burst of music seemed literally to smash the silence. But Calliope Red, whose real name was Bobby Wills, just grinned with sheer joy in the love of his work.

Meanwhile the fast gathering crowd on the bank had not been unaware of the dramatic contest. The prolonged concert had brought most of the village down to the landing, and children of all ages lined the water's edge. Some of them were running up and down, and all of them were shouting and waving at the boats. A dozen dogs had caught the excitement of the occasion, and were punctuating the other noises with staccato barks.

The big WONDERLAND, now silent except for the flailing of the energetic little stern-wheeler pushing her, changed her mind, to continue on down the river to a lower stand. The AMERICAN eased her gangplank into position to welcome visitors and to receive early ticket buyers. Her sign announced,

Tonight at 8

YANKEE DOODLE BOY

With Three Full Vodvil Acts
and
Special Music

————

Admission 60¢, 40¢, 25¢ [1]

[1] Principal Sources: Scrapbooks, manuscripts, interviews, and letters.

XIII

SHOWBOAT ROUND THE BEND

The Bryants

THE BRYANT family and its showboats have received during
recent years much publicity, some of it favorable, all of it significant. For a quarter of a century, first the PRINCESS (1907–1917)
and then Bryant's NEW SHOWBOAT (1918–1942) were making the
river landings both large and small. Since that period Billy Bryant
and his troupe have played extended engagements in the more lucrative river spots, especially Cincinnati, and they have played New York
and Chicago in land theatres. More recently they have staged their
Shakespeare medley in St. Louis for a whole season, they have been
interviewed by the national press and also on nation-wide radio programs, and they have even written a book.

As one becomes familiar with the whole story of the Bryants, one
suspects that their particular brand of showboating was determined
for them years before they ever owned a boat. Samuel Bryant, whose
father had been one of the caretakers in Queen Victoria's Crystal
Palace Gardens, eloped to America with his sweetheart Violet, believing that this was the land of promise. He was twenty-five, his wife
thirteen. They expected generosity from a rich uncle in New Jersey,
but the old gentleman, both in life and in death, disappointed them.

They believed, apparently, that in this new country money would
come, not necessarily from honest labor or value given, but from
cleverness or some magic trick. In such a mood they went West, still
expecting riches, or at least a comfortable subsistence. They acquired
a pair of mules, and sold soap and various sundries from the back of
their conestoga wagon. Violet's guitar—as a child she had traveled
through England with a Gilbert and Sullivan itinerant troupe—and
a hired boy's sleight-of-hand attracted their crowd. Sam Bryant manu-

factured a rheumatism "cure" out of gasoline and red pepper, and rigged up what he called "electric" belts for sale to the gullible. And so the family—son Billy and daughter Florence had been born— "worked" its way across Texas as far as Colorado, with more than a suggestion of insincerity. But the going was hard, for the farther west the wagon went, the less gullible people seemed. At one stand Sam Bryant was even jailed.

By 1900 they were back on the Mississippi, sometimes peddling their fake wares and sometimes entertaining in impromptu fashion, for Violet still had her guitar, Sam had acquired some magic tricks, and the children had learned to sing and dance.

In answer to Captain Price's advertisement in the New York *Clipper* for "vaudeville people in all lines," the "Four Bryants," as they now styled themselves, joined the WATER QUEEN at Augusta, Kentucky, for the most comfortable year since they had left New Jersey. Captain Price welcomed the family, partly because it would have been difficult to find four entertainers more conveniently packaged for accommodation on the boat than this group, and partly because they offered the very numbers that the WATER QUEEN at that time needed. Sam Bryant performed fifteen minutes of magic, climaxed by his turning river water into wine, and then the wine back to water again. Violet Bryant sang "The Fatal Rose of Red," with lantern slides, usually to the accompaniment of audible weeping in the audience. Florence sang "The Wedding of the Lily and the Rose," with a coy little dance at the stanza-ends. And young Billy, after a few well worn mother-in-law jokes, gave them, in his best cocky style, "The Green Grass Grew All Around." The tired and half-starved Bryants became rested and well fed, and they approached New Orleans and the end of the season at Christmas time with regret. As a final gesture of generosity, Captain Price paid their fare back to Cincinnati.

They were "at liberty" again, with the responsibility of making their own way. This strange family still seemed to expect to pull riches out of its bag of tricks. They again sold their pepper-and-gasoline liniment to ready believers, this time in Ohio; they put on their "show" on improvised platforms for mining audiences in Pennsylvania; and finally at the little town of West Hickory, Pennsylvania, they built a barge, and later a gasoline towboat with materials salvaged from the river and from the shipyards. They became shantyboaters, with a little showmanship thrown in. Early spring thaws on the Little

Kanawha River, where they had spent an uncomfortable winter of inactivity, destroyed their boats and all their meager belongings, leaving them destitute. But during that winter Billy Bryant had seen George M. Cohan on the stage and had heard him sing his famous song, "Then I Know That I'd Be Satisfied With Life." He was to remain through the years the boy's ideal of showmanship. Vivid in all their minds, too, was the memory of that comfortable season on board the WATER QUEEN.

The "luck" that the Bryants had been waiting for came at Point Pleasant, West Virginia, in the person of Captain C. C. Bowyer, as typical a product of the American Middle West as the rivers could show. Generous, sympathetic, and energetic, whenever he saw human beings in want he immediately tried to find a remedy. When he heard of this family of four stranded in the old Klein House by the river, he called Sam and Violet Bryant into his bank for an interview. These were show people and they loved the river. That in Captain Bowyer's mind added up to a showboat. A week later he bought for them, for twenty-five dollars, a condemned government dump scow, which he thought might be converted into what they wanted.

To the Bryants that scow—covered with mud and humped up in the middle like a razor-back hog—was a showboat the moment they laid eyes on her. To make that vision a reality they worked almost ceaselessly for the next six months. First, at one end of the sixteen by ninety hull, with waste slabs of lumber given to them at the saw mill, they built a shanty in which to live. Friends in Point Pleasant and Henderson contributed services and materials most generously. Most of the lumber, however, was salvaged from the river. Logs escaped from their owners were snaked to shore, the brands deer-horned off, and the timber dragged to the sawmill. Needed metal—nails, bolts, hog-chains—was purchased with money borrowed from almost every family in town. Painters donated their discarded cans, sometimes with substantial quantities of paint still in them. Sam Bryant proved surprisingly efficient with the few tools that he had brought with him from England. The building of the showboat became a community project, pushed forward by an enthusiasm characteristic of a generous and energetic Midwestern village.

The big news of early spring was that the showboat had been completed. True, the stage had no scenery, the auditorium had no seats and no paint, the windows had no glass, the ticket booth had no door, and neither stage nor auditorium had any lights. Perhaps the

most serious lack of all was a planned program. But the Bryants refurbished the acts they had performed on the WATER QUEEN—Sam's
magic, Violet's sentimental songs, the sprightlier song-and-dance
numbers of Florence and Billy—added several skits for the whole
group, and felt they were ready. Months earlier they had named the
boat the PRINCESS, for as Mrs. Bryant had explained, "That's the way
I'll feel when she's finally built."

And then came the opening night! It proved to be a prophecy of
the Bryants' future, a glowing success built, not on program or acting,
but rather on a lack of these, with the gaping void on the stage filled
by personality and friendship. All the good people of Point Pleasant,
Henderson, and the surrounding territory flocked down to the boat,
carrying with them, in accordance with the request on the posters,
their lanterns and their chairs or boxes. Not more than a third of that
crowd ever got as far as the ticket office. The remainder literally
covered the PRINCESS inside and out, or stood on flatboats tied alongside. Door receipts, $48.50, indicate about two hundred paid admis-
sions, almost twice the normal capacity of the little boat. The spirit of
hospitality and warm neighborly friendship prevailed, and the whole
scene more closely resembled a gigantic house-warming or an old-
fashioned camp meeting than a theatrical opening night.

Quite characteristically, Billy Bryant remembers everything about
that first performance except what was on the stage! Before the last
act, the show was interrupted by the fainting of "a large heavy-set
lady" in the stifling heat. Before it could be resumed, the audience
had pushed back their chairs and boxes and turned the entertainment
into a rollicky country dance. The string band from Point Pleasant
furnished the music, and a Salt Creek six-footer did the calling, who
roared out as he jumped onto the stage, "I can out-dance, outrun, . . .
and lick any man twice my size. I love my licker an' women an' I'm
chock-full of fight. Let's go!"

Perhaps that sudden change in the nature of the entertainment is the
best comment on the stage-offering of the evening.

As the PRINCESS and her little gasoline tow worked their way up the
Ohio system, into the mining districts along the winding Monongahela, through flood and wind and accident—for her owners were
sadly lacking in knowledge of the river—she faced even more serious
dangers. These miners seemed to have fixed standards of what a showboat should offer, and apparently they did not approve of the program
that the PRINCESS was carrying. Furthermore, they did not hesitate

(Above) The COTTON BLOSSOM's Baseball Team (Number 3 is
Captain Emerson); (below) Captain Eisenbarth's Band (Director
High is seated, front center)

The HOLLYWOOD

to express their disapproval with rocks and other weapons. These same men and women for years had witnessed America's best in vaudeville on French's New Sensation, they had listened to Price's Water Queen band, they had been entranced by the melodramas of Markle's Grand Floating Palace, and had seen the acting of artists like Norman Thom. Little wonder that the make-shift program of the Princess seemed to them to deserve nothing but rocks, and with these they were generous. Sometimes they even piled up their missiles in advance, when news of the show had out-traveled the boat. More than once the glass on the pilot house would have needed replacing—only there wasn't any glass there. The Bryants erroneously assumed that their hardy audiences accorded all visiting showboats the same treatment, and were accordingly not unduly disturbed by this rather primitive method of criticism. After all, perhaps they argued, was it not better to get a man's dollar, even though it was followed by a rock, than to get neither the dollar nor the rock? But certainly they must have learned that not all men are so gullible as those who had bought the pepper-and-gasoline liniment. However, door-receipts were good, and as they found their first winter haven up the warm waters of the Kentucky, they felt rich. Enough to pay all their debts at Point Pleasant, and to buy food till next spring!

Their second season was marked by expansion into the field of full-length drama. At Ford, Kentucky, where the boat wintered, a school teacher, who evidently knew his Shakespeare better than he knew the Bryants, recommended "Hamlet." With misgivings, they began rehearsals. Bald father Sam played Laertes, and son Billy the role of Polonius, in addition to doubling in three other parts. Mother Violet did Ophelia, daughter Florence a lady-in-waiting, while an East Side New Yorker did strange things to Hamlet's lines. Both the cast and the audience were amazed. Billy Bryant's own comments on the show are significant: "It's an awful thing to . . . talk for two hours and not know the true meaning of one blessed thing you have said." The audience "seemed to be in a stupor, as if they had been gassed or something." [1] The hopelessly confused faces out front proved more effective criticism for the Bryants than even the rocks up the Monongahela. In those days, it must be remembered, they were playing their dramas "straight," without any of the burlesque that they later introduced. Their version of "Hamlet," without either the king or the

---

[1] When the Bryants later began burlesquing showboat plays, they turned again to "Hamlet," this time in medley form.

queen, with all the characters buried in Ophelia's grave, must have been most incoherent, even to those who had never heard the whole story as Shakespeare wrote it. And then, too, the New York Hamlet was becoming impossibly temperamental, demanding real cream for his coffee and suggesting that the opening curtain be held until he could get in the proper mood for portraying the melancholy Dane. Papa Bryant wisely, in one of his fits of anger, threw both the grave effects and Hamlet over the side.

In a few days, with the help of several hastily recruited additions, the Bryants were ready with "East Lynne," which is, as Billy phrased it, strictly a "suffering and dying" melodrama. The characters died so fast that even multiple doubling could scarcely fill roles fast enough to bury the dead. River audiences liked it no better than they had "Hamlet," and one suspects for the same basic reason that these actors were not able to create their roles. After an especially dismal performance one evening, an old Negro auntie characterized the production as "an old folks' show." As individuals the provincials in those seats out front probably seemed ridiculous to the actors; but as a mass they were an audience, capable of inspiring fear and even awe in those behind the footlights. Therefore for a second time the Bryants heeded river criticism, and sadly shelved their version of "East Lynne."

By next evening they were ready with a substitute. This time it was that rip-roaring western, "Jesse James, the Missouri Outlaw," a copy of which one of the actors happened to have in his trunk. It required few properties except two thirty-eight revolvers, plenty of blank cartridges, and a set-rock. Billy Bryant himself was delighted with it, because, in his own words, "Every time I forgot my lines, all I had to do was to pull my gun and keep shooting until I could think of them again." That statement probably implies the reason that the play did not go too well, though at first it had appeared to be a "knockout." Billy facetiously stated that the play was laid aside because the shooting invariably aroused the sleeping babies in the audience, and these usually succeeded in making more noise than the actors on the stage. The next production, "Dr. Jekyll and Mr. Hyde," chosen because the character-man on board had a great desire to play the lead role, was not much more successful. The hideous death scene in the last act, where the dying villain with a green spotlight on him blew Bromo-seltzer froth through celluloid tusks while fake blood trickled down his white shirt bosom, was certainly one of the worst bits of acting that the rivers had ever witnessed.

Such plays as "Lena Rivers," "The Circus Girl," "Mother," "Little Nell of the Ozarks," and "Tempest and Sunshine" followed each other through succeeding seasons.[2] Door receipts continued to be good, for young Billy Bryant's big job was to keep his audiences satisfied. If the performance was very bad—and it usually was—Billy could offer excuses in his friendly, sparkling manner, and so largely atone for the sins of his cast. He soon found that much of his placating of the audience could be best accomplished long before the last curtain: if the villain's loud bluster shook off his black mustache, Billy would rush forward to retrieve it and present it to the confused owner with the rich elaborateness of mock ceremony; if the hero's gun refused to go off at the moment of his triumph, Billy would leap from the wings to offer a great bowie knife as an effective substitute; if the beautiful heroine forgot her lines in the most touchingly tender scene, Billy promptly appeared with a great tome, *Lessons In Love,* and offered to become her teacher. The blunders of bad acting became the high spots of the show, little unrehearsed comedies superbly set by spontaneous art in a background of drab and unconvincing tragedy. The remedy for the tragic weakness of the performance became its comic virtue. Billy Bryant always performed these little plays within the play so promptly and with such finesse that many an audience believed that they were the most carefully planned portion of the program, and held its breath waiting for another actor to make a blunder. Certainly few audiences ever guessed the great truth of Bryant's stage technique: to do the "kidding" from behind the footlights before it could come from in front of them.

A slight improvement in the program came with Billy Bryant's marriage, the climax of a romance begun, if we are to believe the groom's story, by a note found in a drifting bottle. The "Four Bryants" were now five, and eventually became six. Josephine Bryant was a most attractive addition to the cast, far superior as an actress either to sister Florence or to mother Violet. Best of all she was a gifted musician, and her version of "The Bird on Nellie's Hat" and her medley of Irish songs, as well as her expert piano playing, bolstered up a program that was threatening to sink into unintentional and premature burlesque.

By 1917 the showboat world was in a strangely confused condition. A fully developed movie industry was providing such strong com-

[2] Marked prompt scripts for these and some other dramas played by the Bryants are now in the possession of the Cleveland Public Library.

petition in the cities that the larger boat-shows were driven to the
smaller landings, formerly the exclusive territory of the little boats.
When the big COTTON BLOSSOM or the palatial GOLDENROD threw
down her stage plank by the side of the tiny PRINCESS or the NEW
ERA, the little boat's auditorium remained empty.[3] Some of the operators of the smaller boats went out of business, as did McNair of the
NEW ERA; some hunted more remote territory, still inaccessible to
the big competitors, as did Reynolds of the AMERICA; and some built
larger and finer boats and entered the big-time circuit. The Bryants
chose the last way. Sadly they parted with the faithful PRINCESS at
Parkersburg, West Virginia, and proceeded at once to Point Pleasant,
where they had tediously and painfully built their first boat ten years
earlier, to begin the construction of a boat better suited to the fast
competition of the show world.[4]

Their second boat, ready by the fall of 1917, was bigger than their
first, one hundred and thirty-five by thirty feet, with a capacity of almost nine hundred. But the greatest improvement was in equipment
and decoration. The auditorium was resplendent in white and gold,
with red plush and black tassels draped over the boxes and around the
orchestra pit. Green striped coconut matting padded the aisles, and
red-and-green slips cushioned the reserved seats. Steam pipes provided
heat for winter, and electric fans cool air for summer. The new stage,
with an ample eighteen-foot opening, boasted three sets of scenery,
adequate footlights, and a spotlight operated from the balcony. The
name chosen, simply BRYANT'S NEW SHOWBOAT, suggests a desire to
profit from the many sentimental associations and traditions already
beginning to cluster around the boat-shows. THE VALLEY BELLE,[5] a
converted steam packet formerly operating between Marietta and

---

[3] On at least one occasion the PRINCESS fought back, but to no avail. The
COTTON BLOSSOM's calliope had scarcely cooled when a member of the PRINCESS
cast started the rumor in town that smallpox had broken out on the big boat.
Both boats were promptly quarantined.

[4] The sale was made to Ed Darnold and Lew Kinser, for a sum less than half of
the original cost. "What happens to the value of a boat the minute it is launched?"
Billy sadly complained. In 1922 the PRINCESS, rebuilt, passed into the hands of
Norman Thom.

[5] The E. F. JACKSON, their first towboat, proved not big enough to handle the
showboat; the VALLEY BELLE was purchased through that genial "little giant
broker," John F. Klein. The new showboat had the financial backing of Captain
C. C. Bowyer, the same generous banker who had enabled them to build the
PRINCESS. The Bryants replaced this second boat by two successive duplicates
bearing the same name. Later towboats were the CLAIRMONT and the NEW LOTUS.

Middleport, was purchased to do the pushing, and a new calliope placed on her upper deck.

The opening night was again played at Point Pleasant, and the contrast with the PRINCESS's opening night was in everybody's mind. For this was a very different occasion from that earlier one. Now searchlights played across the sky and the calliope, under the happy hands of Josephine Bryant, announced the gala event. The band, later to double as the orchestra, in white trousers, black shirts, and white bow ties, played "A Hot Time in the Old Town Tonight" just in front of the ticket office. The ushers uniformed in blue sailor suits, were rushing about, seating the capacity crowd. Earlier in the afternoon neighboring Henderson had bought half the seats in a block, and old friends from Point Pleasant swarmed aboard, bringing flowers and other congratulatory messages. Sam Bryant in a new Prince Albert and Violet Bryant in black and rhinestones were tearful with happiness. Yes, their dream had come true, for even the program, "Over the Hill to the Poorhouse," with copious tears inspired by the mother role and comic relief furnished by the versatile Billy, was all that the good-humored audience could desire.

It was the same up the Kanawha, up the Monongahela, down the Ohio, with even an occasional trip on the Mississippi and the Illinois. "Ten Nights in a Bar Room" was an especial favorite, for its simple emotional effects proved easier for the half-trained actors. At Marietta, Sam Bryant purchased a bucking mule, January, from the American Circus Corporation, and offered ten dollars to any who could ride him. The act had to be discontinued in the coal districts, for these hardy miners somehow seemed to stick. Billy Bryant became more and more skilled at turning the weak spots in his show into sparkling bits of personal comedy. He developed, too, a special technique for playing melodrama, with a peculiarly stirring curtain line at the end of each act. Whether Lady Rivers exclaimed, "My God, it's Nellie the cloak model," or the wronged heroine sobbed, "If they call this nobility, thank God I'm a country girl," the curtain always came down on an electrified audience. Or whenever opportunity offered, the over-abundance of sentiment was gathered up at the end of an act in a sudden tableau of gun play. The heavy melodrama was thus, in effect, "jazzed up." It was further lightened by a few excellent vaudeville numbers by professionals, between acts, such as the Mundy and June juggling act, Vic Faust, the Four Mortons, and the Four

Huntings. The Bryant boat-show had at last developed from a make-shift thing into honest entertainment. The show was still further improved by the sudden acquisition of the Cohan plays, all of them comedies. That great good fortune came about in this way. Since childhood Billy Bryant had secretly admired and envied George M. Cohan. Through a series of Cinderella events, the well known playwright and actor learned of this fact, and as a generous gesture of appreciation he gave Bryant all or any of his twenty-nine plays to change or to use as he pleased on the rivers. Bryant chose "Broadway Jones," and proceeded to adapt it to boat-show audiences. He cut it into half, "threw in a half-dozen song numbers, taught a chorus of six to dance to the melodies, and surged down the rivers with 'Broadway Jones' transformed into a musical comedy." [6] For five years the Bryant boat-show played only Cohan plays, with most happy results, for these seemed far better suited to the meager talents of the Bryant players than the heavier dramas. After "Broadway Jones" it was "Adeleine" and "Rosie O'Reilly" and "The Song and Dance Man," through a long list. The portrait of George M. Cohan hung in the office, a symbol, one may guess, that the boat was no longer "faking" entertainment but was dedicating itself to art.

Perhaps ironic fate decided that the change of heart had come too tardily, for circumstances almost immediately forced a return to the old manner, or even a worse manner of entertaining. During the early days of the Depression in 1929, the Bryant boat, in a desperate attempt to find a paying audience, tied up at Cincinnati, her first try at a large city. Bryant was warned when he paid his license fee that his show would probably be razzed out of town. But he was not to be shaken from his resolution to fill his auditorium. In spite of liberal advertising and the loud persuasion of the calliope, the first night three people constituted the audience. The second night nobody came. City dwellers, now the only ones with any money at all, evidently considered the boat-show a relic of the past and frankly preferred a movie theatre. On the third night by accident a society yacht tied up alongside, and the party aboard offered Bryant twenty-five dollars to play "Ten Nights in a Bar Room." The cast attempted a serious "straight"

---

[6] This incident has a New York sequel. Cohan happened to learn about the transformation of his straight play into a musical comedy, and starting with his song "Happy," he tried some transforming himself. The result was "Billie," the musical comedy version that enjoyed a record run in New York. It was named after Billy Bryant.

version of the old favorite. But not so the audience. They wanted their fun, and the more melodramatic the actors became, the more ridiculous to those out front the performance seemed. The parts of the old classic intended to be the most seriously moral or touching drew the biggest laughs. The repentance scene when it passed over the footlights became a high spot of comedy. The more exaggerated the acting, the greater the applause. Blunders on the stage—and there were many—brought ovations. Even Billy Bryant was a bit confused. And then he got the idea: This audience found the old play, with its moral and its sentimentality, as amusingly antiquated as a dress out of style, but they found an ill-timed and exaggerated playing of these old effects altogether ridiculous, a novel source of fun to sophisticated appetites. A tip from Billy and the tragic speeches from the stage became worse and worse, with better and better comic effects in the audience. The worst possible acting, because insincere, was being asked for and was being paid for in money and in applause. The cast responded easily, though a little resentfully.

A newspaper man happened to be among the guests, and next morning all Cincinnati learned about the newly discovered source of amusement. For two months the boat-show did not even need to change the bill, and each night the boisterous fun-makers came, willing to pay for this glimpse of the ridiculous past. They remembered Edna Ferber's *Showboat* and wondered why they had been so slow to come down to the foot of Lawrence Street where the old boat-show had tied up. An astutely timed free performance advertised for "Cincinnati's Crippled Children," and a full auditorium was assured for many nights to come.

Billy Bryant slipped quite easily into the spirit of the new manner, for audacity had always been his greatest asset on the stage. He became almost a Greek chorus for the "melerdrama," constantly prompting, correcting, and commenting for the benefit of the hilarious audience. He presented specialties of his own as interludes, when, with straw hat a-tilt, he would sing the old-time sentimental tunes in a strained tenor, with a background of colored lantern slides that seldom matched the song. His show was an invitation to ridicule and to laugh, and certainly no stage traditions could come between him and the accomplishment of his purpose. During the whole two hours of the performance he was in constant communication with the audience. His business was to make them like what they were getting, whether he was playing a role in the center of the stage or merely acting as "prompter" on its front corner. Here is a glimpse of him in a characteristic role in "Bertha the Sewing Machine Girl":

Of course Bertha's husband was disowned by his rich father, her baby abducted, herself confined in a madhouse, and there were attempted stabbings and poisonings. Things might not have gone well but for Cheatam [Billy Bryant], who intervened when needed. His appearance came to be expected, and once when seemingly delayed the sorority crowd shouted: "Cheatam! Cheatam! Bring on Cheatam!" [7]

From the corner of the stage Billy perfected his curtain speeches. Years before he had begun these as apologies to placate irate audiences with his mediocre performances. Now he found them an excellent means of making friends, and directing and suggesting to those out front. His speech at the end of the performance always included an invitation to come up on the stage to meet the troupe and have pretzels and near-beer. In his longest talk, delivered after the first act or earlier, he would say:

Well, Folks [tilting his straw sailor at the usual rakish angle], we know you came down here to see us murder this play. And boy! We will! All we care for is your money. The sooner you leave, the better we like it. The play gets worse as it goes along. We wouldn't dare to give this kind of thing at Constance, Kentucky. Those audiences are serious. We have to give them modern plays, "The Miracle Man," "The Man from Home," and play 'em straight. Why, we play "Ben Hur" and "Strange Interloode" —yes, we do "St-r-a-n-ge Interlude." We even do musical comedy, except we have to be careful what we wear . . . Now, we know you didn't come here expecting to see grand opera. We want you to hiss the villain, razz us all you like. We don't care. [8]

What an astoundingly frank talk! Like Chaucer's Pardoner of old he was labeling the fake product and still finding buyers. His artistic creed was simply, "Be a ham, and admit it," and this philosophy he carried into the interpretation of all his melodramas, as well as his vaudeville numbers, acting them to the hilt, to exaggerate both movement and lines for comic effects. Professional "hamming" had been born, and the boat-shows, made intensely self-conscious, began to wilt under the slow blight of burlesque.

As if to mark the spot where a century-old institution of service was

[7] The commentator, actually in the audience at Cincinnati, was Clark B. Firestone.

[8] New York *Times*, Oct. 12, 1930.

dying, BRYANT's NEW SHOWBOAT floated for a little while into an unnaturally bright light of public notice. For nine months in the year the boat hovered around her new-found patroness, Cincinnati, but each spring, to keep her good standing as a *bona fide* boat-show, she made the upper rivers as far as Wheeling, West Virginia. Between seasons Bryant and his "all-star river actors" filled lucrative engagements in some of the larger land theatres. In 1931 they revived their Ohio River version of "Hamlet," with the strange addition of "certain strong characters from the other Shakespearean plays," such as Shylock and the Witches, for a special run in Chicago's Cort Theatre. Almost ten years later "the reigning monarch of showboat acting" returned to that city to Forester's Theatre, this time with that indestructible tear-provoking melodrama, "Uncle Tom's Cabin." On that occasion the *Tribune* significantly remarked: "No detailed list of Capt. Bryant's company has been submitted to this desk. We are asked . . . to assume that we need no more reassurance than Capt. Bryant's promise to give a standard river performance." Evidently the city slickers desired, not a play, but the spectacle of the river actors butchering a play. New York's John Golden's Theatre received Billy Bryant frankly as a clown, and laughed at his antics in "Ten Nights in a Bar Room" and "Convict 999." [9] Certain newspaper columnists appeared particularly delighted to contribute generously to the Bryant snowball of publicity, and Billy was not slow to capitalize on it. "The hen that lays a good egg has a perfect right to cackle," he quipped. The Cincinnati creed, "To be a ham and know it," now became "To be a ham and know that it is beautiful." The last large city to receive him was St. Louis, where in 1949 he played his comic Shakespeare medley, "Hamlet," on board Menke's GOLDENROD, to the delight of both the public and the critics. He has proved that expert "hamming" is more entertaining than poor acting.

On his boat Bryant entertained notables of radio and screen, such as Graham McNamee and Walter Connally, as well as a certain sweet little old lady homesick for the river, and always the public found out about his hospitality. First in a book,[10] then from the lecture platform, and last over a national radio network Billy has told America

[9] Prompt scripts are now in the possession of the New York Public Library.
[10] *Children of Ol' Man River* (New York, 1936) is an excellent record of the Bryants. Its implication, however, that this family's experience was typical of the American showboat institution has been rightly resented by all those who knew the Frenches, the McNairs, the Prices, Ralph Emerson, "Double R" Markle, the Menkes, Norman Thom, and the many others like them.

about himself, his family, and his showboat. Ever since that night in Cincinnati when he learned to "ham it up" for the party on board the society yacht, he has been exploiting showboating, selling the relics rather than the realities. And it has been a lucrative business, for at long last the hoped-for miracle has paid off. In the old days the Bryant family sold fake gasoline-and-pepper liniment to an ignorant and gullible public. In later years Billy Bryant has sold fake acting and the relics of showboating to a fun-making and sophisticated public willing to pay for its laugh.[11]

[11] Billy Bryant's father Sam Bryant died at the age of 92 at Gallipolis, Ohio, in 1948; he had retired in 1924 to his home in Point Pleasant, West Virginia, where his wife Violet died in 1949. BRYANT'S NEW SHOWBOAT was sold during the Second World War to Charles Slepski, who temporarily converted her into a wharf boat at Huntington, West Virginia.

Principal sources of this chapter include: Billy Bryant's *Children of Ol' Man River*, federal and municipal records, interviews, manuscripts, letters, posters, and newspaper files.

Other Sources: Items listed in the bibliography under Robert Allen, Kyle Crichton, Clark Firestone, Ethel Leahy, G. W. Piddington, Horace Reynolds, Frederick Simpich, Cecil Smith, Sidney Snook, Wesley Stout, and James Wallen.

XIV

Enchanted Water

Actors and Audiences

EARLY IN APRIL a showboat picked up her new recruits, usually at Elizabethtown, Illinois, or often at Paducah, Kentucky, or sometimes at Cincinnati. Always it seemed a heterogeneous group. There were sure to be a few hold-overs from the year before, and these got the pick of the tiny bedrooms. The Captain assigned married couples and single women to the none-too-spacious quarters on the showboat, while the single men lived on the steamer tow. The tiny cubbyholes behind the stage, usually entirely separate from the bedrooms, were assigned as dressing rooms, or sometimes chosen by lot.

In the palmiest days of the business the large boats carried from twenty-five to thirty-five people, about equally divided between stage entertainment, including music, and other duties, such as running the boat and cooking. The smaller boats were family affairs with a few pick-ups added. Salaries were low, especially for actors. While the engineer would be drawing $60 per week and the cook $40, the villain would be getting $12, the fetching little ingénue perhaps as much as $15, and a competent team, usually man and wife or sisters, as much as $20. These salaries represented clear money, however, for food and room were furnished, with no hotel bills, no tips, no traveling expenses of any kind. Very little wardrobe was needed. Furthermore, landings afforded slight opportunity for spending money—no night clubs, no attractive stores, no social life. Many a seasoned trouper, in debt for years, has been amazed at his accumulated savings at the end of his first showboat cruise.

Actors were on a showboat for an infinite variety of reasons. Some, with or without talent, were the owner's children, and from babyhood had been fitted into convenient niches in the programs. Some were tired professionals from the bright lights, some were dancers, acrobats, and magicians from sideshows and carnivals, seeking rest and relaxation for one season. Some were "ham-actors," dragged in by that alluring advertisement run in the *Billboard* every spring, men and women as restless as migratory birds. A few were country boys and girls lured by the glamor of the stage and the freedom of the river. Couples were preferred, for in crowded living quarters matrimony was both convenient and socially safe.

As soon as members of the cast gathered on board, they selected one of their own number as director, whether the program was to be vaudeville, a play, or a combination, and then rehearsals began. The next two or three weeks saw the hardest work of the season, though the boat remained tied up where it had wintered. Parts were memorized and practiced, with the old-timers patiently teaching and drilling the inexperienced. The hours were from ten in the morning till ten at night. Costumes were prepared and properties made ready. Great rivalry existed if more than one boat happened to winter at the same location. Gradually, as the grueling days slipped by, tunes became recognizable, dances set into patterns, cues and entrances matched, and acrobats learned to gauge the stage limits. As the program began to take form, everybody relaxed, to find himself in a congenial group which marked the boundary of all his activities—his work, his amusement, his meals, even his sleep must be with these same. After a day of rehearsals in full costume and a few trial performances for the home town, they were ready for the rivers. The boat, too, had been prepared, with replacements and new paint.

A well equipped showboat starting out in the spring of 1896 from Cincinnati was likely first to go up the Ohio to the mining regions along the Kanawha and Monongahela. These patrons were not hindered by muddy roads or spring rains, for most of them lived in close-packed little settlements called "patches" near the river. Then during the summer the boat would play down the Ohio, dipping into the Kentucky, the Wabash, the Tennessee, and especially the Green. Then she would pass by Cairo to turn up the Mississippi, stopping at landings and towns rather than cities. Certainly she would devote extra time to the Illinois River, rich territory for showboats. These people sometimes trailed the show in boats or wagons to see as many as three repetitions of the performance. Then followed the less lucrative trip up the Mississippi, perhaps even as far as Hastings, Minnesota. But October was sure to find the showboat once more below St.

Louis, ready to take advantage of the cotton picking and sugar cane season on the lower rivers. Only a few showboats ventured into the turbulent Missouri, and still fewer into the White, the Arkansas, and the Red. The boats needed most of the winter months for the lower Mississippi. Christmas was usually celebrated in the Bayou Districts of the Atchafalaya, and the season ended early in February at New Orleans.

Once en route, the whole procedure settled into a comfortable routine. As the showboat edged in toward a stand about eleven o'clock in the morning, whether it was a mere landing marked by a tree and a light, or a full-sized town, the calliope player started a lively concert ten minutes before the boat tied up, the official musical announcement to the countryside that a boat-show had arrived. A crowd was beginning to gather even before the gangplank was down. Then if the stand was a town or village and the date before 1915, the band went ashore for the parade, accompanied by all hands. Everybody marched, for the size of the parade became the popular index to the worth of the show. A free band concert followed at the busiest corner in town, during which standards, handbills, posters, and announcements advertised the show. Captain French was in the habit of doing much clowning on such occasions, and the nervous little Captain Price doubtless performed just as comically, though unintentionally. Both drew big crowds. After the parade, which was the most irksome incident of the day, mail was delivered on the boat, and then the cast was free until the evening performance.[1] No rehearsals after the first few busy weeks, for the same play and the same vaudeville acts satisfied a thousand miles of audiences. No matinee, because patrons had no time to attend, and in the Bible Belt no performance on Sunday. During the long afternoons one could fish from the sunny side of the boat, shoot alligators, hunt ashore,[2] or swim. Or one could sit on the cool side of the deck, and sew, read, gossip, or just dream. The living quarters, especially on the larger boats after 1900, were quite comfortable, with steam heat, electric lights, and hot water. Breakfast was usually served about ten o'clock, in time to allow preparation for the parade; dinner came at four o'clock, and a hand-out snack followed the evening performance. On most showboats records indi-

[1] Often one man would be designated to call at the local Post Office immediately after the parade and deliver the mail to the boat, for which service he collected a fee of ten cents per week from each person.

[2] At least one inexperienced Nimrod returned with a turkey buzzard instead of a wild turkey (Keeler's *Vagabond Adventures*, p. 193).

cate that food was abundant and wholesome but plain.[3] Quantities of produce and fruit were received in exchange for tickets.

No scurry of train or road travel, no packing, no lodging problems, no landladies, no hangers-on at stage doors. Parade duty from eleven to twelve in the morning, stage and other duties—ushering, candy-selling or selling tickets for the aftershow—from seven to ten at night, and the remainder of the twenty-four hours belonged to one-self and the river! It was an easy, but usually a well-ordered life. Married actors always played counter to their wives, perhaps a practice more in the interest of social tranquility than good art. There was no drinking. No other rules were needed, and, except on the Eisen-barth boat, no others were posted. Before 1920 showboat girls did not smoke except in the pages of fiction, but there was no rule about it. Even the gentle art of "chasing"—escorting local belles to their homes after the performance—was winked at by most captains, pro-vided the young actor could get back on the boat without bringing with him a hailstorm of rocks from jealous village swains. If he wished, he was free to roam the town until daybreak and unless, as Captain Menke phrases it, he got a little drunk or landed in jail, no-body worried. To highlight the routine existence on board and on shore there were the occasional vital moments—a birth, a death, a marriage, or even an inspired hour on the stage—to wrench one's life into an unexpected direction. Sometimes an important visitor appeared in the audience—Flo Ziegfeld, Fay Bainter, Dick Powell, Fifi D'Orsay, Walter Hampden, or a talent scout. In general, living conditions on board closely resembled those of the well behaved middle-class family of the Middle West. Any other social pattern would not have been acceptable to the clientele.

True, there were a few flies in the ointment of happiness. The "shakes" or river fever sometimes dragged one helpless to his bed for days or even weeks at a time. Mosquitoes and willow bugs were seasonal pests dreaded more than the dangerous floods of spring or the sawyers and sand bars that knew no season. Minor troubles, too, were certain to appear, as the friction between the cast and the crew in regard to sleeping hours. For the cast disturbed the crew with their stage performance in the early night hours almost as much as the crew

[3] Surviving accounts of one of Emerson's showboats in 1900 show large pur-chases of chickens at fifteen cents each, butter at ten cents a "pat," hams at one dollar each.

disturbed the cast by their early morning activities in getting the box-like showboat under way before the impeding winds rose.

Every showboat cast was sure to include certain typical characters that came to be associated with the business.

The little ingénue, pretty, innocent, and big-eyed, plays the female leads. Between acts she is the singing soubrette, clasping a big bouquet of roses, artificial unless it happens to be rose season, as she sings songs that she perhaps only half understands. She is single, and therefore under the watchful chaperonage of the Captain's wife, who knows her parents, the quite respectable operators of a junk boat below Cairo. She will tell you that she did not really intend to be an actress . . . that she expects each year to start to college—but every spring when she hears the calliope . . . And she will add, "Can you believe me when I tell you that we stop at some places where they don't even have ice cream?"

The villain is likely to be the best-natured person on the boat, a little voluble both on and off stage. Because of his experience and maturity, he is often chosen by the members of the cast as their director. He is quite fortunate if his own mustache is still black enough for stage purposes. Besides playing the "heavy" in the melodrama, he also may do "chalk-talk" in the aftershow, when all his sketches of women resemble his own comfortable wife. She is the right wing of the chorus and plays mature female roles, and sometimes fills in with Stephen Foster songs. Both are proud of their son, aged fifteen, lately become the drummer. Coatless but swelling with pride, this young man begins whamming away at his drums almost before he reaches his seat in the tiny orchestra pit, and continues to bounce up and down in time to the music like a jockey on the back of a rough-gaited nag. Each time just when he reaches the point of complete abandon, when one thinks he will surely soar through space, the music always ends.

The leading man of the cast, sometimes called the juvenile lead, is somewhat like a bridegroom, necessary but not much talked about. He may be a Norman Thom of the PRINCESS or a Tommy Windsor of the HOLLYWOOD, an actor of real talent. He is likely to be young and handsome, as meticulous in his dress as funds will permit, and he combs his hair back in a full pompadour. If single, he usually thinks he is in love with the little ingénue, who plays opposite him in the melodrama. He is likely to take himself, and life in general, very seriously, and will discuss his problems of histrionic art with anyone willing to listen.

The comedian is seldom a jolly person, for it is his business to make others laugh, and he works hard at his job. He need not be comically ugly, but he is almost sure to have that big nose, those prominent cheek bones, that narrow-eyed sad expression that make the perfect setting for clown's paint. He may be an Ernest Vevea who can pull yards of paper tape out of his immense snout, or can pull off his trousers before a shocked audience, only to reveal an underlying pair. He may be a Victor Faust, who can do the best acrobatics on the rivers in the funniest possible manner. He may be a Ralph Keeler in blackface, whose dance steps and impersonations, especially the female roles, are better than his jokes. He may even be a Billy Bryant, who can combine clowning with publicity. No matter what particular branch of his gentle art he specializes in, the comedian is aware of the heavy cargo of sentiment and tradition that his boat is carrying, and he therefore confines his fun to the borderline of propriety, and adjusts it nicely to the relief of the strained emotions of melodrama. Naturally the audience is more grateful to him than is the cast.

The cook and calliope player are likely to be the most temperamental of the group. On the larger boats the cook is usually a man, on the smaller ones often a woman. The man-cook invariably demands a stage part, one suspects in order to keep caste, and if he is a good cook he gets what he asks for. He seems always partial to female impersonation numbers, as Charles Bruslé on the HOLLYWOOD, who delighted to make himself appear more feminine than any woman on the boat. The cook often has a special yearning for pets, sometimes even white rats. His fellow travelers demand good food of him, and it is his pride and joy to sustain his own reputation on the rivers by making what he serves both delicious and wholesome. After that, they merely hope that he may be also clean—that is, unless a Callie French happens to be in the Captain's cabin.

The calliope player is the other most spoiled person on board, for everyone feels that much of the success of the boat depends on this man who controls the musical airways for miles around. He is energetic and likes to handle his music in large lumps. He has considerable courage, too, for he is willing to risk parboiling at his steaming monster twice or even three times a day. If he is an old-timer, like Ray Choissier or Bobby Wills (Calliope Red), he scorns such affectations as canvas gloves and sheet music, both of which, he will inform you, belong to

Eisenbarth-Henderson FLOATING THEATRE

Courtesy Frederick Way, Jr.

Bryant's Showboat

the other kind of player, like Mrs. Thom. In the vicinity of a rival showboat, it falls to his lot to defend the reputation of his craft. He must never commit the unpardonable sin of playing his giant music box out of hours.

Various other types are common on showboats. The comedienne who secretly longs to play lead roles but who knows her aging face and angular form forbid. The band leader who bemoans the public's taste in music and considers his men as "comrades in suffering." The country fiddler, with the gray dust of age settling over him, who valiantly advertises for a challenger and yet half-dreads the appearance of a real master in his rustic art. Half a dozen dependable but uninspired actors who always double in a strange assortment of vaudeville numbers, ranging from flame-swallowing to tumbling. The funny little man who prints the handbills on the press in the corner of the dining room under the stage, and who in his leisure moments runs errands for the Captain and plays the big alto in the band. The advance man, who makes his presence felt, like a benign ghost, leading the boat to audiences.

The busy Captain brings harmony and efficiency from this heterogeneous crowd. He hires and fires, he keeps the peace both behind and in front of the footlights, he makes the *thank-you* speeches, he provides food, he plays host to important local people (including the sheriff, upon occasion), he looks after the money, and does the worrying for everybody. He has a host of friends in every town. The frontier long since has taught him versatility, and in time of trouble, whether it is drought or flood, he can turn his floating theatre into a freighter, or a ferry, or a rescue boat.

A force even bigger than the Captain molds that motley crew into a co-operative, clannish family. It is a double power, both of the river and of the stage. As the boat slips farther and farther down the broad rippled path between the swerving shore lines, the stage becomes more and more the magic means of creating a life different from ordinary existence. Before long the feeling of isolation and of glamor creates a restricted private world, separated from the vast public shore world by the river, and centered in that spot of make-believe, the stage, where life and patterns for it can be created at will. This is the two-fold magic of water and of art, known to every showboater, which welds that strangely assorted gathering into a clan capable of working, sleeping, eating, loafing, and playing together for months in living quarters smaller than the space of a tiny bungalow.

The stage nuisance chiefly responsible for the mediocrity of many a showboat performance was doubling. This was the practice of one actor carrying more than one part. In one of his best excuses and worst puns old Sol Smith remarked, with tongue in cheek, "We play mostly from the Dublin edition." Doubling was one of the adaptations which the frontier demanded of the dramatic artist. Very seldom could any actor devote himself exclusively to the stage, even though he might be playing several roles in the play. Most actors "doubled in brass" (band) or doubled in the vaudeville between acts or the aftershow. Some even divided their time between engine room or ticket office and stage. Of course everybody doubled in the parade when there was one. Even the calliope doubled, for in its silent moments it was distilling drinking water.

The smaller the boat the more prevalent doubling necessarily became. Some extreme cases of the practice are on record. Catherine Reynolds, on the MAJESTIC, often acted three roles in the melodrama, played both the calliope and the piano, sang sentimental songs between acts, danced in the afterpiece, sold candy, and ushered, all in one evening. Doubling sometimes meant not only multiple assignments but also conflicting parts. An actor might simulate a marble statue in "Don Juan" one minute, and the next be dancing hornpipes, without a change in make-up. The beautiful Lena Rivers could be reduced to helpless weeping by the evil doings of her vicious uncle, and yet when the curtain had barely dropped on the first act, she would come dancing gaily out from the wings in a vaudeville number, in the same costume, in the arms of this same hateful villain, both happily smiling. Unsophisticated audiences were obviously puzzled and sometimes even shocked by such unfortunate combinations, and found emotional adjustment for the remainder of the play rather difficult. The dying hero in "Kentucky Sue" sometimes found it convenient to fall with the upper part of his body well within the wings so that he could play his own death music on the fiddle while the rest of his body lay dead upon the stage. Burlesque lay only one step away from such ridiculous necessity.

Showboat audiences might seem, at first glance, as mixed as the cast itself, for they were cross-sections of American life. They changed gradually, like the rest of the country, with the passing of generations, and they changed constantly and more noticeably with the different localities visited. But always they were American. As the showboat slipped between the willow-lined shores, the mining shacks and factory "patches" changed with the passing days into cornfields and pastures, and these in turn, with the passing weeks, into cotton and sugar cane plantations, glimpsed through gnarled cypresses and moss-draped live oaks. And in about the same succession, miners, factory workers, farmers, backwoodsmen and stockmen, laborers, plantation people, and *cajuns* filled the auditorium. Family groups were prominent, some of them of three and four generations. In the mining districts of West Virginia and in the backwoods of Kentucky and Tennessee many pockets bulged with guns and whiskey bottles, and these were the trouble spots of the rivers. But most audiences were well behaved, from the Negroes in their section of the balcony to the teen-age blades in the front boxes.

The small landing usually produced as big an audience as the town, for most of these people came from the back country. Groups of families and neighbors arrived in wagons, surreys, and buggies, and many after 1915 in Fords. Some rode horseback or walked. All of them were much in earnest, for to them the showboat was what the first theatre must have been, a place that magically transported one to a realm where dreams came true in a splendor of vicarious achievement, with love triumphant and evil foiled; and, best of all, where one could cry or laugh unashamed, and give way to emotions long repressed. These audiences were responsive rather than critical, and so completely identified emotionally with the action on the stage as to be removed from reality. Many stories tell how spectators have tried to take part in stage situations and, with difficulty, have remembered that they were not looking at real life. When William Chapman was playing "Metamora" at Natchez back in 1839, he records that at the mention of *eagles* in the play an unkempt eager-eyed young man arose from mid-audience to remind him that those birds must have been buzzards, since there were no eagles thereabouts. When the GREATER NEW YORK was playing "The Red Dagger" at Commerce, Missouri, just as the renegade villain was about to kidnap the innocent and weeping heroine, he heard a voice from the box at the end of the stage saying, "You make one more move toward that little gal, and, damn you, I'll kill you." And the startled actor looked up to see a whiskey bottle poised ready to crash down on his hapless head. When a showboat was playing a town in which was located a state prison, the warden engaged the troupe to put on a matinee for the inmates. When the "heavy" slapped the pretty little heroine in Act III, as per stage directions, a burly six-footer shouted from the second row,

"Kill that son-of-a-bitch," and a near-riot followed. The poor villain became the meekest man in the cast.

In Tennessee during the Depression when showboats were in bad repair, a hero was dying on the stage one rainy night, when a leak in the roof began to drip water on his head. A kindly colored lady seriously climbed to the stage to hold her umbrella over him, remarking righteously, "I ain't goin' see no pore boy dyin' with his neck all wet."

The strangest case of all happened at a Kentucky landing. A gambler's family was portrayed on the stage as starving, when a substantial farmer rose in his seat to propose taking up something for the neglected wife. Someone whispered to him that it was all a sham, but he insisted on expressing his opinion of the worthless gambler, and, throwing a dollar on the stage to start the collection, he advised the woman not to let her rascally husband know about the money. Then, with what must have been a divided mind, he said as he sat down, "Now go on with the play." That is what the actors of that day meant when they spoke of picking up an audience into their arms!

At the close of the program, only half relaxed from emotional tension, these showboat goers filed to the back of the auditorium and out the door. One would say, "Right good play, wasn't it?" And another, "That fellow sure can handle the fiddle!" And another, "Can she sing and dance, though!" As they passed on to the gangplank, and clambered up the steep bank beyond in the half-light of kerosene flares and lanterns, they ceased to be the entranced audience that had the minute before occupied the auditorium. Suddenly they became tired men with sleepy babies in their arms, fat women that had known only drudgery, solemn-faced girls worn out before they were old enough to marry, stoop-shouldered boys with inadequate lanterns in their hands . . .

They were returning to their world of reality.[4]

[4] Principal Sources: Manuscripts, letters, interviews, and newspaper files.
Other Sources: Items listed in the bibliography under Hamilton Basso, Billy Bryant, Lucien Burman, M. W. Childs, Thoda Cocroft, Kyle Crichton, Frederick Dayton, Meigs Frost, Paul Gilbert, Jan and Cora Gordon, Ralph Keeler, Constance Rourke, Lyle Saxon, Sol Smith, Sidney Snook, Wesley Stout, A. H. Tarvin, and James Wallen.

XV

Where All Good Showboats Go

The Menke Brothers

Sooner or later, most of the big showboats came into the hands of the Menke boys. The New Sensation (French's last boat), the Greater New York (formerly the New Grand Floating Palace, Markle's first love and Price's "beautiful thing"), the Sunny South (for a while called the Hippodrome), the Hollywood (formerly Steve Price's Columbia), the Dixie Queen (that nostalgic gesture of Al Cooper), and the palatial Goldenrod (Markle's last dream) all eventually tied up at the Menke dock. All these great boat-shows at the end of the story are gathered together as patly as the summary of an old book.

There were four of these Menke brothers—John William (Bill), H. J. (Harry), B. F. (Ben), and C. J. (Charley). They were associated with showboats for more than forty years, for they went into the business as young men. In 1904 Bill and Ben were watchmakers in Jersey City. That summer they built a thirty-eight-foot gasoline launch, named her the Cincy after Cincinnati, where they had been born, shipped her by rail to Pittsburgh, and set out down the river for their native city. The ice caught them at Uniontown, Kentucky, where French's New Sensation was also frozen in. The boys lost little time in going aboard, for they had never before seen a show-boat. Captain Callie French and her genial manager John McNair proved hospitable hosts, and before the week was out, they had engaged the Menke boys and their speedboat as advance agents for the coming season. During the next eight years, for one or another of the boat-show captains—for McNair, for Price, for Markle, for Cooley, for Emerson—they pasted posters and distributed handbills from Pittsburgh to New Orleans. This was their introduction to the great showboat fleet which in later years they were to own. When the two older boys made enough to buy a boat, the two younger brothers came West to take their places as advance agents. New Jersey lost a Swiss family of watchmakers, and the river gained four of its most substantial showboat men. These Menkes were cautious as well as substantial, and they were careful therefore to heed the ironic old river adage, "Except you go broke too slowly, then buy two showboats." In the early years of their career they owned their boats in succession, never two at once. Their first three ventures could scarcely be called successful.

Early in 1911 they acquired their first showboat, the SUNNY SOUTH with her steam tow WABASH, from Captain Markle.[1] They changed her name to the HIPPODROME, and enjoyed three mildly successful seasons on the lower rivers. Moderate success was not enough, however, for their boat was still heavily in debt to the Pope Dock Company. Because of this financial pressure, the owners resolved upon the most daring venture that an American showboat ever attempted: they steamed out into the Gulf of Mexico, into Mobile Bay, and up the Alabama to Montgomery and the Tombigbee to Demopolis, virgin territory and therefore rich, they believed.

They found they were wrong in both suppositions. The cotton crop was good, just as they had heard, but the price was the lowest in history. It was 1914, one of those "buy-a-bale" years, when men bought cotton as a patriotic duty. Wages for picking were correspondingly low, and door receipts disappointingly meager.

Their hope to be the first boat-show to penetrate the region also ended in disappointment, for both the DOVE and the LILY LOU had preceded them. The latter had sunk, or, in the romantic phrasing of the region, "the river had closed his tawny arms about her." The DOVE had met an even more dramatic fate. Floods stranded her five miles inland, where for years she was an object of curiosity and awe, until the river rose again and drew her back for a final wild ride. Menke and his cast found that both boats had already become legendized. The LILY LOU, especially in the minds of the wealthier classes, stood for romantic ecstasy, a symbol of pure sentiment as sharply separated from the real life about her as was the cool river from the

---

[1] For the earlier history of the SUNNY SOUTH, see p. 100. Ben Menke, in association with Brad Coleman, was probably mainly interested in this first venture, but little attempt has been made to ascertain the individual interests of the four brothers in their various enterprises. Ben captained the later HOLLYWOOD, and Bill the GOLDENROD.

sultry bank. In actual existence and the realm of the intellect, slow troubles and unfulfilled promises seemed to drain away happiness along with life; but on the LILY LOU a world of pure sentiment, unadulterated by the drudgery of living, created for them an enchanting moment of refuge, where problems were instantly simplified into happy endings. And all for fifty cents! The DOVE, Menke found, had been even more completely idealized, especially by the Negro populace, who were confidently expecting the return of this ghost ship of happiness. And while they waited for her to come back they were remembering hours of pure rhythmic joy, when they seemed translated by their own music.

To the public in these regions, all showboats must be like those two mythical craft that had succeeded in escaping into sentiment and rhythm. Because Menke and the HIPPODROME soon realized what was expected of them and made an earnest effort to respond to the wishes of their patrons, their adventurous trip assumed significance. As they worked their way up the crooked Alabama, lined with the homes of planters who had only half forgotten the Civil War, they laid aside "Under Western Skies," and "Jesse James," and substituted "Tildy Ann." As they played it, the drama was divorced completely from reality, idealized into the realm of pure emotion. The characters could have been named Love, Good, Evil, and Triumph, the stage could have been labeled Human Feelings. The LILY LOU herself (whose records have been lost) could not have produced shows that escaped more successfully from the world of facts and the intellect into the realm of pure sentiment. It was a dramatic feat that would not have been possible in any other region.

As the HIPPODROME turned up the Tombigbee, which penetrates deep into the "black belt," she laid aside "Tildy Ann" and took on several Negro musicians. As the colored patrons listened to the haunting syncopations of their own beloved music, and watched in fascination as the juba and the buck-and-wing were created before them on the little stage, many a one was hypnotized into believing that the DOVE had returned to bring joy again to the black man. Here in the region close to the birthplace of jazz, music and dance furnished to the Negro the readiest escape. On the Mississippi the HIPPODROME had produced Americana of the Middle West; on the Alabama, Americana of the Old South; on the Tombigbee, pure Africana.

Such versatile responsiveness received, because of economic conditions, smaller reward than it deserved, and the discouraged owners began their return trip across the Mississippi Sound. Several miles out a sudden squall caught the boat and blew her far into the Gulf. Thomas Stone, engineer on the towboat, tells the story:

> It was plain as the nose on your face that we couldn't save the boat. Lifeboats couldn't live in the rough water . . . Finally I hit on the idea that we could make headway if we backed the boat [thus *pulling* the showboat] against the wind. Deer Island near Biloxi was only a few miles away. If we could reach it before the steamboat shipped too much water we'd be safe for a time behind the island. So the crew started pumping and from one o'clock in the morning till three the next afternoon we heeled back the WABASH till we got her safely behind the island where we laid for two whole days waiting for the squall to settle.[2]

The storm over, the HIPPODROME limped into Biloxi, which had never before beheld a showboat. At the request of the citizens, Menke staged here a week of melodrama to full auditoriums, and this "providential" stop financed the otherwise disastrous trip. But the crew, anxious to reach familiar inland water, headed for the Mississippi, and made straight up it and the Ohio to Parkersburg, West Virginia. Here Menke and Coleman sold the HIPPODROME to Jim Bonnelli.[3]

The Menke brothers had even worse luck with their next boat. In September, 1917, they bought the GREATER NEW YORK from Captain Price (formerly Markle's and then Emerson's NEW GRAND FLOATING PALACE) up on the Green River. Five days later, when they were preparing to rebuild, a storm sank her on the Ohio, near Newburgh, Indiana, along with her tow the ROBERT DODDS, which Menke had leased from Price.

The solid Menkes were not unduly disturbed by the disaster, for this they had learned was the way of the River. During that fall they towed enough corn down to New Orleans to recoup their fortunes, and early in the spring of 1918 they bought another boat from Captain Price, this time the historic FRENCH'S NEW SENSATION.

Bill Menke insisted that the SENSATION continue to play only musical comedy and vaudeville, for that had been the treasured tradition of the boat since the days of Captain French. The boat-show had not only never changed its name, but it boasted a succession of four

---

[2] Louisville *Courier-Journal*, Oct. 26, 1941.
[3] Bonnelli in turn sold to John Fultz, who changed the name back to the SUNNY SOUTH. Ice sank the boat on the upper Monongahela during the winter of 1917. A smaller SUNNY SOUTH operated 1929–1933.

earlier SENSATIONS reaching back to 1878. Since the days when the Frenches had "purified" river entertainment, that name NEW SENSA-TION had stood for clean shows, and also for big, enthusiastic audiences. Menke was anxious to foster all the old boat's traditions.

One practice, however, he proceeded at once to upset. He began to pay royalties for his musical comedies, and royalties had never been a part of the boat's normal expense. In 1925, his most successful season with the SENSATION, he bought the river rights to the musical comedy, "Andy Gump," knowing well that the popularity of Sidney Smith's cartoon strip would bring the crowds. When the script arrived, Director James Bonham, who had got his experience under Charles Hunter on board the JAMES ADAMS the year before, believed it too sober for river audiences, and proposed to liven it up with snatches from half a dozen old minstrel acts and afterpieces. "That will be fine," agreed Menke; "all I want is the name." The name, the music, and Andy's nose were about all that resembled the original when Bonham had finished. Menke had been right, for the crowds came.

Since crew and cast combined numbered only twenty on the SENSATION, actors in the comedy also doubled in the vaudeville. Cooper (Andy Gump) and Shaw (right-wing girl in the chorus), as well as the comedians Scott and Lamar, were vacationing from the big-time circuit. Director Bonham and his wife (Min Gump) gave a blackface song-and-dialogue act. Norman Kester (Chester Gump) and his wife (left wing of the chorus) were billed as "Jack and Jill" in a trapeze act. Charles Bruslé, female impersonator supreme, did soubrette roles as convincingly as Ralph Keeler almost a century earlier. One of the chorus girls played old melodies on bells disguised as flowers and on saws and combs, for the fifth and last act of the vaudeville. On his posters and handbills, Menke always emphasized "A fast stepping chorus"—six dancing girls, who wore tight-fitting bodices and elaborate knee-length ballet skirts. An observer in the audience in 1925 wrote of them:

Their costumes are not many, but they are neat and pretty; their steps are not intricate, but they dance earnestly, well, and in unison. When Harry Sutton comes down hardest and fastest on the piano their fast-flying feet literally rock the boat. . . . A tall, taciturn, and handsome girl who has no line to speak is David Graham Phillips' heroine to the life. The illusion is so strong that you expect her momentarily to step out of line and sing in a sweet, untrained soprano "Suwanee River" and "The Blue Alsatian Mountains," as did Susan Lenox . . . and you wonder if, like Susan, she is headed up the unpaved road to Broadway and to stardom.[4]

Prosperity continued to follow the NEW SENSATION, for she was playing the small towns, from Louisiana to Pennsylvania, where the movie theatre was likely to open its doors only two nights a week. Sometimes the night's stand was merely a tree to tie to, where a narrow dirt road came down to the river. Wherever the calliope announced the arrival of the SENSATION with the "Blue Alsatian Mountains," her theme-song for two generations, the crowd was sure to gather. For Harry Sutton was master of the giant instrument, and could send the musical summons floating miles in all directions.

The faithful old boat in her battle with the rivers had experienced many adventures. As early as 1925 she had hit a snag off New Madrid, Missouri, but the Menke Brothers raised her and continued operations. Five years later she struck a submerged piling at Franklin, on the Bayou Teche in Louisiana. When Menke went below he found the water pouring in through a hole in the bottom of the boat as big as a tree trunk. The SENSATION would have been at the bottom in a matter of minutes. Bill Menke wrapped a blanket around his body and let himself down feet-first into that geyser of cold river water, as far as his rotund stomach, and there he stopped, a human plug that could not squeeze down any further. Re-enforced with hot coffee and whiskey (which he seldom drank), his body remained for hours stuffed into that hole until the crew could build a box around the breach. Once more the SENSATION had been saved. Greater love hath no man for his boat!

Her last accident occurred at Mound City, Illinois, where she had been run up on the ways for repairs. Bill Menke at the time was on board his GOLDENROD in St. Louis, when the telegram came: "SENSATION entirely demolished by storm." The intrepid Captain Billy, inured to the iniquities of the river, proceeded with his rehearsal of "The Trail of the Lonesome Pine." Next morning, however, he

---

[4] Wesley Stout, who had evidently been reading David Graham Phillips' novel *Susan Lenox*, wrote the best article on showboats ever published, "Tonight at the River-Landing" (*Saturday Evening Post*, Oct. 31, 1925). Mr. Stout writes: "I had intended calling my article 'Showboat,' but a dodger I picked up on the levee at Wickliffe advertising that night's performance gave me the one I chose instead. . . . When I learned from Hunter [the JAMES ADAMS] that Edna Ferber had been a guest for a week on his boat and already was well into her novel, I hurried my piece into print that fall."

ordered the SENSATION stored in the old Navy Yard at Mound City, where she remained until 1931, when she was salvaged for storage costs. Strangely enough, at almost the very moment the wreck was being dismantled, the Cincinnati *Billboard*, "the river man's Bible," was announcing that the SENSATION, after a thorough overhauling, would soon begin the new season, and even predicted that Menke would take this symbol of the showboat world to the Chicago Fair in 1933.[5] Instead, she became a part of the mellow tapestry of history.

Meanwhile the Menkes had purchased another showboat, the COLUMBIA, the last of the Price boats. This had originally been the AMERICAN, distinguishable by a wide-flung American flag on her deck, composed of over seven hundred colored lights. She enjoyed also the distinction of possessing one of the most powerful calliopes on the river. Her builders, the Needham Amusement Company, transferred her to the Thompson brothers (of Missouri River fame), these sold her to Captain Emerson, and he to Captain Price, who changed her name to the COLUMBIA and gave her into the hands of his son Steve. After his son's death, Price, the same little temperamental Captain that had worked with French in the 1880's, sold her to the Menkes.

The first concern of the new owners was to rebuild her. She was given a new hull, though her size remained one hundred and twenty by thirty-two feet. Her originally exquisite equipment was repaired, and she was renovated and redecorated throughout. The sprawling flag in lights was removed, but the huge calliope retained. Of the dozen boat-shows then on the rivers, she was by far the trimmest and best equipped, with the sole exception of the big GOLDENROD. She was re-christened the HOLLYWOOD, and put in charge of Ben Menke. She was given the queen of towboats, the CHAPERONE.[6]

Unlike the NEW SENSATION with its musical comedy, the HOLLYWOOD emphasized drama, gathering up the traditions left by the SUNNY SOUTH of the earlier decade. Ben Menke selected good plays, such as "The Hoodlum," "The Vulture," and the favorite "Tildy Ann," highly romanticized and scrupulously clean. Between the acts

[5] The *Billboard* (Cincinnati), April 25, 1931, p. 24.
[6] First she was assigned the ROBERT DODDS (which had been raised after the tragedy with the GREATER NEW YORK), then the WENONAH (formerly with the NEW SENSATION), and finally the CHAPERONE (also at one time with the NEW SENSATION). This little steamer, built in 1904 by C. E. Lamb, a millionaire lumberman of Clinton, Iowa, was luxuriously equipped with hot and cold water, private baths, electric lights, telephones, hardwood floors, and comfortable wide berths.

he interspersed vaudeville numbers resembling those of French's earlier years. On that first trip South she carried a total of twenty-eight persons: ten in the cast, eight in the band-orchestra, and ten in the crew and management. Among the actors probably the most valuable man was Tommy Windsor, who had seen service with Norman Thom on the PRINCESS. Early in 1928 he worked aboard the WATER QUEEN until she changed hands, and then on Hitner's COTTON BLOSSOM until the heavy overhead caused that big boat to discontinue for the season. He joined the HOLLYWOOD in midsummer for thirty-four weeks as her attractive and versatile leading man. Between acts he did a chalk-talk number, with a little paper cutting thrown in, and he carried the whole aftershow with his clever magic.[7]

Drama on the HOLLYWOOD was played "straight," with no invitation to ridicule, exactly as in the days of French, McNair, and Price, when the boat-show was an institution of service to faraway places. In fact the whole atmosphere of the boat was a little self-consciously pointed toward the past, with a quick readiness to take advantage of the fascination people feel in the old-fashioned ways of by-gone days. This tendency was discernible not only in the emotional presentation of the dramas, but also in her music, largely restricted to Stephen Foster; in her candy-selling, which, patterned after the practice on the early Markle boats, became almost a show in itself, with coatless young men galloping up and down the aisles with their prize-getting wares; and in the florid little *thank-you* speeches following the show, evidently modeled after Captain French's after-talks of the preceding century. Even some of the HOLLYWOOD's adventures remind one of the dangerous days of French and McNair, as the occasion when suddenly a waterlogged tree trunk, moving swiftly with the current, pierced the hull and the stage, to protrude into the center aisle of the auditorium. Her route, too, was like that of the older boats, for she covered the Ohio, the Lower Mississippi, the wild White River, the Tennessee, and Bayou Teche. She was the last major showboat to make the Southern rivers, reaching New Orleans both in 1928 and 1929.

The great change came in 1930 when the HOLLYWOOD tied up for repairs at the Louisville docks. Captain Menke advertised "Tildy Ann" for one evening, thinking to compensate himself in a small way for large repair bills. The response from the Louisville public was

[7] Mr. Windsor, master magician and popular entertainer, now has studios in Marietta, Ohio (See the Columbus [Ohio] *Citizen*, Oct. 1, 1950).

so enthusiastic that the engagement lasted twenty-one weeks, with the auditorium filled to capacity each evening. At first the evident careful preparation of the cast, combined with the strange fascination of the past, commanded the serious consideration of the audiences, and they frankly enjoyed the melodramas, played honestly and "straight," as delightful sentimental journeys to realms of unreality. Little by little, however, the spirit of making fun crept into the audiences, with a corresponding change back of the footlights. With actors already schooled to play up the past, the transition on this stage from straight drama to burlesque was easier than on most boat-shows, though even here it was resented. By the end of the engagement these actors, like those of BRYANT'S SHOWBOAT the year before at Cincinnati, had been forced to learn the gentle art of "hamming," though they lacked a trainer as skilled as Billy Bryant.

The experience of tying up at a city dock had proved so remunerative that the HOLLYWOOD repeated it the next season, this time at Nashville, where no showboat had performed since the days of the redoubtable Noah Ludlow, with his NOAH'S ARK, a century before. When Menke's boat arrived at the foot of Broad Street early in April of 1931 for a thirteen-week stand, it staged its full repertoire of favorites, including "St. Elmo," "The Fighting Parson," "Mysterious Intruder," "The Woman Pays," "The Sweetest Girl in Dixie," "The Old Homestead," "Tildy Ann," "The Skin Flint," "The Rio Grande Romance," "East Lynne," and "Lena Rivers," every one a melodrama. Cheers for virtue's triumph mingled with hisses for the villain, as the pages of time turned back. "It is the age of innocence again," the Nashville *Tennessean* (April 11, 1931) assures us, "and though innocence is ever on the brink of danger and disillusionment, it is by some miracle always safe, and triumphant, of course!" The cast was no longer attempting sincere acting, but was substituting a shoddy burlesquing of the past demanded by the audience.[8]

The Menkes' most successful showboat venture has been the mammoth GOLDENROD, which is still (1950) in operation. This was the FLOATING PALACE which in 1909 climaxed "Double R" Markle's dreams of what a showboat could be. She passed from Markle in 1913 through the Pope Dock Company to Ralph Emerson in 1914, to become the special charge of Captain Bill Menke in 1922. She was not only the biggest showboat ever built, with a hull two hundred by

---

[8] The HOLLYWOOD continued operations until 1941, when she was crushed by the ice in the Clark River about four miles above Paducah, a total loss.

forty-five feet and an original seating capacity of fourteen hundred; she was also the best equipped and most comfortably furnished of all boat-shows. With steam heat for winter and a cooling system for summer, she played a twelve-month season, and with her large, well-equipped stage and a well-appointed auditorium, she could compete on even terms with any land theatre. Living quarters for actor-couples were entirely separate from the dressing rooms back of the stage, the most distinctive feature of her arrangement. Though a part of an old tradition, she approached modern efficiency.

For the first fifteen years that the GOLDENROD was owned by the Menkes, she trouped the Western rivers exactly as her predecessors had traveled them for a hundred years. Her dependable steamer-tow pushed her usually into fifteen different states each season, with frequent stands on the Monongahela, the Ohio, the Kanawha, the Illinois, the Wabash, the Tennessee, and the Mississippi.[9] She never went south of Memphis, however, after 1926 because of the rapidly diminishing audiences in the Southern agricultural belt. Her practice was to follow a week behind the NEW SENSATION, as long as the Menkes were operating that boat, the first carrying a full cargo of musical comedy and vaudeville, the second mainly drama.

Bill Menke knows the river and he knows the show business, but he is not an artist, as he himself fortunately has realized. At the beginning of each season the cast has selected one of its own troupe as director, who has been responsible for stage matters. Probably the most successful of directors so chosen has been Harry Owens, who, in his own right, has been called "the perfect villain of the wheezing type." The big boat-show has been successful with several past Broadway hits, notably "The Spook," which brought Menke his biggest season in 1926, and "The Cat and the Canary" down the rivers in 1927, and "Main Street Folks" up the rivers the same year. Menke followed carefully the practice set by Captain Emerson of giving his audiences near-current plays, for the small towns and rural landings clearly preferred modern drama. Meanwhile his advertising became more and more simplified, perhaps because Bill Menke himself had served as the advance man for many boat-shows. The GOLDENROD had received so much publicity as "The World's Greatest Showboat" that she could afford often to content herself with a simple announcement of her arrival. For her cast, there was never any high-noon parade

[9] The steamers LIBERTY, WENONAH, and CROWN HILL (her favorite) successively towed the GOLDENROD.

and no band concert on the streets. For a few years an advance agent traveled in a Ford a week ahead of the GOLDENROD with the "paper." Menke discontinued both him and the calliope in 1927, and came to depend largely on announcements inserted in newspapers and framed posters set up on the wharf or a nearby street, much as the movie theatre does. The need for economical management was stripping showboating of its traditional sources of glamor. The laying aside of the calliope was also an adaptation to the city environment, which objected to this noisily melodious instrument.

Menke had no choice except to follow the boat-show tactics used by Bryant, the pattern the age demanded. During the summer of 1930 the GOLDENROD tied up at Aspinwall, a suburb of Pittsburgh, for a stand of seventeen busy weeks, and she repeated the procedure the following summer. The city audiences, as on other boat-shows, demanded burlesque, and proceeded so to interpret all that was presented from the stage. For a while the cast continued to play straight drama, much to the onlookers' amusement. To make matters even more confusing, iron workers and other non-sophisticates still composed a considerable proportion of the audience, and these insisted on taking their drama intensely seriously. This group resented any suggestion of burlesque from either the stage or the other half of the audience. One such man in Pittsburgh suddenly jumped onto the stage one evening, scooped up the villain in his powerfully muscled arms, and heaved him, false mustache and all, into the river. On the other hand, if the cast put their hearts into a serious presentation of "East Lynne," "From Rags to Riches," or even "Tempest and Sunshine," the majority in the audience considered the performance ridiculous and insisted on making fun of both play and actors. For a while Bill Menke tried rather desperately to keep order, walking up and down the aisles, "wanting to conk them all," as he will now tell you. But at last he became resigned to the ill-timed applause and the hissing, and recognized an unpleasant fact by tacking up a sign on the boat inviting this strange form of appreciation: "Hiss the Villain All You Please—We Want You to Enjoy Yourself." About the same time a new sign appeared on the boat's side, announcing "Old Time Melodrama." The cast, be it said to their credit, resented both signs, but they loyally co-operated with the management. The last big showboat had been forced into burlesque.

The GOLDENROD finally tied up at St. Louis. Her stopping seemed a mere coincidence, for she first went there for repairs. The New

York *Times* (Sept. 6, 1937) even announced that she would not long remain, and certainly would not show there for "city slickers," but soon would head for remote bends and bayous where her melodrama and candy were still appreciated and where there were no ordinances against wooden theatres. Surprisingly enough, the GOLDENROD announced a performance of "East Lynne." When she attempted to put down her gangplank at the foot of Locust Street, she was met by a posse of policemen, who insisted that she must go *much* farther down the river. The imperturbable Bill Menke drifted a few yards down, took time to get a Federal Court ruling that the Mississippi River did not belong to any city, nosed the GOLDENROD back to the Locust Street landing—and there he has remained for the last thirteen years.

The citizens and transients of St. Louis have proved far more hospitable than were its officials. More than two million have visited the old boat, many of whom, especially during the war years, had never before seen a showboat. Her programs present the old favorites in melodrama, from "Lena Rivers" and "Traffic in Souls" to "Pollyanna" and "A Thief in the Night," with old-time vaudeville numbers to relieve the tension—Swiss bell ringers, chalk artists, and cakewalk dancers. Her most recent and most publicized program presented in 1949–50 a screamingly funny concoction by Billy Bryant entitled "Hamlet and Yeggs." This scrambling of three Shakespearean plays, pepper-and-salted with the New York underworld, is substantially the same version that Bryant's company played years before in the land theatres of Chicago, New York, and Philadelphia, as well as on board his NEW SHOWBOAT at Pittsburgh. The GOLDENROD's cast, with its clever doubling, conveys some idea of the show:

HAMLET
AND YEGGS
In 3 Acts and 5 Scenes
by
Billy Bryant and Wm Shakespeare

———

Cast of Characters

Larry, A Guard
Francisco, Player King, Witch .... Frank Anton
Alibi Eddie, Bernardo
Polonius, Grave Digger .... Ed Ford

"Hamlet" on the GOLDENROD

Courtesy Capt. J. W. Menke

The GOLDENROD, towed by the CROWN HILL

Harry the Bug, Player
Witch, Grave Digger, Frog Ears .... Malcolm Collins
Lippy, Marcellus, Shylock
Lucianus, Laertes .... Bill Rochester
Fish-Eye Kelly
Horatio, Witch .... Robert Ellsworth
Edward Dawson, Warden
Ghost, King .... Eustace Fletcher
Red Light Annie
Queen .... Blanche Forbes
Light Fingered Rosie
Ophelia .... Vida Sedgwick
Hamlet .... Jack Fletcher
Mrs. Buffington
Player Queen, Lady in Waiting .... Mary Meeker

Though this Shakespearean medley has attracted unusually large audiences, it has probably been the GOLDENROD's least commendable production, for both her cast and her atmosphere are at their best, not in garbled art, but in the more simplified patterns. Certainly the melodrama has been Menke's best field. He has probably brought more dark villains face to face with hissing audiences than any other man living. Recently it has all been done in a mild spirit of burlesque, it is true; but these audiences at St. Louis have somehow been different from those jeering crowds in the auditoriums of BRYANT'S NEW SHOWBOAT and the HOLLYWOOD. It is as if the GOLDENROD and the matter-of-fact Bill Menke, when they found that they had outlived their original mission of carrying entertainment and civilization to remote places, had decided, instead of dying, to undertake a new job—that of interpreting to the present the entertainment of the past. Menke has through these last years been fortunate in securing a cast capable of playing melodrama "straight," as our grandmothers liked it, without making it ridiculous. They have performed in their melodrama, in their vaudeville, even in their candy-selling, a dramatic feat, the sympathetic reproduction of outdated entertainment. The atmosphere of the past has permeated the boat like incense in a shrine. And so it is that these audiences seldom jeer, but merely laugh understandingly or even grow a little thoughtful as they applaud and hiss at all the right places.

The aging GOLDENROD, the last of her kind, has gathered through the years a rich accumulation of story and legend, like the hero of an old saga. Those who have sought to encrust the old boat with her own romance will tell you that she has assisted in catching bank robbers, that she has made strange trips into the Gulf, that she has become so much a part of the river that fish have flopped from the water directly onto her stage. They will even add that Captain Bill is a great river fisherman, a story that must be compared with Menke's own statement that he never caught a fish in his life and that his one attempt was in salt water.[10] There are also the stories, more credible, of how Captain Billy threw aside a telegram from Edna Ferber asking for an interview when she was gathering material for *Showboat*, and of how, after the publication of her book, he tacked her request on his office door. To add to the accumulation of stories, the public has transferred to this old boat, in true epic fashion, many of the adventures experienced by other boats.

The old showboat still exerts her spell. As one sits comfortably in Captain Menke's auditorium, one can easily imagine that he is on the NEW SENSATION or the gorgeous old COTTON BLOSSOM tied up at Plum Point or Sunshine Landing. If he thinks back a little, of course he will miss the calliope and its echoing concert, and he will miss, too, the dozens of lanterns that in those days starred the black shore, as they lighted zigzag paths down to the river. But not far over the side there is the same half-noisy dark water, and the brilliantly lighted boat surrounded by the vast night has the same fascination as of old. On the stage there is that same simplified dramatic battle between good and evil, and some of the same vaudeville acts that "Toby" Vevea delighted in. There is only one big difference—the audience has changed. The imagination must indeed be agile to translate that gay, much amused sorority group now witnessing the GOLDENROD's "East Lynne" into the Monongahela miner's family who, with gaunt, tense faces, followed that same play in the 1880's; or even to transform the well-fed banker and his sophisticated, pleasantly amused wife, now across the next aisle, into the substantial plantation couple, fascinated as the romance unfolded, who sat in those same seats a generation ago. These people now are being entertained by an amusing glimpse of the past; those others were tensely living by proxy a life that reality denied them.

By sunlight much of the fascination of the old boat disappears, for

[10] Leslie Lieber and Maurice Elfer (see bibliography) have presented the GOLDENROD in a highly romantic light.

one suspects, in spite of the recently acquired steel hull, that she will never again travel the rivers. Her top deck has swagged a little in the middle, the white and gold paint is not new, and the red plush is moth-eaten. The old queen has survived both herself and the frontier she served, to become a symbol of the past. It is a comfort to know, however, that she is to remain in the substantial hands of the genial, honest, and altogether solid Bill Menke—who is himself beginning to age a little.[11]

[11] Principal Sources: Interviews, letters, manuscripts, handbills, federal and municipal records, and newspaper files.

Other Sources: Items listed in the bibliography under Harry Brundidge, Lucien Burman, Thoda Cocroft, Kyle Crichton, Maurice Elfer, Alvin Harlow, Robert Hereford, Leslie Lieber, H. H. Niemeyer, Sidney Snook, Wesley Stout, A. H. Tarvin, and Paul Twitchell.

XVI

ECHOES OF THE CALLIOPE

Decline and Exploitation of Showboating

TIED UP in many a little creek along the Ohio and the lower Mississippi are discarded showboats in various stages of decay. Once they were palaces of glory. Now they seem odd-looking structures, even on the river, where strange sights are common. The smaller ones look like old-time packets with their smoke stacks knocked off, and the larger ones like two-story Pittsburgh apartment houses. Some, with the paint gone and the wooden gingerbread falling off, are doing duty as dance halls, movie theatres, or glorified shanty boats. A few, in worse condition, are inhabited only by rats, and seem waiting for the next big rise to sweep them away in the river's house-cleaning.

The oldest of these boats were usually called *Floating Theatres* or *Floating Operas*. After the Civil War the more common name was *Showboats*. During the last generation the popular word was *Boat-Shows*, though the inverted phrase was seldom painted on the vessel's side. Occasionally a *Showboat* appeared in the 1840's, and likewise a *Floating Theatre* sometimes in the 1890's. There is, therefore, no dating of these relics of the past, for the showboat changed little in appearance with the passing years. Nor are all discarded showboats moored in secluded coves. Others have been converted into light freight barges, merchant boats, and even menagerie boats, and are still plying the rivers. Some have been dismantled, and their materials built into other structures.

In 1910 there were twenty-six identifiable boat-shows on the Middle Western Rivers. By 1928 the number had dwindled to fourteen, and by 1938 to five. By 1943 only the GOLDENROD [1] was doing

---

[1] The MAJESTIC was later temporarily revived (1948–1949) by college groups, and BRYANT'S NEW SHOWBOAT also resumed activity for a short period.

business, tied up at St. Louis, where she remains. General dilapidation of survivors accompanied the decrease in numbers.

Back of this rapid decline was one fundamental cause, the passing of the frontier. The showboats had come into being to serve a region where civilization had been slow to penetrate, especially where the non-physical forms of entertainment, such as the drama, and the social niceties of living were retarded by the environment. As larger towns achieved better social and entertainment conditions—theatres, schools, musical organizations—the showboats followed the under-privileged classes farther and farther into the backwoods. At last when these remote districts had also either received the means of cultural sustenance, or had provided themselves with easy transportation to sections so blessed, the showboats had no further function to perform. They turned back toward the cities, where they were neither needed nor appreciated, to compete, on unequal terms, with land entertainment and its limitless resources. The moving picture theatres not only had the advantage of Hollywood's millions for production, but also were exempt from dock fees and, since they were permanent installations, from ordinances against wooden theatres. The Depression of 1929 struck simultaneously with the disappearance of the river frontier and did much to hasten the showboats' frantic search for a new and unnatural clientele in urban centers. In 1930 every large showboat on Western rivers tied up for a long stand at a city pier.

Thus any invention or condition which assisted in transforming the near-frontier regions into socially and culturally privileged territory contributed its share to the decline of the showboats. The Ford motor car was low in price and well adapted to rough terrain. County and state governments were opening new and better roads even into remote river districts. Moving picture theatres, affording gaudy glimpses of sophisticated life at low prices, sprang up in both the city and the small town. Those three—cars, roads, and movies—interacted to spell doom for the floating shows. The railroads began linking the river frontiers with the larger towns to contribute their share to the decline of the boat-show institution, and even the lowly phonograph and juke box, and later the radio played their parts.

Not all the causes of the showboats' decay came from the outside. In adapting themselves to the frontier, they had acquired certain characteristics which unfitted them to survive in any other environment. Their captains had to be, first of all, expert rivermen. Of all these

hardy heroes, only two—Chapman and Norman Thom—were primarily artists and theatre men. The excessive doubling made necessary
by their small casts, their one-night stands, the lack of expanding opportunities for actors on the rivers, and the meager properties and
scenery usually available were further hindrances to art on their
stages. Audiences once nurtured on picture shows found it impossible
seriously to accept the conventions and limitations necessary to showboat programs. This meant that their productions were acceptable
only in the absence of more sensitively rendered entertainment, and
that, unable to meet competition, they would therefore prove the
ready victims of progress.

Furthermore their environment had forced the cleansing of the
boat-shows, both as to entertainment and as to the personal lives of
performers. Since the early days of Captain French, they had been
models of virtue and had vehemently preached this same doctrine
from their stages. Here again the picture shows had the advantage
of them, for these new arrivals were not similarly restricted. Villagers
found immensely attractive on their screens what they would not
have tolerated on the homely showboat stage, for sin, even by proxy,
has always proved more alluring to human beings than virtue.

In general the entertainment on the boat-shows trailed a little behind the fashions prevailing elsewhere. Before the Civil War, comedy,
back-to-nature plays, the circus and exhibits of freaks, and vaudeville
were popular. After the War vaudeville with minstrel numbers and
nostalgic, sentimental songs filled most showboat programs. During
the gay 'nineties and the following decade the melodrama, with a
slight sprinkling of tragedy and musical comedy, took over their
stages. Of all dramatic forms, the melodrama proved best adapted
to showboat casts and best suited to the needs of genuine showboat
audiences. In the following decades a few hardy souls, such as Ralph
Emerson and Bill Menke, tried the new plays of social criticism. But
royalties came high and boat casts found the new roles difficult. Showboat audiences did not want to see themselves portrayed—the truest
function of dramatic art—and shunned indigenous materials in favor
of the faraway. Most showboats, therefore, preferred to retain their
melodramas, already outmoded on other stages. That choice marks
the decline of their programs. Their audiences came to expect only
melodrama of them, and at last demanded of them the burlesquing of
melodrama. The showboat, as if embarrassed at being caught outside
the environment that had nurtured it, turned backward, toward the

past. The burlesque demanded by city audiences brought disintegra-
tion to their programs exactly as the disappearance of the river frontier, coupled with the Depression, brought economic extinction. Both
science and art were creating a life with a quicker tempo, and the
showboats were not able to keep up.

As soon as the institution of showboating, as American as our
frontier itself, began slipping into the past, opportunities for exploitation became numerous. A certain coffee company during much of
the 1930's broadcast its radio program of sentimental songs and advertising from "a Mississippi showboat," with exaggerated effects of
romantic incident and atmosphere. Major Bowes and his amateurs
toured the rivers one summer on board the GOLDENROD with a full
assortment of vaudeville numbers. The city of Lowell, Michigan,
before the Second World War, celebrated a showboat festival, when
a barge fitted out as a floating theatre pulled in to the landing to deliver
to the waiting populace, besides a band and a hundred-voice chorus,
also lumberjack fiddlers, cakewalk dancers, harmony singers, boxing
cats, clowns, tumblers, and, most appreciated of all even if slightly
out of the tradition, a nationally known dance orchestra. Catlettsburg,
Kentucky, has more recently made showboating the motif for its
centennial celebration. So much sentimental enthusiasm was generated for the dying institution that an agency of the Federal Government at one time considered financing a return of the Ohio River
boat-shows, and private capital has attempted a revival in foreign
waters.[2]

The *Billboard* (Cincinnati) in 1931 decided that New York's millions "were dying for a chance to witness" a performance of a real,
old-fashioned showboat. Local promoters and society matrons immediately provided various opportunities, such as the PERIWINKLE
(Long Island), the BEAR MOUNTAIN (Hudson River), and the BELGEN-
LAND (New England Coast). By 1936 seven of these pseudo-showboats
were operating from the Battery and at least one from the West 42nd
Street landing in New York. Such boats sometimes tied up as stationary playhouses, as did the BUCCANEER; but more frequently they combined excursions and dancing with the show. Either affectation or
burlesque marked every recorded performance. The case of the BEAR
MOUNTAIN is typical of these society-boat ventures. The sponsor, a
society matron, insisted that the boat be painted pink because she

---

[2] Louisville *Courier-Journal*, Aug. 28, 1936. New York *Times*, July 12, 1931.

thought she remembered that the Mississippi river-boats of her youth had been thus decorated, and, she argued, without pink the spirit of the Mississippi could not be recaptured. The Captain refused to subject his boat to such a color, but as a compromise he painted the smoke stack pink. It is altogether probable that such enterprises derived more of their profits from the business of their bars than from admission charges. Certainly they did not represent the true showboat of the Middle West in any respect except their false label. Billy Bryant and Norman Thom were the only *bona fide* showboaters to take the New York bait, and both of these performed in that city only in land theatres.[3]

A few colleges have realized the close association between early American dramatic history and showboating, and have attempted to revive or to duplicate the old institution. The dramatic club of the Carnegie Institute of Technology (Pittsburgh) put a class of students aboard the GOLDENROD during the season of 1931, to tour the rivers with their own musical comedy and variety numbers. The program was excellent, and the students were hard-working and efficient, some of them even richly talented. But the Depression and inadequate advertising seriously cut down the audiences, and after a few weeks the project was discontinued. More recently, 1948–1949, Kent State University (Ohio) and Hiram College (Ohio) chartered Tom Reynolds' MAJESTIC, Captain, calliope, and all, as a laboratory for classes in drama. The twenty-nine students enrolling for the course, called *Operating Theatre*, after paying a small fee, shared in the boat work, acting duties, musical features, directing, and advertising. Along the Kanawha and the Ohio this version of the old-time showboat played alternately the old temperance drama "The Drunkard, or The Fallen Saved" (1844) and Norman Krasna's more recent "John Loves Mary," with a good student orchestra and five acts of vaudeville. The experiment attracted much attention, more as an honest attempt to duplicate show conditions of the past than as present-day entertainment. Fortunately certain groups, including local schools and the national press, co-operated to furnish full auditoriums and at least temporary success. But the experiment can in no sense be thought of as a revival of showboats.

Other universities have modeled their playhouses after showboats.

[3] *Billboard*, Jan. 17, 1931; New York *Times*, Feb. 2, 1930; May 20, 1930; April 15, 1931; July 12, 1931; June 5, 1932; June 2 and 15, 1933; April 29, 1934; May 12, 1934; June 1, 1935.

One of the best of these is the University of Washington's Showboat Theatre, in a unique marine setting on the campus waterfront at the foot of Fifteenth Avenue, Seattle. The theatre, built in 1937 with the help of the Works Progress Administration, is a modernized showboat, constructed on a permanent foundation of piling. The auditorium seats two hundred and twenty spectators, and the stage is efficiently and beautifully equipped, with a revolving disc to permit quick change of scenes, a permanent sky-dome, and an elaborate switchboard for remote control.

Literary exploitation of showboats has also begun. In fact it began with Mark Twain's unforgettable quacks, the Duke and the King, and their river productions of Shakespeare "for men only." This satire, directed both at foreign actors and at boat-shows, was penned before the revival of the true showboat. It must be remembered that after the Chapman boat ceased operation in 1845 and before the Frenches "cleansed the rivers" in 1878, all local entertainment had fallen into the hands of charlatans, rascals, and the money-monger circuses. The Civil War swept away even the circuses, leaving the field entirely in the hands of poverty-stricken rovers who combined their pseudo-entertaining with many worse activities. The great humorist's picture is dramatically true if it is confined within the years he knew.

Unfortunately later writers of fiction, working long after river entertainment had changed, continued to rely on tradition rather than on current facts. To these it was both convenient and dramatic to consider showboats and those who worked on them as permanent symbols of evil.

Turnbull's "Showboat," a short story of the 1920's, presents just such a perverted and popular view of river entertainment.[4] In this story, more cheaply melodramatic than any showboat play ever was, Eunice Darling, the repressed but innocent daughter of the Rector, has stage aspirations. When the calliope announces the arrival of the showboat at the small Monongahela town, Aunt Sarah, the sister of the minister, speaks of it with "the shocked inflection which she reserved for references to drunkenness, gambling, and immoral ladies," and the high school boys wink and nudge each other. Nevertheless Eunice, desperate for release, slips away to board the showboat after the night performance, carrying her little bundle of clothes. There she easily convinces the black-mustached owner that she can be a

---

[4] A. S. Turnbull, "Showboat," *American Magazine*, CI (Feb., 1926), 28–31.

useful employee, and he assigns her a private room where he himself hopes to enjoy some pleasant hours in the future. When Eunice is preparing for bed, she suddenly remembers her prayer book, and she at once asks permission to return for it. Her dissipated and villainous employer, with an unwonted twinge of conscience, not only grants her request but personally escorts her to her home. In the early morning hours on the rectory steps he whispers, "Do you know what you've done tonight? You've shown me that I have gone clear to the devil!" Then he kisses her (those kisses, we are assured, awaken something in her), and leaves her—to quit the evil showboat business forever! From such false pictures the public has derived much of its impression of showboats.

Novelists have done little better, even as good a writer as David Graham Phillips. His *Susan Lenox* (1915) devotes three chapters to the Burlingham Floating Theatre. The heroine, seventeen, beautiful and wronged, herself a love-child, is escaping on the showboat from marriage to a drunken farmer. Before the Theatre sinks, splintered by a coal barge, the innocent Susan learns from the pretty coarse lips of one of these "veterans in the unconventional life" many of the facts of life. Phillips' portrayal belongs to a period fifty years before other scenes in the book. He too has substituted the old tradition of evil for the facts that he did not know.[5]

Edna Ferber, the most successful of all the literary exploiters, has also largely followed tradition in her best-seller novel, *Showboat* (1926). She has sought to paint, not the reality, but rather a symbolic showboat, daubing into her picture only the traditional colors. Along with the familiar legend of moral evil she has emphasized most a flimsy but all-enveloping sentimentality. From beginning to end her story reeks with melodrama far less convincing than the worst ever acted on a showboat stage. Magnolia, the daughter of a rawboned virago New England school teacher and a lovable but eccentric little river captain, grows up on board the Cotton Blossom Floating Palace during the 1880's and 1890's.[6] Here with her parents she wit-

[5] George Hobart's stage adaptation, "The Fall and Rise of Susan Lenox," was first produced at the 44th Street Theatre, New York, June 9, 1919.
[6] In some later printings and in the screen versions of the book the name was changed to Cotton Palace because of a suit brought by the owners of the Cotton Blossom. Thomas Taggart, Democratic leader in Indiana, also threatened a $100,000 suit because of his involuntary appearance in the book, and his name was deleted after a few copies had been sold. (See p. 120; also the New York *Times*, Sept. 2 and 3, 1926.)

nessed a strange panorama of imagined showboat life. Apparently Miss Ferber loaded on that one showboat all the most melodramatic incidents at her command, without much regard to usual or probable occurrence. In one chapter the little Magnolia sees a sheriff come aboard to arrest an actor whose crime is living with a wife who has a few drops of Negro blood in her veins (here is the tragic pretty-quadroon story bundled into a scant three pages); the little girl sees the husband suck blood from a puncture in his wife's thumb, and hears him swear that therefore he too has Negro blood in him; she sees the pilot at the dramatic moment come down from his house atop the texas to report what he has seen taking place on the lower deck— a physical impossibility on a river showboat. After Magnolia grows up, she falls in love with a cavalier villain, and elopes with this attractive gambler who has somehow charmed the rivers as a snake hypnotizes a frog, all with the conniving co-operation of her wise father. (Here are all the gambling legends of the river draped on one rather inadequate figure, a tradition that seldom actually touched showboats). And then her beloved, eccentric father, as if to pay for his sin, tumbles into the river and is drowned, an end that history does not record for a single showboat captain. After her elopement, Magnolia lives, sweet and pure, on the fringe of Chicago's underworld until, opportunely deserted by her reprobate husband, she jumps meteor-like into national stardom in vaudeville. In the meantime she has placed in a convent the little daughter who is eventually to soar, peculiarly without hardship or pain, to a first place among American actresses—a strange distortion of the success story of a very few showboat actors. And to cap it all, the old termagant of a mother when she dies leaves Magnolia not only the showboat but also half a million dollars in cash. This bizarre conglomeration of melodramatic incidents, skimmed from river legends and traditions, is entitled *Showboat!*

Evidently Miss Ferber forgot that on a showboat melodrama occurred much more frequently on the stage than in the bedrooms and on the deck. When she was collecting her material she perhaps forgot, too, that most river captains love to make a good yarn out of what they relate, and also that they are prone to neglect in their reminiscences the humdrum everyday existence on board their boats. As a result she has told a story which is a distorted dream of boat-show life, done in symbols of melodrama, but she has not created an authentic showboat.

Apparently she had no first-hand acquaintance with any river show-boat when she wrote her novel, though claims have been erroneously made that various boats were her original, among them the COTTON BLOSSOM, the GOLDENROD, and the HOLLYWOOD.[7] In 1925 she sent a telegram to Captain Bill Menke of the GOLDENROD, requesting his itinerary, evidently with the intention of visiting his boat. Since Captain Bill had never heard of Edna Ferber and has always disliked letter writing, he never answered her telegram, and she never visited his boat. Oddly enough, after the publication of her book, Captain Menke tacked her message on his office door, with a belated desire to share some of the highly favorable publicity.

Miss Ferber was more successful in her effort to communicate with the JAMES ADAMS FLOATING THEATRE, and she was a guest on this Atlantic coast vessel for four days, to enjoy the only showboat experience she ever had. Here she learned much from the manager, Charles Hunter, and her gracious hostesses, Mrs. Adams and Mrs. Hunter. Later she visited Hunter in his home at Ironton, Ohio, to hear more of the showboat way of life. Miss Ferber probably did not realize that the coast boat differed greatly, both in structure and in ideals, from the river type. And so she unsuspectingly launched her fictitious COTTON BLOSSOM, patterned largely after the JAMES ADAMS, on inland waters.

Most of the river stories and traditions, and even some of her characters, Miss Ferber may have learned about from Captain Hacker, who during the summer of 1925 was running a ferry at Cairo, Illinois. For two months, it is said, she rode back and forth on that boat, listening to all the anecdotes and river stories that the old Captain could tell. These were numerous and rich. For Hacker's steamer the NEW IDEA had towed the Eugene Robinson FLOATING PALACE (later French's fourth NEW SENSATION) in the 1890's, and he had known the Frenches, the Prices, and the McNairs. Miss Ferber caricatured Captain Price into her eccentric Captain Hawks, she stripped Callie French of all her lovable qualities and created the iron-like Parthenia Ann Hawks, and perhaps she started with one of John McNair's daughters when she pictured the little Magnolia Hawks. On these

[7] Miss Ferber has said that she wrote all her books without first-hand knowledge of the scenes or background materials. As late as 1939 she stated in her autobiography that she had never been on the Mississippi. For some of the claims made for various boats see Beal, *Through the Back Door of the Circus*, p. 7n, and the New York *Times*, Sept. 11, 1932, and July 3, 1933.

three Miss Ferber apparently draped every melodramatic story and sentimental anecdote that the old Captain could remember.

The novel first appeared as a serial in *The Woman's Home Companion*, May–September, 1926, and was then almost immediately published in book form by Doubleday. It leaped into sensational popularity to become a best-seller, and the young Book-of-the-Month Club selected *Showboat* as one of the nine books distributed during its first year. Those who knew the rivers were inclined to be derisive. Captain Bill Menke accused Miss Ferber of taking her showboat overland part of the time, and Captain Ralph Emerson did not quite understand how the fictitious COTTON BLOSSOM could navigate the rivers twenty-five years before the actual COTTON BLOSSOM was ever built. Wesley Stout, the decade's best authority on boat-shows, could not forgive Miss Ferber for her willingness to write a novel about an Ohio-Mississippi showboat when she had never seen one. Such criticisms Miss Ferber had intended to forestall by her "Introduction," which begins, "*Showboat* is neither history nor biography, but fiction."

A few novelists have written of showboats without seriously distorting the spirit of truth. Such men as Ben Lucien Burman in *Blow for a Landing* and *Big River to Cross*, and Pete Martin in "River Singer" [8] paint authentic, though sometimes meager, pictures of showboats. Even in writing fiction, they have found artistic truth—not necessarily factual truth—more desirable than melodrama. The most elaborate true picture of showboats in fiction today is Rose B. Knox's *Footlights Afloat*, unfortunately aimed at juvenile readers. Except for changed names, a manipulated plot, and a telescoped timing, the story is a surprisingly accurate account of life on board French's NEW SENSATION (here the NEW WONDER). After Miss Ferber's melodrama, this book becomes a wholesome as well as a delightful experience.

The film companies were not slow to see possibilities in showboats. Paramount made the first substantial effort in 1925 with Gloria Swanson in "Stage Struck." Most of the scenes could be handled in the studios, but a few of them seemed to call for a genuine showboat—or at least so said Paramount's publicity man. Representatives offered Otto Hitner a thousand dollars a week for the lease of his COTTON BLOSSOM, but the hardy old Captain refused because he could not be

---

[8] Martin's short novel appeared in the *Saturday Evening Post*, August 16, 23 and 30, 1947.

assured the right to censor the film. Roy Hyatt was not so fussily solicitous about the reputation of his boat, however, and gladly leased them his WATER QUEEN. New Martinsville, West Virginia, was selected as the scene of operations, and brakemen on the Baltimore and Ohio Railway began announcing the town as "Hollywood on the Ohio." So many visitors streamed in that the Governor sent state troops to direct the traffic. Soon after film-shooting started, the director asked for volunteers to serve as extras the next day. Anticipating some shyness, as an inducement he offered to use the first applicants conspicuously. At eight o'clock the following morning nearly nine hundred men, women, and children—among them the Mayor and his family—were crowded around the little Riverview Hotel, and the director had to use them all. Apparently the public enjoyed the making of the picture more than the finished production, for the film, even with the attractive Gloria, was not a notable success. The show-boat scenes were so much cut that they did not have great significance. But long after the public had forgotten the picture, the brakemen were still announcing "Hollywood on the Ohio," and Captain Hyatt was still calling his boat the GLORIA SWANSON.

In less than a year after its publication, the film producers pounced upon Edna Ferber's *Showboat*. It had everything they wanted: a background both American and romantic, and melodrama galore. Best of all it had already sold three hundred thousand copies, and was still going strong. Carl Laemmle of Universal bought the screen rights and set about the creation of a silent motion picture, with the beautiful Laura La Plante as Magnolia, Joseph Schildkraut as Ravenal, and Otis Harlan as Captain Andy Hawks. Before the film could be completed, however, Florenz Ziegfeld had bought the stage rights and in 1929 produced his magnificent musical comedy, the songs by Oscar Hammerstein II and the unforgettable music by Jerome Kern. Laemmle wisely decided that, in the face of the tremendous success of the stage production with its brilliant color and deeply emotional songs, it would be foolhardy to release the silent film for the inevitable comparison. To complicate matters further, "The Jazz Singer" finally demonstrated before a surprised world what sound, especially songs, could do for a moving picture. Universal executives were quick to realize that if, with sound possible, they launched a silent "Showboat," they could expect nothing but failure. At great expense they bought some of the sound effects from the Ziegfeld production, especially five of the most popular songs, which they tacked on as a prologue.

"Ol' Man River" furnished background music for all the most dramatic scenes. They added to the film also two other songs, a Negro spiritual called "Lonesome Road" and "We Could Make Believe," which appeared to be sung by Laura La Plante and Joseph Schildkraut. But since neither of these could sing, voices were substituted—and "dubbing in" was born. The patched-up result was not entirely satisfying to anybody. One reviewer remarked, "You might like 'Showboat' if you could see it in an unwired theatre, with an orchestra, or even a good piano. The sound effects had such a disjointed, irritating effect that this reviewer was not even able to enjoy the truly fine performance of Miss Laura La Plante—the only good thing in the picture." [9]

In 1936 after sound had been perfected, Universal tried "Showboat" again, with somewhat happier though too elaborate results. This time Kern and Hammerstein lent their full co-operation from the beginning. Hammerstein based the script on the Ziegfeld musical show rather than on the Ferber novel. The tale plunges into the dramatic romance of Magnolia and Ravenal, and follows closely the theme of their love, the joy of parenthood that blesses it, their separation, and their happy reconciliation—most of which does not at all resemble what Miss Ferber wrote, and most of which does not necessarily associate itself with showboats. The four new songs added by Jerome Kern do happily remind one occasionally that the set is on the rivers. A few actual showboat scenes were photographed on board the old WATER QUEEN, found at Plum Point, Tennessee, doing duty as a dance pavilion. Irene Dunne plays Magnolia, Allan Jones is Gaylord Ravenal, Paul Robeson sings "Ol' Man River." There are fifty dancing girls, two hundred voices, and thirty-five hundred extras. Certainly this later film, though only dimly associated with real showboats, is better entertainment than the indifferent part-sound effort of 1929.

The musical shows based on *Showboat* have been far superior to the film versions. These Hammerstein-Kern song-fests, the first one in 1927 and revivals in 1932, 1946, and 1948,[10] have tended more and more to de-emphasize the unconvincing incidents of the Ferber story, and to preserve the characters—the dashingly handsome gambler, the deserted wife who troupes to stardom, the pretty mulatto who tries to "pass"—as mere symbols of romantic hokum. The boats and

[9] A. M. Sherwood in the *Outlook* (New York), May 22, 1929.
[10] Still another is scheduled for 1951.

the river have become the harmonizing mood, the rich backdrop for the melting, affectionate melodies.

Edna Ferber's novel, with the films and musical comedies based on it, seemed for a little while likely to check the decline of the show-boat business. During 1930–1931 boats like the HOLLYWOOD, BRYANT'S NEW SHOWBOAT, and the GOLDENROD could tie up to a city dock and fill their auditoriums. With all the free advertising, the old Palaces seemed to be floating back into public favor and perhaps into revived usefulness. But it was a false glow that, on account of its very nature, could not last. The basis of this revival was insincerity, for these audiences were different from those of former days. Most of these "city slickers" came, not to be genuinely entertained, but to scoff and to be amused at the past. Such audiences, in spite of both gallant effort and painful compromise on the stage, soon grew bored and dwindled away, to leave the showboats empty, an institution of the past without a present duty. The River has already taken most of them.[11]

[11] Principal Sources: Letters, magazine and newspaper files, interviews, manu-scripts, and Film Year Books.

Other Sources: Items listed in the bibliography under G. B. Beal, Lucien Bur-man, Thoda Cocroft, James Cunningham, Edna Ferber, Wolcott Gibbs, Rosa-mund Gilder, Rose Knox, Leslie Lieber, Pete Martin, David G. Phillips, A. M. Sherwood, Wesley Stout, A. H. Tarvin, S. A. Turnbull, Richard Watts, and Euphemia Wyatt.

APPENDIX

PARADE OF SHOWBOATS

*A List of the Principal Showboats
Arranged Chronologically*

Chapman's FLOATING THEATRE. Built in 1831 at Pittsburgh by William Chapman, Sr. Seated 200. Name changed in 1836 to the STEAMBOAT THEATRE. Lower Mississippi and Ohio system. After Chapman's death in 1840, operated by his wife under the name CHAPMAN'S FLOATING PALACE. Sold to Sol Smith in 1847, and in the same year collided with a steamboat and sank.

Butler's MUSEUM BOAT. Operated by Henry Butler, 1836–1850. Seated 200. The Erie Canal.

HURON. A minstrel boat of the early 1840's. Seated 200. The Little Miami Canal.

TEMPLE OF THE MUSES. A converted man-of-war, operating in 1845. Seated 1800. The Hudson River.

BANJO. Minstrel boat, 1849–1859. Owned by G. R. Spaulding. Seated 200. The Upper Mississippi.

Spaulding and Rogers' FLOATING CIRCUS PALACE. Circus boat built at Cincinnati in 1851 for Gilbert R. Spaulding and Charles J. Rogers. Seated 3,400. Mississippi and Ohio system. Confiscated by the Confederates in 1862 for use as a hospital boat at New Orleans.

UNITED STATES AID. Circus boat of the 1850's. Owned by Tour Leathers. Seated 500. Ohio River.

NEW SENSATION. A. B. French's first showboat of that name. Built by French in 1878 at Cincinnati. Seated 89. Lower Mississippi and Ohio system. Operated by French until 1887, when she was dismantled for the construction of the second NEW SENSATION.

TWENTIETH CENTURY. Owned and operated by Frank Rice (Kruse) from 1882 to 1905. Seated 140. Yazoo River.

[197]

NEW SENSATION. A. B. French's second showboat of that name. Built in 1887 at Cincinnati. Seated 200. Lower Mississippi and Ohio system. Sold in 1890 to Orke, McNair, and Armstrong, and renamed the VOYAGEUR.

Dan Rice's FLOATING OPERA. Built by Dan Rice in 1886 at Cairo, Illinois. Seated 440. Mississippi and Ohio system. Ceased operations in 1887.

Price's FLOATING OPERA. E. A. Price's first showboat. Built at Paducah in 1887. Seated 100. Lower Mississippi and Ohio system. Sold in 1891 to Matt Clinger of Spottsville, Kentucky. Later converted into a liquor boat.

VOYAGEUR. Formerly French's NEW SENSATION (his second showboat of that name). Operated by Orke, McNair, and Armstrong, 1890–1892. Seated 200. Lower Mississippi and Bayous. Sold to Troni Bros. to become a dance hall at New Iberia, La.

THEATORIUM. Built by C. F. Breidenbaugh in 1889 at Hawesville, Ky. Sold in 1890 to A. B. French to become NEW SENSATION No. 1, French's third showboat of that name. Seated 624. Mississippi and Ohio system.

NEW SENSATION No. 1. A. B. French's third showboat of that name. Formerly Breidenbaugh's THEATORIUM. Purchased by French in 1890. Seated 624. Mississippi and Ohio system. Sold in 1900 to E. A. Price to become successively the NEW OLYMPIA, the WATER QUEEN, the GREATER PITTSBURGH, and again the WATER QUEEN.

Price's FLOATING OPERA. E. A. Price's second showboat. Built in 1891 at Paducah. Mississippi and Ohio system. Sold in 1901 to become a dance hall at Smoke Bend, La. In 1901 sold to J. E. McNair, and by him sold to the Levee Board at Thibodeaux, La.

Robinson's FLOATING PALACE. Built by Eugene Robinson in 1893 at Jeffersonville, Indiana. Seated 759. Mississippi and Ohio system. Sold to A. B. French in 1894, to become NEW SENSATION No. 2, French's fourth boat of that name.

NEW SENSATION No. 2. A. B. French's fourth showboat of that name. Formerly Eugene Robinson's FLOATING PALACE. Bought by French in 1894 at auction in Louisville, Ky. Seated 759. Mississippi and Ohio system. Burned at Elmwood Landing, La. in 1900.

NEW SENSATION. A. B. French's fifth showboat of that name. Built by French and McNair at Higginsport, Ohio, in 1901. Seated 960. Mississippi and Ohio system. Operated by Callie French and John McNair until 1907, when sold to E. A. Price. Sold to J. W. Menke in 1918. Disabled by storm at Mound City, Illinois, in 1930, and dismantled in 1931.

NEW OLYMPIA. Formerly French's NEW SENSATION No. 1 (French's third showboat of that name). Purchased in 1900 from French by E. A. Price. Seated 624. Mississippi and Ohio system. Sank in 1900 at North Bend, Ohio. Raised and repaired at Leavenworth, Indiana, to become Price's WATER QUEEN.

WATER QUEEN. Price's repaired NEW OLYMPIA, renamed WATER QUEEN in 1901. Seated 624. Mississippi and Ohio system. Leased to Otto Hitner as the COTTON BLOSSOM No. 2. Half interest sold to Jim Bonnelli and Bill Paden, who operated her as the GREATER PITTS-BURGH. Sold to Roy Hyatt, and name changed back to WATER QUEEN. Demolished by ice on Kanawha River in 1936.

Lightner's FLOATING PALACE. Built by J. P. Lightner in 1900. Seated 300. Lower Mississippi and Bayous. Sold to Ralph Emerson and E. A. Price and renamed the NEW ERA.

NEW GRAND FLOATING PALACE. Built by the Pope Dock Company for W. R. Markle, 1901. Seated 952. Mississippi and Ohio system. Sold to R. W. Emerson, 1905. Sold to E. A. Price, 1907, and name changed to GREATER NEW YORK.

GREAT AMERICAN WATER CIRCUS. An equestrian circus boat operated from 1901 to 1905 by W. P. Newman of Charleston, W.Va. Carried forty horses and fourteen parade wagons. Seated 800. Ohio system. Discontinued in 1905 because of objections of S.P.C.A.

EISENBARTH-HENDERSON FLOATING THEATRE—THE TEMPLE OF AMUSEMENT. Built by Eugene Eisenbarth and his wife in 1901. Seated 600. Mississippi and Ohio system. Rammed by the steamer SPRAGUE in 1903, and sank.

EISENBARTH-HENDERSON FLOATING THEATRE—THE NEW GREAT MODERN TEMPLE OF AMUSEMENT. Eugene Eisenbarth's second show-boat of that name. Built in 1903 for Eisenbarth by the Pope Dock Company. Seated 900. Mississippi and Ohio system. Sold in 1908 to Steiner and Needham and renamed the COTTON BLOSSOM (the original boat of that name).

NEW ERA. Formerly Lightner's FLOATING PALACE. Renamed NEW ERA by Emerson and Price in 1904. Sold to the McNairs, 1906 (half interest) and 1910 (half interest). Seated at first 300, later 450. Mississippi, Ohio, and Bayous. In 1917 converted into a beached movie house at Houma, La.

SUNNY SOUTH. Built for W. R. Markle in 1905 by the Pope Dock

Company. Seated 1200. Mississippi and Ohio system. Sold to Coleman and Menke in 1911, and renamed the HIPPODROME.

JAMES ADAMS FLOATING THEATRE. Officially the S.S. PLAYHOUSE. Ocean-going showboat. Built at Little Washington, North Carolina by James Adams, owner, 1906, and operated by Charles Hunter. Seated 700. Chesapeake Coastal Region. Sank in 1937.

WONDERLAND. Built in 1906 for James Hagen and John W. Cooley by the Pope Dock Company. Seated 900. Mississippi, Ohio, and Missouri system. In 1908 Hagen sold to Cooley, and Cooley sold part interest to Norman Thom and Walter Pell. Sank in 1918.

GREATER NEW YORK. Formerly Markle's and then Emerson's NEW GRAND FLOATING PALACE. Seated 952. Sold by Price to J. W. Menke in 1917, and sank five days later.

PRINCESS. Built by Samuel and Billy Bryant in 1907 at Point Pleasant, W.Va. At first seated 140, later 300. Mississippi and Ohio system. Sold to Ed Darnold and Lew Kinser, and by them to Norman Thom in 1922. Dismantled by Thom in 1928.

COTTON BLOSSOM (the original showboat of that name). Formerly Eisenbarth's FLOATING THEATRE . . . TEMPLE OF AMUSEMENT (Eisenbarth's second showboat). Sold to Steiner and Needham in 1908, rebuilt, and renamed COTTON BLOSSOM. Identified by the dish-pan front filled with lights. Seated 900. Mississippi and Ohio system. Sold to R. W. Emerson in 1909. Half interest sold to Roy Hitner in 1914. Crushed by ice in 1917.

GOLDENROD. Built for W. R. Markle in 1909 by the Pope Dock Company. Seated 1400 (later 980). Mississippi and Ohio system. Sold to R. W. Emerson in 1913. Sold to J. W. Menke in 1922. At present (1950) tied up and showing at St. Louis.

HIPPODROME. Formerly Markle's SUNNY SOUTH. Purchased by Coleman and Menke in 1911, and renamed the HIPPODROME. Seated at first 1200, then 900. Mississippi, Ohio, Alabama, and Tombigbee Rivers. Sold to Jim Bonnelli. Sold to John Fultz, who changed the name back to SUNNY SOUTH. Sunk by ice on the Monongahela River in 1917.

DIXIE. In operation 1911–1916. Seated 300. Lower Mississippi and Bayous.

AMERICAN. Built for Walter Needham at Cincinnati in 1911. Seated 780. Mississippi, Ohio, and Missouri systems. Sold to Thompson Brothers, 1916. Sold to Ralph Emerson, 1917. The same year sold to E. A. Price, and renamed COLUMBIA.

ILLINOIS. A picture-show boat owned and operated by Tom J. Reynolds, 1913–1916. Seated 200. Ohio River system. Burned in 1916 at Foster, Kentucky.

AMERICA. Built by Tom J. Reynolds in 1917. Seated 300. Ohio River system. Sold in 1923 to F. M. and William Reynolds. In 1933 beached as a club house at Curdsville, Kentucky, on the Green River.

COLUMBIA. Formerly the AMERICAN. Purchased from Ralph Emerson by E. A. Price and renamed COLUMBIA. Seated 780. Mississippi, Ohio, and Missouri systems. Operated by Steve Price until 1928, when sold to Menke Brothers to become the HOLLYWOOD.

COTTON BLOSSOM PAVILLION (the second COTTON BLOSSOM). Converted from a grain barge in 1917 by Otto Hitner. Seated 500. Mississippi and Ohio system. Converted into a dance boat in 1918.

COTTON BLOSSOM No. 1. Otto Hitner's third boat of that name. Converted from the barge PRINCESS. Seated 1200. Mississippi and Ohio system. Sold for debt in 1931, and converted into a freight barge.

BRYANT'S NEW SHOWBOAT. Built by Billy Bryant in 1918 at Point Pleasant, W.Va. Seated 880. Mississippi and Ohio system. Two later duplicates successively built and operated under the same name. The last one sold during the Second World War to Charles Slepski, who converted her into a wharf boat at Huntington, W.Va.

VALLEY. Built by Harry Hart, 1918. Seated 400. Ohio River. Sank in 1932 when rats gnawed holes in her hull.

RIVER MAID. Owned and operated by Captain Hi, 1918–1929. Seated 300. Ohio River system.

MAJESTIC. Built by Tom J. Reynolds in 1923. Seated 450. Mississippi and Ohio system. Tied up at Point Pleasant during the Second World War. Leased by college drama classes, 1948–1949.

FUN BOAT. Operated by Doc Bart, 1927–1928, on the Green and Ohio Rivers. Seated 300. Converted into a freight barge, 1929.

HOLLYWOOD. Formerly the COLUMBIA. Sold by Price in 1928 to Menke Brothers, and renamed the HOLLYWOOD. Seated 780. Mississippi, Ohio, and Missouri systems. Demolished by ice on the Clark River, four miles above Paducah, 1941.

WATER LILY. Built and operated by the Farnsworth Shows, 1931–1942. Seated 200. Movies and vaudeville. Ohio, Muskingum, Allegheny, and Monongahela rivers.

COTTON BLOSSOM (Fourth showboat bearing the name). Built by R. W. Emerson on the Chicago River in 1932. Seated 300. Burned in 1933.

DIXIANA. Built under the direction of R. W. Emerson in Sturgeon's Bay, Wisconsin, in 1933 for the Century of Progress Exposition in Chicago. Seated 600. Converted in 1934.

COTTON BLOSSOM (Fifth showboat bearing the name). Built by Jim Bonnelli in 1939. Seated 700. Sold by auction to Oscar Bloom in 1941, and burned the next year.

DIXIE QUEEN. Built by Al Cooper in 1939 for the Kansas City territory. Seated 600. Sold in 1943 to Oscar Bloom, who converted her into an excursion boat.

A Selected Bibliography

The principal sources of information for *Showboats* have been personal interviews, manuscripts, logbooks, letters, albums, scrapbooks, unidentified clippings, diaries, newspaper files, and various official records, which, because of their nature, cannot be listed here. Anonymous articles and advertisements also are omitted from this bibliography.

Abdy, Harry Bennett. *On the Ohio*. New York, 1919.

Albright, E. Deacon. "First Time in 90 Years . . ." in *Billboard* (Cincinnati), LV (Aug. 7, 1943), 28.

Allen, Robert H. "Still Another Phase of Show Business," in New York *Times*, Oct. 12, 1930.

Ambler, Charles H. *History of Transportation in the Ohio Valley*. Glendale (California), 1932.

Aylward, William James. "Steamboating through Dixie," in *Harper's Magazine*, CXXXI (Sept., 1915), 512–522.

Baldwin, Leland D. *The Keelboat Age on Western Waters*. Pittsburgh, 1941.

Banks, Bert. "Career of Showboat that Burned at Memphis," in the *Waterways Journal* (St. Louis), LVI (March 13, 1943), 13.

——. "Original Cotton Blossom," in *Waterways Journal* (St. Louis), LVII (April 10, 1943), 12.

Basso, Hamilton. "Cotton Blossom, the South from a Mississippi Showboat," in *Sewanee Review*, XL (Oct., 1932), 385–395.

Beal, George B. *Through the Back Door of the Circus*. Springfield (Mass.), 1938.

Brown, Charles E. *Old Man River* (Pamphlet). Madison, 1940.

Brown, Maria Ward. *The Life of Dan Rice*. Long Branch (New Jersey), 1901.

Brown, T. Allston. *History of the American Stage*. New York, 1870.

Brundidge, Harry T. [Menke and the GOLDENROD] in St. Louis *Star-Times*, Aug. 13, 1932.

Bryant, Billy. *Children of Ol' Man River*. New York, 1936.

Buckman, David Lear. *Old Steamboat Days on the Hudson River*. New York, 1909.

Burman, Ben Lucien. *Big River to Cross*. New York, 1938.

———. *Blow For a Landing*. New York, 1946.

———. *Steamboat Round the Bend*. New York, 1946.

Carmer, Carl L. *The Songs of the Rivers of America*. New York, 1942.

Carter, Hodding. *The Lower Mississippi*. New York, 1942.

———. "The Mississippi," in *Holiday* (Philadelphia), March, 1949, pp. 34–63.

Childs, M. W. "Showboats Still Carrying Drama . . ." in St. Louis *Post Dispatch*, Aug. 18, 1929.

Cist, Charles. *The Cincinnati Miscellany*, 2 vols. Cincinnati, 1845.

Clarke, Asia Booth. *The Elder and the Younger Booth*. Boston, 1893.

Clemens, Samuel L. (Mark Twain). *Life on the Mississippi*. New York, 1883.

———. (Mark Twain). *Huckleberry Finn*. New York, 1885.

Clurman, Harold. "Old Times," in *New Republic*, Sept. 27, 1948, p. 38.

Coad, Oral S. and Edwin Mims. *The American Stage* (Vol. XIV of "The Pageant of America"). New Haven, 1929.

Cocroft, Thoda. "The Floating Theatre Thrives," in *Bookman*, LXVI (Dec., 1927), 396–398.

Conner, Edmon S. "The Birth of Jim Crow," in New York *Times*, June 5, 1881.

Crichton, Kyle. "Showboat 'Round the Bend," in *Collier's*, CIV, No. 3 (July 15, 1939), pp. 19, 40.

Crowther, Bosley. "Showboats Are Coming," in New York *Times*, July 5, 1936.

Cunningham, James P. "Showboat," in *Commonweal*, XXIV (May 8, 1936), 48.

Curtis, Joe. "Dan Rice's Showboat is Remembered Today," in Memphis *Commercial Appeal*, Sept. 8, 1938.

———. [Showboats] in Memphis *Commercial Appeal*, July 3, 1938.

Dayton, Frederick Erving. *Steam Boat Days*. New York, 1925.

DeCasseres, Benjamin. "Showboat," in *Arts and Decoration* (New York), XXXVII (Sept., 1932), 43.

Devol, George H. *Forty Years a Gambler on the Mississippi River.* New York, 1892.

DeVoto, Bernard. *Mark Twain's America.* Boston, 1932.

Dorsey, Florence L. *Master of the Mississippi.* Boston, 1941.

Dunn, Esther Cloudman. *Shakespeare in America.* New York, 1939.

Eaton, Walter P. *The Actor's Heritage.* Boston, 1924.

Elfer, Maurice. "Famous Showboat," in *Inn Dixie* (New Orleans), June, 1948.

Eskew, Garnett L. *Pageant of the Packets.* New York, 1929.

Eustace, Edward J. "Showboat Must Go On," in New York *Times,* May 10, 1936.

Favrot, J. St. Clair. "Visit of Cotton Blossom," in Baton Rouge *State Times,* Feb. 25, 1930.

Ferber, Edna. *A Peculiar Treasure.* New York, 1939.

———. *Showboat.* New York, 1926.

Firestone, Clark B. *Flowing South.* New York, 1941.

———. [Showboats] in Cincinnati *Daily Times-Star,* May 28, 1927.

———. *Sycamore Shores.* New York, 1936.

Foster, T. Henry. [Editions of *Uncle Tom's Cabin*] in *Book Collector's Packet,* IV (1945), No. 5.

Free, Joseph M. "The Ante-Bellum Theatre of the Old Natchez Region," in *Journal of the Mississippi Historical Association,* V (Jan., 1943), 14–27.

———. *The Theatre of Southwestern Mississippi to 1840.* Thesis at the University of Iowa, 1941.

Freeman, Lewis R. *Waterways of Westward Wanderings.* New York, 1927.

Frost, Meigs O. "Mississippi Showboat Girls . . ." in New Orleans *Times-Picayune,* Aug. 19, 1934.

———. [Mrs. Callie French] in New Orleans *Times-Picayune,* Feb. 27, 1935.

Gaisford, John. *The Drama in New Orleans.* New Orleans, 1849.

Gamble, J. Mack. "The River Showboat," in *Ohio River and Inland Waterways Magazine,* Dec., 1922.

———. "The Showboat Survives," in *National Waterways Journal,* Jan., 1929.

Gibbs, Wolcott. "Nice to Have Back Again," in *New Yorker,* XXI (Jan. 12, 1946), 40.

Gilbert, Paul T. "King of the River," in Chicago *Sun,* May 10, 1945.

Gilder, Rosamund. "Showboat," in *Theatre Arts* (New York), XXX (March, 1946), 138.

Gordon, Jan and Cora. *On Wandering Wheels*. New York, 1928.

————. "Two English Tourists on a Showboat," in *Literary Digest*, XCIX (Dec. 29, 1928), 38–41.

Goulder, Grace. "Showboat Majestic," in Cleveland *Plain Dealer*, July 11, 1948.

Green, Margaret A. "Showboats," in *History of Bolivar County, Mississippi*. Jackson, Miss., 1948.

Greenbie, Marjorie B. *American Saga*. New York, 1939.

Gross, Sarah C. "Some Notes . . . For a Study of Showboats," in *Broadside* (New York), VIII (Feb., 1947), No. 1.

Hall, James. *The West*. Cincinnati, 1848.

Haller, Grace. "Showboat Season Is On," in Cleveland *Plain Dealer*, May 9, 1937.

Hardesty, Corinne. "Here Comes the Showboat," in New Orleans *Item-Tribune*, Aug. 25, 1929.

Harlow, Alvin F. "Showboats," in *Dictionary of American History* (New York, 1940), V, 76–77.

Hereford, Robert A. "Captain Billy's Showboat," in *American Weekly*, Sept. 11, 1949.

Hobart, George V. *Fall and Rise of Susan Lenox. A Melodramatic Pilgrimage in Three Acts and Ten Scenes*. (Play). New York, 1919.

Holliday, Carl. "American Showboats," in *Theatre Magazine* (New York), XXV (May, 1917), 246.

Hornblow, Arthur. *A History of the Theatre in America*. Philadelphia, 1919. I, 348.

Howells, William D. "Ralph Keeler," in *Atlantic Monthly*, XXXIII (March, 1874), 366–367.

Hudson, Arthur P. *Humor of the Old Deep South*. New York, 1936.

Hughes, Glenn. *Story of the Theatre*. New York, 1928.

Hulbert, Archer. *The Ohio River*. New York, 1906.

Hutton, Laurence. *Curiosities of the American Stage*. New York, 1891.

Ireland, Joseph N. *Mrs. Duff*. Boston, 1893.

————. *Records of the New York Stage*. 2 Vols. New York, 1866.

Jefferson, Joseph. *Autobiography of . . .* New York, 1889.

Johnson, Clifton. *Highways and Byways of the Mississippi Valley*. New York, 1911.

Judd, "Doctor." "The Water Days of the Drama," in *Theatre Magazine* (New York), Aug., 1903, pp. 202–203.

Kane, Harnett T. *Bayous of Louisiana.* New York, 1943.

Keeler, Ralph. "Three Years a Negro Minstrel," in *Atlantic Monthly*, XXIV (July, 1869), 71–85.

———. *Vagabond Adventures.* Boston, 1870.

Kelm, William E. "The People's Theatre," in *Palimpsest*, IX (March, 1928), 89–105.

Knox, Rose B. *Footlights Afloat.* New York, 1937.

Koch, Felix J. "Ho! For the Floating Opera," in *Drama* (Chicago), XI (Jan., 1921), 114–115.

Kussart, S. *The Allegheny River.* Pittsburgh, 1938.

Langehennig, Laura. "The Steamboat, . . . in the Fifties," in *Missouri Hist. Review*, XL (Jan., 1946), 205–214.

Lawren, Joseph. [Showboats] in Philadelphia *Inquirer*, Aug. 9, 1942.

Leahy, Ethel C. *Who's Who on the Ohio River.* New York, 1931.

Leavitt, M. B. *Fifty Years of Theatrical Management.* New York, 1912.

Lieber, Leslie. "Last of the Showboats," in New York *Tribune*, Aug. 11, 1946.

Lloyd, James T. *Steamboat Directory.* Cincinnati, 1856.

Ludlow, Noah M. *Dramatic Life As I Found It.* St. Louis, 1880.

M'Clure, W. Frank. "A Floating Theatre," in *Scientific American* (New York), CX (Jan. 9, 1904), 24.

MacGowan, Kenneth. *Footlights Across America.* New York, 1929.

MacMinn, George R. *The Theatre of the Golden Era in California.* Caldwell (Idaho), 1941.

Madison, Frank H. "Floating Theatres of the Mississippi River," *Green Book Album.* New York, 1926.

Martin, Boyd. "Sunday to Sunday," in Louisville *Courier-Journal*, May 10, 1936.

Martin, Harry. "Stranded Showboat Troupe . . ." in Memphis *Commercial Appeal*, Jan. 1, 1940.

Martin, Pete. "River Singer," in *Saturday Evening Post*, Aug. 16, 23, and 30, 1947.

Mathews, John L. *The Log of the* EASY WAY. Boston, 1911.

Matthews, Brander. *A Book About the Theatre.* New York, 1916.

May, Earl C. *The Circus from Rome to Ringling.* New York, 1932.

Meeker, N. C. *Life in the West or Stories of the Mississippi.* New York, 1868.

Merrick, George B. "Genesis of Steamboating on Western Rivers," in *Proceedings of the State Historical Society of Wisconsin,* LXIX (1911), 97–151.

———. *Old Times on the Upper Mississippi.* Cleveland, 1909.

Mims, Edwin and Oral S. Coad. *The American Stage* (Vol. XIV of "The Pageant of America"). New Haven, 1929.

Morgan, Deck. "The Showboat Era Ended," in New York *Times,* May 13, 1934.

Nevin, Robert P. "Stephen C. Foster and Negro Minstrelsy," in *Atlantic Monthly,* XX (Nov., 1867), 608–616.

Niemeyer, H. H. [Goldenrod Showboat] in St. Louis *Post-Dispatch,* Oct. 24, 1932.

Odell, C. D. *Annals of the New York Stage.* New York, 1931. Vol. V.

Olmsted, Frederick. *A Journey Through Texas.* New York, 1857.

Petersen, William J. *Steamboating on the Upper Mississippi.* Iowa City, 1937.

Pettit, Paul B. "Showboat Theatre," in *Quarterly Journal of Speech* (Detroit), XXXI (1945), 167–175.

Phillips, David G. *Susan Lenox.* New York, 1917.

Piddington, G. W. "Showboat Days and Nights," in *Everybody's Magazine* (New York), LV (Aug., 1926), 70–75.

Pinkerton, Allan. *Mississippi Outlaws and the Detectives.* New York, 1882.

Porter, Marion. "Here Comes the Showboat," in Louisville *Courier Journal,* June 11, 1939.

Power, Tyrone. *Impressions of America.* Philadelphia, 1836.

Pratt, Helen T. "Souvenirs of an Interesting Family," in *California Historical Society Quarterly,* VII, 282–285, and 406.

Quick, Herbert. *Mississippi Steamboatin'* . . . New York, 1926.

Quinn, Arthur H. *History of the American Drama.* New York, 1923.

Reynolds, Horace. "All Gone, Cap'n!" in *Christian Science Monitor,* Nov. 14, 1942.

———. "Billy Bryant, Master of the Ohio," in New York *Times,* Nov. 14, 1937.

(Rice, Dan)? *Sketches from the Life of Dan Rice.* Albany, 1849.

Rice, Edward Le Roy. *Monarchs of Minstrelsy.* New York, 1911.

Robinson, Gil. *Old Wagon Show Days.* Cincinnati, 1925.

Rourke, Constance. *American Humor.* New York, 1931.

Saxon, Lyle. *Father Mississippi.* New York, 1927.

———. *Old Louisiana.* New York, 1929.

Schick, Joseph S. "Early Showboat and Circus in the Upper Valley," in *Mid-America*, XXXII (New Series, XXI), 211–225.

Sherwood, A. M. "Showboat," in *Outlook* (New York), CLII (May 22, 1929), 155.

Simpich, Frederick. "So Much Happens Along the Ohio," in *National Geographic Magazine* (Washington), XCVII (Feb., 1950), 177–212.

Skinner, Otis and Maud. *One Man in his Time*. Philadelphia, 1938.

Smith, Cecil. "Billy Bryant Presents . . ." in Chicago *Tribune*, May 23, 1943.

Smith, Soloman F. *Sol Smith's Theatrical Apprenticeship*. Philadelphia, 1854.

———. *Theatrical Management in the West and South For Thirty Years*. New York, 1868.

Snook, Sidney (Mrs. Miles Haman). "The Showboat Drifts Downstream," in *South Atlantic Quarterly* (Durham, N.C.), July, 1942.

Sparks, W. H. *The Memories of Fifty Years*. Philadelphia, 1870.

Spears, Raymond S. "The Mississippi Boat Theatres," in *Harper's Weekly*, LIII (Sept. 4, 1909), 13.

Stout, Wesley W. "Tonight at the River-Landing," in *Saturday Evening Post*, CXCVIII (Oct. 31, 1925), 16–17.

Striker, Hopper. "Cruising Theatres of the Long Ago," in *Literary Digest*, LIII (July 22, 1916), 189.

Tarvin, A. H. "Trekking Backward," in Louisville *Herald-Post*, June 29, 1930.

Tousley, Albert S. *Where Goes the River*. Iowa City, 1924.

Trollope, Frances. *Domestic Manners of the Americans*. London, 1832.

Turnbull, S. A. "Showboat," in *American Magazine* (New York), CI (Feb., 1926), 28–31.

Twitchell, Paul. "He Towed a Showboat Across the Gulf," in Louisville *Courier-Journal*, Oct. 26, 1941.

Venable, William H. *Beginnings of Literary Culture in the Ohio Valley*. Cincinnati, 1891.

Wallen, James A. "Billy Bryant—Showboatman Supreme," in *West Virginia Review* (Charleston, W.Va.), Sept., 1937.

Walsh, G. E. "The Floating Theatre," in *Theatre Magazine* (New York), XVI (Aug., 1912), 48.

Watts, Richard, Jr., "Showboat Sails Again," in *Saturday Review of Literature* (New York), XXIX (Jan. 26, 1946), 30–32.

Wemyss, Francis C. *Chronology of the American Stage From 1752 to 1852.* New York, 1852.

Wilson, William. *The Wabash.* New York, 1940.

Winter, William. *The Jeffersons.* Boston, 1881.

Wittke, Carl. *Tambo and Bones: A History of the American Minstrel Stage.* Durham (N.C.), 1930.

Wright, G. Harry. "About Early Showboats," in *Waterways Journal* (St. Louis), March 5, 1949.

——. [Showboats] in *Dramatics* (Cincinnati), Oct., Nov., Dec., 1948, and Feb., March, and April, 1949.

Writers' Program. *Michigan.* New York, 1941.

——. *Missouri.* New York, 1941.

Wyatt, Euphemia. "Showboat," in *Catholic World*, CLXII (Feb., 1946), 456.

——. "Showboat," in *Catholic World*, CLXVIII (Oct., 1948), 77.

Wyman, Walker D. "Missouri River Steamboatin'," in *Nebraska History Quarterly* (Lincoln), April, 1946.

Zuber, Charles H. "Curtains Down," in Cincinnati *Enquirer*, Nov. 3, 1935.

Index

Bibliographical sources, rivers, and fictitious characters are not included.

Blank Verse, 23n

Blondin, Charles (Jean Gravelet), 31

Bloom, Oscar, 115n, 139

Bloomer Girl Baseball Team, 95, 110n, 111

"Blue Alsatian Mountains, The," 47, 53, 62, 81, 173, 174

"Bob Lively et al," 90

Bonham, James, 173

Bonnelli, Jim, 93, 115n, 120, 172n

Book-of-the-Month Club, 193

Booker, John, 31

Bonnett's Mill, Mo., 96, 141

Booth, Edwin, Sr., 10, 11

Boston, 2, 130

Bowery Theatre, N. Y., 10

Bowes, Major Edward, 187

Bowyer, C. C., 147, 152n

Breidenbaugh, C. F., 50, 55, 58, 60, 67, 120

Brewer, Clair and Daisy and Velma, 137

"Brewster's Millions," 113

Broad Street, Nashville, 177

"Broadway Jones," 154

Brooklyn, 26

Brown, Cyrus, 9

Bruslé, Charles, 164, 173

Bryant, Billy: on the WATER QUEEN, 87-88, 146; on the PRINCESS, 146-152; on NEW SHOWBOAT, 152-158; reputation, 145, 164; western tour, 146; marriage, 151; in burlesque, 154-156

Bryant, Florence, 88, 146-158

Bryant, Josephine, 151, 153

Bryant, Sam, 88, 121n, 145-158

Bryant, Violet, 88, 145-158

BRYANT'S NEW SHOWBOAT: description, 152; opening night, 153; melodrama, 153, 154; program, 154-155; with burlesque, 154-157; revived, 184n; 201

BUCCANEER, 187

Buck-and-wing, 171

Buffalo, N. Y., 24

Bull, Ole, 28

Bullard, Artemus, 37n

Burlesque, 17, 26, 48, 122, 124, 129, 149, 154-157, 166, 176-177, 179-181, 186, 187

BURLINGHAM FLOATING THEATRE, Phillips', 190

Burman, Ben Lucien, 193

Butler, Henry, 24-25, 197

Butler's MUSEUM BOAT, 197

"By Killarney's Lakes and Hills," 47

Cairo, Ill., 23, 39, 45, 48, 59, 73, 83, 160, 163, 192

Cajun, 63, 64, 91, 119, 167

Cakewalk, 180, 187

California, Ky., 123

"Call of the Woods," 105

Calliope, 30, 53, 53n, 54, 60, 61, 62, 65, 75, 78-82, 88, 107, 109, 110, 122, 124, 126, 128, 129, 134, 137, 141-144, 163, 165, 166, 174, 175, 178, 179, 182, 188

Calumet Plantation, Columbia, Ala., 74, 77

Canal Street, New Orleans, 45

Candy Sales, 99, 126, 128, 176, 181

Cape Girardeau, Mo., 23, 120

Carnegie Institute of Technology, Pittsburgh, 188

Caseyville, Ky., 35

"Cat and the Canary, The," 178

Catfish, 14, 41, 73

"Catherine and Petruccio," 5, 7

Catlettsburg, Ky., 187

Century of Progress Exposition, Chicago, 116, 175

Chambers Street Theatre, N. Y., 17

CHAPERONE, 175, 175n

Chapman, Bernard, 9n

Chapman, Caroline, 9, 11, 15, 17, 20n

Chapman, Elizabeth, 9n

Chapman, George, 9, 11, 15

Chapman, Harry, 9, 11

Chapman, Mary Ross Parks, 9n

Chapman, Phoebe, 9, 15

BIGGER AND BETTER THAN EVER!

THE SWALLOW & MARKLE FLOATING PALACE

REPRESENTS MORE CAPITAL, BRAINS AND ENERGY THAN ALL OTHER SHOWS OF ITS KIND.

A show organized by the very brains of the show world. Placed before the public without fear of competition. One that travels solely on its merits, and a well and favorably known reputation, asking no favors and courting honest criticism. Constructed with a view of giving every comfort to our patrons. By a special system of ventilation and aided by countless electric fans, the theatre is kept unusually cool and refreshing.

BOLD BANK ROBBERY.

Most Sensational, Exciting and Thrilling from Start to Finish. The Greatest Production in Motion Tableaux.

The Moving Picture Machine Projects apparently Living Pictures and Actual Scenes, as well as some Strange, Startling and Bewildering Illusions. You will see the same pictures that are exciting so much interest among people in the largest cities

BOLD BANK ROBBERY
COPYRIGHTED 1904 BY S. LUBIN

VAULT

·····FOR DATE AND PLACE SEE FIRST PAGE·····